EARLY COMMENTS

From Robert Lacey, author of *The Kingdom, Inside the Kingdom, The Year 1000,* the three-volume *Great Tales from English History,* and bestselling biographies of Henry Ford, Meyer Lansky, Queen Elizabeth 11, and Princess Grace of Monaco:

I devoured *Second Sight* at a sitting. This is original contemporary history at its best. As someone who has lived in Saudi Arabia for many years, I was greatly impressed by the sharpness of David Paton's Arabian observations—and was green with envy at his charmed access in high places. As someone who lives and dies a professional author, I marvel at Paton's narrative command and pace. And as someone whose own gift of sight is threatened by the disease that stole my dear father's vision, I am deeply moved by Paton's dedicated medical crusade to cure and protect the eyes of others. I wholeheartedly recommend this memoir—insightful in every sense.

From Barbara Bush, former First Lady of the United States and longtime champion of ORBIS:

In the beginning many thought ORBIS was a great dream… but an impossible dream. Dr. David Paton had that dream. Through great persistence on David's part that dream came to fruition and he gave the world a gift of sight with global instruction in ophthalmic surgery. George would say he is a true Point of Light.

From James A. Baker III, 61ˢᵗ U.S. Secretary of State:

Dr. David Paton has crafted a most compelling memoir—an interesting, informative, and extremely well-written story of a man born to privilege who chose to devote his life to restoring sight to people around the world, particularly those in developing countries. The book becomes an irresistible read as he not only acknowledges his successes but describes the impact of failure and the subsequent replenishing of his career with undiminished energy. I have known him most of my life but never as well as I know him after reading this intimate account of his life, the life of a unique American.

Printed by CreateSpace, An Amazon.com company
www.secondsightbook.com

LCCN: 2011903307
ISBN: 1456474863
ISBN-13: 9781456474867

THIS BOOK IS DEDICATED TO

DAVID TOWNLEY PATON

WHO MAKES HIS FATHER FOREVER PROUD

CONTENTS

INTRODUCTION

A life in medicine offers a broad array of options which can be conceived of as a series of genes arranged along an imaginary chromosome. In this image, each gene represents a potential career thrust, ranging from fundamental biomedical research at the one extreme, through clinical research, clinical care, teaching and training efforts, administration and/or institution building, health systems architecture and public health, to health-related policy activities and, finally, catalytic impacts on institutions or other elements of the medical enterprise. To carry the genetic image further, these latent possibilities can be thought of as located on the long arm of the medical career chromosome, while on the short arm are a variety of important potential facilitating factors, especially personal characteristics, the realities of academic politics and professional societies, a group of interests and talents that might be embraced under the term academicism, and the potential broadening effects of friendships, hobbies and travel.

The analogy can be carried further. Epigenetic factors are modifiers, promoters or inhibitors of the expression of the genetic material, and might include, in this model, the influence of significant figures in the education of the nascent physician, colleagues, the ambiance of the academic medical centers in which education and training occur, faculty mentors, institutional roles, and others. Yet further, as the medical career expresses itself, some analogs of messenger RNA, the translating mechanism in gene expression that leads to gene products, also obtain, for example in the form of publications, presentations at scientific meetings, impact on students, trainees, faculty and other colleagues, and through participation on professional boards and program committees and consultations and other service at the various levels of government.

For most of those entering medicine the choice is made early, the chief gene activated, as it were, remains the track pursued, the pathway to a useful and fulfilling professional life. In most instances that pathway primarily involves clinical care, the traditional engagement of the individual physician with the individual patient. For a few who choose this path, things evolve or broaden with the passage of time along related or derivative avenues. Such individuals have in important instances blazed new trails from the clinic to the laboratory as Banting did in discovering insulin and its application in the treatment of diabetes, or as in the case of MacLeod and McCarty who as clinicians concerned with pneumonia as a leading cause of death, joined with Avery in studying the pneumococcus and discovering that the genetic substance involved in the transformation of pneumococcus was DNA. Others have broadened from clinical interests to major teaching responsibilities as chairs of departments or deanships or yet further into efforts to broaden the engagement of medicine in health matters, for example David E. Rogers, who went from the chair of medicine at Vanderbilt University to the deanship of the Johns Hopkins School of Medicine to the presidency of the Robert Wood Johnson Foundation. Least commonly, a few pursue the demanding trajectory that goes from the clinical care of individual patients in academic settings to the invention of systems that take needed interventions to entire populations for whom such care is unavailable. Such a choice was made and acted upon by David Paton in the course of his extraordinary career, and is described in this volume.

Dr. Paton's pathway is a modern adventure story. From a privileged educational and training background in medicine he moved energetically into a full time faculty career that combined patient care with teaching and with publication of original observations and clinical innovations. It was clear early that he was exceptionally talented, and in fact he was named chairman of the department of ophthalmology at the Baylor College of Medicine at age 41, only seven years after completing a year as chief resident physician at the Wilmer Eye Institute of the Johns Hopkins Hospital.

It was also clear quite early that Dr. Paton was an innovator. In his first year on the faculty at Johns Hopkins he founded a surgical research laboratory in the Wilmer Institute and over the ensuing years founded the Ophthalmic Systems Research Laboratory and the Glaucoma Service and Research Laboratory at Baylor, as well as the

EXCEL Foundation, a non-profit enterprise focused on disease prevention. Most importantly, in 1970 he founded Project ORBIS, Inc., an imaginative not-for-profit public corporation organized to bring modern techniques in eye care to countries where they were not available by teaching ophthalmic surgery and other treatment modalities on refitted jet aircraft. Beyond the nearly incredible difficulties involved in making that dream a reality, the multiplier potential of the idea was immense, involving as it did the training of indigenous ophthalmic surgeons, primarily in the developing world, in the latest surgical and related techniques for the relief of blindness. Moving from a traditional academic track in medicine to an effort to address in an innovative manner the staggering global burden of visual disorders required a scope of vision and an investment of energy possessed by relatively few people. Some idea of the challenge may be derived from World Health Organization figures, which estimate at least 37 million blind people worldwide and another 124 million have low vision, more than 90% in developing countries. Further, WHO estimates indicate that some 75% of all worldwide blindness is avoidable through prevention or treatment. The international lack of access to trained ophthalmologists and issues of surgical cost have prevented most affected people from receiving adequate care.[*] ORBIS was an inspired addition to the efforts of the WHO, other international entities and governments to construct effective approaches to those problems.

Dr. Paton's idea came into being and grew through the development of an engaged, energetic volunteer board and through his intelligence, imagination and drive. Over time the ORBIS curriculum has expanded to include not only teaching surgical skills to ophthalmologists but also enhancing the skills of nurses, ophthalmic assistants, public health workers and biomedical engineers. The overall object has been to leave behind in the country visited a sustainable program that would have a capacity for indigenous growth. Now, some thirty years after its founding, ORBIS continues to flourish, on the basis of annual funding from the private sector. Its flying eye hospital, now

---

[*] Oh DM, Oh KT: Disabling Visual Disorders in: Wallace RB, Kohatsu N (Eds): Wallace/Maxcy-Rosenau-Last (Eds): Public Health and Preventive Medicine, 15th Edition, McGraw Hill 2007.

a converted DC-10 aircraft, continues to visit developing countries. The basic model of providing exposure to the latest techniques in eye care has been supplemented by year-round programs in Ethiopia, Bangladesh, China, India and Vietnam, with offices in these countries run by local staff, and with ongoing efforts to combat visual disorders with a particular focus on the treatment and prevention of childhood blindness, cataract, trachoma and corneal disease. A partial idea of the dimensions of the effort can be garnered from the fact that the total revenue of ORBIS in 2008 exceeded $79 million. A more astounding picture emerges when one considers that, in that year alone, ORBIS trained more than 6000 doctors and 3300 nurses, paramedics and rural health workers, screened almost 3½ million people, did more than 156,000 surgeries and implemented 90 international projects.

Numerous honors have of course come to Dr. Paton over the course of his distinguished career. They have included honorary degrees, membership in most of the senior and honorary societies in ophthalmology in this country and elsewhere, medals, decorations and awards. One of these, membership in the American Society of the Order of St. John, is particularly apt. The Knights Hospitallers of St. John of Jerusalem, founded in the 11th century to provide medical care for European pilgrims traveling to the Holy Land by establishing hostels, precursors of the modern hospital, along the routes they traversed. From the beginning, an oath was taken by every Knight on his admission to the Order: "The brethren of the Hospital should serve our Lords the sick, with zeal and devotion, as if they were serfs to their Lords."* The sick were thereby ennobled, raised in a sense to the Peerage. Centuries later their leaders were still proclaiming, "We make a promise which no other people make, promising to be the serf and slave of our Lords the sick."* That ancient service ethic is deeply embedded in the life trajectory described in this book, as is another, taken from the seal of the New York Hospital, where Dr. Paton interned. On the hospital seal, around an image of the Good Samaritan, are inscribed the words, "Go And Do Thou Like-

---

* Jonsen AR: Our Lords the Sick in Barondess JA, Roland CG (Eds): The Persisting Osler II. Selected Transactions of the American Osler Society, 1981-1990. Malabar FL, Krieger Publishing Co., 1994, 3-8.

wise." Both the promise of the Knights Hospitallers and the injunction on the hospital Seal continue to echo the traditional commitment of the physician, however deeply embedded in the complexities of modern scientific medicine or the panoply of technologies it uses, or in the convoluted structure of modern practice. They continue to find individual expression in the traditional clinical activities of doctors as well as in attempts to bring modern healing techniques to populations in need. Dr. Paton's career offers a dazzling instance of both. It is still possible for one person to change the world.

Jeremiah A. Barondess, M.D.
President Emeritus, The New York Academy of Medicine
William T. Foley Distinguished Professor in Clinical Medicine (retired), Weill Medical College of Cornell University

and veiled women, I wondered if the job descriptions of those men required that they be eunuchs. Townley and I were seated in the last row on the aircraft, windowless and adjacent to a rest room in constant demand. I was getting my own sense of place in the Kingdom, but being essentially anonymous on that trip was a welcome change of pace from my responsibilities in Riyadh.

Dr. Fateah had preceded our departure to make sure all was in readiness for Her Highness when she arrived at her summer villa. He was there to greet us in Nice with more than a dozen antique cars from the collection of Prince Mohammad, the King's Number One son, all in mint condition with liveried drivers. In style, therefore, all seventy-seven of us passengers were driven high into the hills behind the city of Cannes to a chateau commanding an impressive view of the Mediterranean.

Since the royal eye seemed to be doing just fine, HRH's persisting grumpiness suggested she was merely reluctant to have her surgeon go back to Riyadh. On the first night after our arrival, a dinner was given at HRH's villa for "the doctor." In her enormous dining room was a single long narrow table, lined with seventy-seven chairs. The table was covered with white linen cloths, on which rested all the accoutrements of luxury dining—china displaying the royal emblems, gold and silver services, large, highly stylized floral arrangements, and two wine glasses at each place setting—a scene fit for a king, even though the wine glasses were intended for nothing stronger than fruit juice.

There was a menu compromise that evening. In honor of the American doctor, the main course was hamburgers, with the buns offered on the side. And at every one of the seventy-seven place settings stood a pristine bottle of Heinz ketchup. The hamburger tasted like minced lamb, but the ketchup made the meal palatable enough to me. So unexpected were the hamburgers that I cannot remember anything else on the menu, but I suppose there was the usual assortment of rice, nuts, veggies and sweets by the handful, served on gold-rimmed platters.

Yet this opening act was nothing compared to the next night. We received word that dinner was to be held at a nearby villa owned by a Lebanese gentleman, a friend of Prince Mohammad's. His chateau also had a magnificent view of the harbor and featured an extensive grass courtyard between the house and a low stone wall at the outer limits of the property, where the hill dropped off into dark oblivion. The lights from boats in the harbor and the city of Cannes far below combined with a profusion of stars to make this a romantic setting. There were some fifty people at dinner, most of them men, and they typically chose to talk to me about their eye troubles or their need for new glasses, making it for me more like a busman's holiday than an elegant dinner party.

When we had finished our dolmas, followed by a curried chicken conglomeration of eggplant and rice patties and I do not know what-all-else, it was entertainment time. Our host invited Townley and me to sit next to him on the stone wall, looking back across the courtyard toward his enormous chateau. As we waited there to find out what was up, we heard a distant sound of rhythmic clicking, slow at first, then picking up tempo. It stopped, then started again, louder and faster as it was joined by some kind of reed instrument combined with the beats of a hand-struck drum and bursts of tambourine shivers. Soon a full-bodied, black-haired beauty appeared from behind the chateau and undulated into the courtyard, slowly dancing to the recorded music. Unrushed, uninhibited, surely untamed.

Over a spangled costume, she was loosely ensconced in veils, one of which partially covered her head and none of which did much to hide her magnificent body. She danced barefoot, with anklets of strung coins that made soft metallic sounds as her castanets defined the action and the spirited passion of her performance. So exotic, so Old World! She had a partly open, full-lipped mouth, golden skin and dark eyes enlarged by a heavy surround of kohl, used for centuries throughout the East to transfigure the organs of sight into organs of sexual attraction. I was unable to look away from her while my host maintained a constant chatter into my left ear, oblivious to my distraction.

No one could suspect then that those doctors were living at the threshold of the fastest and most inclusive advances in science in mankind's history, or that medicine would soon be moving from manual to automatic, from simple systems to complex alternatives, and—from forthcoming intrusions of business and law—to a decrease in medicine's self-determination. But not since Hippocrates had doctoring been awarded such an elevated position in society as it was receiving in Baltimore, Boston, Philadelphia and a few other leading medical centers in the 1930s.

A theatrical producer might have seen those white-clad men as spot-lit actors on an otherwise bleak stage. They were fully aware that they were eye-catching standouts in the institution that dominated the neighborhood. More direct lighting would have revealed a contrasting cast of darker-skinned characters swarming across the background of row houses and streets that stretched for miles on all sides of the hospital's enclave, essentially living out on the house steps and streets in the sulfurous summer evenings, crowded into the houses when the weather changed. From that great multitude of Baltimoreans came and went the hospital's pedestrian patients, moving with the deliberate caution of sickness, age, or both, to *their* hospital, their sole source of care, the only collection of large brick buildings for at least a mile in every direction. Little could they realize how essential their role was in creating the greatness of that institution. An abundant population of local patients was as necessary to the teaching hospital as was wind to power the few remaining classic schooners in the nearby harbor.

Of course, it is also true that the hospital provided patient care for the needy community. Either way, it was a successful symbiotic relationship, without tensions or anger. The cluster of white medical families was safe and sound, nestled against the black multitude of Baltimore's inner city. There was no violence between these rarely introduced neighbors. We lived front to back, with the white folks out front on Wolfe Street and the others clustered in houses connected by alleys on the far side of our backyards. It would be some time before any racial tensions would surface in Baltimore and even then it was almost never between medical families and their black neighbors.

By the 1930s, Johns Hopkins was often affectionately referred to as the "Medical Mecca" by admirers up and down the Atlantic seaboard—although possibly not as far north as Boston, where Harvard University had its own sanctum sanctorum in the medical school that had been established even before Hopkins and remains to this day either the first or the second most famous medical complex in America, depending on where you come from.

For the Baltimore intelligentsia, at least, the senior physicians at Johns Hopkins had names that were the city's equivalent of opera stars, orchestra conductors, leading actors—or names of contemporaries such as Aldous Huxley, John Maynard Keynes, Franklin Roosevelt, Mahatma Gandhi, and John Barrymore. Such was the power granted to the early Hopkins medical idols. I refer to such doctors as William Osler, William H. Welch, William S. Halsted, Harvey Cushing, William H. Wilmer, Walter E. Dandy, J. Whitridge Williams. The list goes on. For the medical profession, those were god-equivalents, with clinical medicine as their principal skill and teaching and research as their unique characteristic. I know from many evenings of chat with my great Aunt Lilian whose husband, Dr. Lewelllys Barker succeeded Osler, that although these men may have appeared as aloof if not haughty to the general public, to medical academia they were almost sacrosanct and, without exception, overflowing with the most recent knowledge of a flowering profession. They were the beacons of their school—and they held no false modesty as to the importance of that role.

My graduation from fetus to infant arrived at four in the morning in a Hopkins delivery room on August 16, 1930. The nine months of gestation had been a breeze—for me, that is. No maternal distresses or excesses, just laid-back, first-class incubation until it came time to go out on my own. The chairman of the Department of Obstetrics, Dr. Whitridge Williams, who was my mother's obstetrician, announced to her that her second-born was a boy. He then sent word to my father that he had a son. As a physician-in-training, my father had requested, but was denied, being present in the delivery room for the actual delivery. The only male in attendance was Dr. Williams himself. Not even male orderlies were allowed in the vicinity of "giving birth." According to hearsay, Dr. Williams grabbed me by the head with his forceps and pulled me into the world, promptly delivering a routine sharp slap on my rump. That was the technique he taught his students as essential in getting the lungs to start fully functioning if the baby was not yet crying. It may seem a shame to have to start life under protest but it is probably good for everyone to be forced to raise some dander, even on Day One.

Mid-summer was sweltering in Baltimore; even the tarred black roads characteristically softened from their own sweat. There was no air conditioning. Instead of refrigerators, there were iceboxes laden with huge chunks of ice delivered by a man wearing a rubber shoulder pad and carrying a gigantic ice tong. Our wall-mounted telephone was on a party line extended from the hospital. Ford's Model T's had only preceded by a few years the cars that were honking and chugging on the streets, and flat tires were a predictable part of almost every lengthy motor trip.

The Paton family of four—my older sister, Joan, my parents and I—lived on Wolfe Street across from the hospital compound in a narrow, three-story brownstone that was virtually identical to the neighboring houses, also occupied by married interns and residents and their families. The houses' ubiquitous white front steps were constructed from piled up rectangular marble slabs, once ballast for empty cargo ships that had sailed from Europe to Baltimore to pick up American exports. The front doors were at the top of those stairs, well above the sidewalk. There were three pairs of windows on the houses' fronts, and their flat roofs were covered in tar paper, with stove pipes and other hardware jutting out above the coping. On Mondays, there were full clotheslines on all the roofs, missing only the doctors' white suits, which were washed and starched by the hospital laundry.

Our family had a domestic staff consisting of three women: Virginia, a pleasantly plump black cook; Goldie, a black housemaid with a prominent gold front tooth; and Betty, a white nursemaid who cared for my older sister Joan and me for the five years she was with us. Mother was what baseball calls a "utility infielder;" she could fill in for most jobs when they were vacated by illness or vacations, except for cooking, which was her Waterloo. She also did the clothing and the grocery shopping for the family. Fathers in those days did not share the daily minutiae of bringing up children, and our's certainly didn't. Nor did our mother often have to cope with what was euphemistically termed "changing the linens." When necessary, I was simply handed over to the nurse for cleaning, powdering and rewrapping. The cotton diapers were washed, then hung out to dry on the roof or strung across the backyard.

When I was growing up, African-Americans in Baltimore were called—and called themselves—"Negroes." My maternal grandparents, however, referred to them as "darkies," and their children as "dear little piccaninnies." I hate to think how those good people referred to us but there were no race riots, and the city was more at risk from its white inebriates than from its poverty-stricken blacks. In fact, those who worked in my family were held in high affection and they knew it. My parents bore responsibility for their illnesses and misfortunes, along with their basic needs.

Joan and I grew up in those early years with the comfortable monotony of the usual milestones, closely attended by our pediatrician. He was as modern as one could get in those days. For example, he was opposed to breast feeding, instead ordering bottles of boiled, fortified cow's milk and boiled water, to be sucked through sterilized rubber nipples. Little did it matter that babies throughout the world flourished on mother's milk and tap water—or lake water, or river water, for that matter.

Our nurse, Betty Foerster, was our warden but also our advocate for any wants that were considered reasonably within the range of indulgent upbringing. She favored the second child with a weenie stem that constituted his man-sized birthright and who sought the spotlight like a moth on hormones. There definitely was some extra indulgence extended to the only child likely to assume the family's medical mantle, for girls in the 1930s were groomed to become wives—perhaps mid-wives—but only rarely physicians. My older sister graciously yielded the advantages of her seniority on her way to becoming the sibling saint whom everyone would recognize as the perfect child, patiently watching her brother's antics and mimicry or whatever it took to steal the show. Betty monitored our meals,

despite the intent of President Woodrow Wilson in 1912 to see "justice done to the colored people in every matter," things had not worked out that way. In the 1930s, the Negro vote wasn't even being counted in the South, and in the North, their participation in voting was still rudimentary.

Despite the recent Great Depression, due to America's growing prominence internationally there existed a mood of commercial optimism, scientific expectancy, and an almost palpable sense of growing national satisfaction. Women were still limited in what they could do in the workplace, however. For example, Pan American Airways, also known as "Juan Trippe's airline," began its soon-to-be-famous, lengthy-but-luxurious seaplane flights from San Francisco to Hawaii, but it would be another14 years before "air stewardesses" (always young and glamorous) were hired by Pan Am, owing to the perceived risks of long flights and a dearth of hotel rooms for single women.

Our family was not only venturing into the spunky environment of showy Manhattan but also taking a big step up the social staircase—that is, if one measures "up" by wealth, power, and—damnable word—exclusivity. We learned to say "to-mah-tow" instead of "to-may-tow" and were exposed to the lilt-deprived intonation of eastern lockjaw, spoken with clenched teeth and a thrust jaw and very present on the upper East Side during that period. Shortly after we moved into an apartment in a high-rise on Park Avenue at 75th Street, a succession of well-turned-out women—some wives of affluent patients and some friends of the family—came to call, wearing white gloves and leaving calling cards if my mother was not at home. Such a call had to be returned in kind, of course.

Our name was soon included in the New York Social Register, which in those days implied entrance into the chic Old Money-Old Family circle—society's Eastern Establishment--that permitted a few borderline candidates without intrinsic prestigious wealth to identify with them under certain conditions. The métier and character of the breadwinner had to be well-respected; the family had to have substantial local roots in the region; and its behavior by reputation and social performance had to reflect "good breeding." Though these prerequisites might have come straight out of an 18th-century comedy of manners, and though it was, in effect, a caste system—one that was not much written about in America's early twentieth century--the unwritten rules existed, paradoxical though they were to the city's increasing modernization.

My mother possessed not only the requisite Manhattan roots but also the social graces that made our family welcomed additions to the circle, and a medical doctor was no threat to any of the captains of industry or Wall Street. Helen and Townley Paton, like their parents, were Republicans and were resolutely opposed to Roosevelt's government—a position shared by the majority of their influential new friends on Manhattan's Upper East Side. Political like-mindedness was as useful in their adaptation to their new surroundings as was the selection of clothes, the location of housing, enrolling their children in the "right" schools, and introductions to the wielders of social power.

Although not "churchy" people, both my parents were from Protestant—Episcopalian and Presbyterian—families, which qualified them as WASPS. It apparently did not matter that my mother's remarkably capable father, Frederick L. Meserve, had begun life too poor to afford college until he could earn the money to pay his own tuition. He did that by becoming a land surveyor in Colorado and, later, a draftsman for the Elks Hotel in Colorado Springs. Neither he nor others in the immediate family had money, but both grandfathers were successes in non-financial ways. Stewart Paton, my father's father, was a neurologist-turned-psychiatrist. After medical training at Columbia University in New York, he studied and did laboratory research in Germany and Italy, later writing books, consulting, and serving as a student counselor on the campuses of first Princeton, then Yale and Columbia. The Paton family was "middle class, medical" and I would contend that the "medical" designation had a somewhat higher ranking than "legal" or "intellectual" at that moment in history, so great was the level of appreciation and admiration for the medical profession then, and for a couple of decades to follow.

The moneyed population—especially the Old Money-Old Family segment—became the staple of my father's referral practice. His office was fashionably located at 927 Park Avenue, at 80th Street.

Professor Wilmer delivered an astonishingly heavy flow of patients from Baltimore and elsewhere, often prominent New Yorkers who had seen him in consultation in Baltimore and accepted his advice to have one of his own trainees in New York assume their further eye care. My father's first-class training, fine surgical results and agreeable personality led to a burgeoning private practice in a matter of months. He saw all fellow physicians and their families free of charge, and treated many poor people without a fee. Such courtesies were expected of doctors in that era, and most could well afford to offer them.

My dad's fellow trainees in ophthalmology began to tease him about his "carriage trade" practice. One old friend even telephoned the office and in a disguised voice said he was the millionaire and philanthropist, J. Pierpont Morgan, Jr., and that he wanted an eye examination as soon as possible.

My father responded politely, "Certainly, Mr. Morgan, I would be glad to see you at any time. I'll work you into my schedule when you arrive."

Hearing that bit of gratuitous hat-doffing, my father's friend burst out laughing and told my father that he was taking himself entirely too seriously. They had a good laugh and a chat about old times, then set a date to have lunch.

Not long thereafter, my father got a similar call. "Dr. Paton, this is Pierpont Morgan. I have been referred by Professor Wilmer in Baltimore. I have a problem I hope you can help me with as soon as possible. My horse in Connecticut has injured her eye and it's left her with a cataract. She needs cataract surgery and Wilmer thought you were the right man for the job."

Dad was not to be fooled again. "Get off it! If you're Morgan, I'm the Tooth Fairy."

There was silence on the other end of the line. Then, "In that case, maybe extracting a tooth would be more to your liking than removing a cataract."

Something about his tone made my father realize he was talking to the real J. Pierpont Morgan. Hastily apologizing, he made arrangements for the cataract surgery, with a veterinarian administering the anesthesia.

My mother, too, found an active life in New York. She became an enthusiastic, non-credentialed interior decorator by studying magazines and books about design while also befriending one of the city's leading decorators, Walter Johnson. He was a bachelor of unusual charm, who sang annually as a lead in the Gilbert and Sullivan operettas put on by the Blue Hill Troop—an amateur company made up of lawyers, businessmen, artists and others with time in the evening for practice and a love of singing on stage. Our duplex apartment on the 7th and 8th floors of 823 Park Avenue became a beautiful, rather formal, but very comfortable place in which to live and entertain.

In addition to decorating, my mother loved stylish clothes. Designer garb was generally beyond a doctor's budget but this did not faze her in the least. We had a cook, a refugee recently arrived from Central Europe who lived in our apartment with her two fine daughters who were in their twenties and unable to speak English. They needed employment and they knew how to sew. Mom helped them get jobs as seamstresses at Mainbocher, one of the most prominent designers of women's clothes in America. The girls learned all the requirements and tricks of the Mainbocher house and reproduced at home the designer's dresses, suits and jackets for my mother, using material that she bought at fabric stores. She became a notably well-dressed woman. Pretty, poised, slender and joyful, my mother had warmth and charm that made her the family's drawing card, while my Dad was the family ace.

Money was not abundant enough to support a New York lifestyle that included a domestic staff of two employees and private school for two children. As a result, my mother decided to become a shop owner. She opened a business called Helen Paton Wool Luxuries on the second floor of a building on the northeast corner of Madison Avenue and 60th Street. Every article in the store was made of high-quality English wool, including throws, small blankets and booties. To advertise her business, Mom's sister, Dorothy Meserve Kunhardt — who, before becoming a successful Civil War co-author with her father, wrote popular children's books, including *Pat the Bunny,* which was one of the first books to use interactive elements—designed and created a flyer to be mailed to existing and potential customers.

told me that Mr. Duques had called to say that he would be too busy to continue the lessons.

I was stricken, and even more so when I learned what he had really said: "Mrs. Paton, I am a professional musician and, like many musicians, I have to give lessons to make ends meet. However, as much as I need the work, I decided after your son left my studio that I could not proceed with someone who has absolutely no sense of notes or scale, no ability to hear incorrectness, no gift for music--no ear, Mrs. Paton, no ear at all."

Thus my musical career came to an abrupt end.

CHAPTER THREE

I became a fledgling preppy while attending The Buckley School in New York, a two-block walk from home. The dress code was brown leather shoes, dark blue knee stockings, grey flannel shorts, a white shirt that buttoned into the shorts, a dark blue tie, a dark blue flannel jacket, and a dark blue beanie with a white B above a diminutive visor.

Buckley was a fine school, still is. My teachers were savvy middle-aged women. Athletics consisted of either class exercises in the basement gym, or volleyball on the caged-in roof, or football and track on Randall's Island, reached by bus. City boys in my day had cuts and bruises all over their arms and legs from sidewalk tussles, and our school clothes caught plenty of the action, chronically in need of repair before being outgrown. We were in a continual state of frustration from the constricted quarters of our lives--not being permitted to ride a bicycle on the streets or having a backyard at home for climbing trees or hitting balls.

When I was seven, a patient of my father's, Lydia Field Emmet, one of the foremost portrait painters in the country, suggested a barter between professionals: If Dad would commission one portrait, she would do a second one free of charge in return for his surgical services. Joan's portrait was decided upon, with mine to follow. The portraits were to be done in oil, each over a period of three consecutive weeks of afternoon sittings in the painter's studio. The painting of Joan turned out fine—a beautiful work of art showing a graceful young girl in a tea-dipped pima cotton party dress with a wide blue sash. The job of painting me probably wasn't easy for Ms. Emmet, but it was total agony for me. Sitting still was close to impossible, but even that was not the worst part. The worst part was the clothes.

I came to the studio wearing my school clothes and was told to sit down on a rectangular piano stool, whereupon the artist placed a piece of brown velvet corduroy over my shoulder and across my lap.

In 1938, when Joan was ten and I was eight, our sister Pamela was born, a wonderful surprise for my parents and a welcome addition to

our family.   More quickly than seemed possible, she grew into a beautiful teenager with a fun-loving disposition and a captivating friendliness that won over even the stodgiest of acquaintances. She was our parents' bond with youth, their amulet of family love—invoking just by

her existence the coziness parents thrive upon as older children begin to go their separate ways. I cannot recall a single moment when Pam was cross, moody, disobedient or unhappy. We all loved her immensely, each in our own way, but she was especially adored by our Dad.

St. James was a beautiful spot: sixteen wooded acres on a bluff high above Stony Brook Harbor. The white clapboard house was set back from the bluff by a small field, with a lawn bordering the house on two sides. There were six bedrooms, two of which were for "the help." After several years, my parents had a tennis court built where the scrub oak woods had been. The court became the recreational and social focus of our lives in St. James. Many neighbors and visiting friends joined the almost continuous daily play on the tennis court. Gussie Moran, the popular tennis star, twice came to practice on our court. It was she who introduced sex appeal to the sport by wearing underpants with lace trim that showed beneath her daringly short shorts, generating no end of newsprint and generating many new tennis fans. It was on that court that I learned to play tennis well enough to qualify for subsequent school teams.

As idyllic as those summers were, there were some drawbacks. There were no females my age in the vicinity and the few boys who were around lived too far away to permit much socializing. I had summer jobs as soon as I could ride a bicycle on the main road the few miles to Long Island Sound, where I raked the stony beach at the Nissequogue Point Beach Club, and tended the umbrellas and chairs. Home life was strictly enforced; together we gardened, painted the row boat, polished the car, raked the driveway, watered the lawn and played tennis.

In 1943, with the war in the Pacific at full pitch, Dad volunteered for military service, signing up for an Army commission as Major. That appointment fell through when he flunked a physical exam, the result of finding evidence of potentially active pulmonary tuberculosis on chest X-rays. But by the time he discovered that he would have to remain in New York, both Joan and I had already been admitted to boarding schools in order to permit my mother to join my father at the base in California where he'd expected to be sent; instead, once we had gone off to school and his military commission was denied, they moved to a smaller apartment on 79th Street. I was leaving Buckley at thirteen and Joan was leaving her school, Brearley, at fifteen. She entered Miss Porter's School in Farmington, Connecticut, where she did well, being everyone's friend and no one's critic.

With my parents, I visited a succession of the aforementioned boarding schools for boys that were so popular with the Eastern Establishment but decided instead on The Hill School in Pennsylvania. The other schools—particularly Groton, St. Mark's and St. Paul's—were relatively small and accommodated almost exclusively boys whose Establishment parents believed that no other schooling was acceptable for their offspring. There were far more applications than places for qualified applicants. It was rumored that upon learning a newborn child was male, the first thing an Establishment father did was enter the lad in one of those elite schools, even before going off to the hospital to congratulate his wife.

As much as I had come to appreciate the privileges of life among the fine, intellectually sharp, widely traveled persons of the Establishment, something told me it was time to edge away from the eastern cloister. The Hill School had no airs and few heirs, although some of the boys did have fathers who had been students there. It was for boys only, true then of almost every Eastern boarding school of

any worth. The Hill was located in a Pennsylvania town called Pott-
stown, after the Potts family who founded the school. On the fringes
of an industrial city, it was five hours from New York by car or by
two trains, with a changeover in Philadelphia. I had never heard of
The Hill and it offered no trace of the verdant campuses characteristic of the New England boarding schools but I felt being there would
suit me just fine.

The Hill's total enrollment was approximately 450 students, most
from Pennsylvania but some from various surrounding, and a few distant, states. Many came from blue collar families, but there were
no African-Americans or other minorities represented that I can recall. There were, however, some Jewish students, which may not have
been true of the Buckley enrollment or of the New England boarding
schools in the early 1940s. I never knew who was or was not Jewish at
The Hill because it was a subject that never came up. It did not occur
to me at the time that the unbreakable requirement of daily Christian
chapel attendance must have been difficult for them to comply with,
but I don't recall chapel waivers ever being issued.

The school campus was quite compact. In addition to several large
classrooms and dormitory buildings, there was an unusually large
gymnasium. On the first day of school, new boys were issued their
fall athletic equipment, which included their first "jock," a landmark
acquisition on the order of the first razor, but even more reassuringly
glandular. The housing for most of the new boys was in several old
clapboard cottages at one end of the campus, where they were billeted
with stringent rules about cleanliness and noise. As school initiates,
every new boy was required to wear a black beanie (skull cap, or dink)
when outdoors, for the entire first year. That beanie was almost identical to the one I had worn in my years at Buckley and would wear as
a freshman in college.

Every new boy was to be tested for possible selection for the chapel choir. I told the choirmaster up front that singing was not my
forte but he was adamant. "Sorry, son, you have to be tested." One
afternoon the new boys were lined up and, one by one, our voices
were appraised. The choirmaster sat at a piano and played a few
starting notes to the hymn he had selected for me, "Nearer My God

to Thee." He gave me a nod as he started to play the melody, my cue to begin singing. As soon as I burst out with the first few words of the lyric, he lifted his hands from the keyboard and stared at me as if I had profaned the Lord. "Thank you, that will be all." For the remaining five years I was at The Hill, if I was crammed into a pew in chapel with a serious singer I would clam up totally. To have to stand silently mouthing words when everyone else is belting their lungs out is thoroughly dispiriting but more humanitarian than the alternative.

Another requirement of the school was the daily "work-job." This referred to a forty-five minute period following breakfast when each student had a job assigned him, such as sweeping the halls of a dormitory, keeping the walks clean on the campus, drying the silverware after meals, setting the dining room tables, rolling the tennis courts in season, cleaning up the classrooms before classes started in the morning, and on and on. The faculty was assigned as monitors to see that the jobs were done well and demerits were handed down to those who were absent or were out of line in one way or another. To my knowledge, none of the other schools I had visited had any such menial work requirement, nor do they to this day. Yet, in retrospect, it was probably one of the most valuable disciplinary experiences a school could offer.

The Hill was delightful in most aspects, but on the down side, it was an eight-months-a-year imprisonment without girls. The popular rumor that the school's milk was laced with saltpeter to quell our hormonal longings was probably accurate in the early 1940s, although such milk dosing was later determined to be ineffective. My parents had always avoided the slightest mention of human sexual behavior; they did not consider it their job to teach us the facts of life. My somewhat taciturn father was a modest man with Scottish blood who disliked being seen with bare feet, even within the family; so in childhood I had to resort to hearsay in the playgrounds for information about anything relating to sex. At the adolescent level I learned from tales told by boastful classmates freely spiced with fantasy and wishful thinking. Biology teachers--all-male "masters," as we knew them—had a way of making sex seem about as thrilling as amoebas in division.

I don't want to embarrass my classmates by naming them but Baker and I are in all four pictures; Janie at far left, below

Often my grades were high enough for the honor roll; to achieve this required as much effort as I could put out without being labeled "a grind," the antonym for "hanging loose," the image a BMOC (big man on campus) would want to portray. Walking the thin line between a teacher's idea of an outstanding student and a student's idea of being in vogue was a subconscious balancing act. As my studies intensified, continuing to maintain high grades became increasingly challenging for me. In particular, I found math difficult and geometry and algebra a trial, and I was a decidedly slow reader. I began to realize that the other students could absorb content more quickly than I could. Unlike them, I had to formulate each printed word, unable to take the short cut of having visual images from the page go directly into comprehension. It would be years before I identified the dysfunction that was holding me back as a moderate degree of dyslexia.

Science was my favorite subject. Once in science class, our teacher asked us what it was about science that appealed to us—expecting answers like "dissecting frogs" or "looking at Mars through a telescope." I told him that I liked science because it stimulated my imagination. To explain what I meant, I described the plot of a mystery story I hoped to write some day that was based on something he had taught us about the earth's magnetic field. To illustrate the effects of magnetic fields, he had said that in the northern hemisphere toilets flushed in a clockwise direction, whereas in the southern hemisphere, the water left the bowl in a counter-clockwise fashion. My novel had to do with a hero held hostage by Interpol criminals being able to determine to what part of the world he had been taken simply by observing the direction of the flush in a toilet once he had arrived there. Recently I read that directional toilet flushes are not as reliable as my fiction assumed but for me at the time science was providing an enjoyable flight of fancy.

Along with my newfound friend, Jim Baker, who came to The Hill for the last two years of high school, I played on the varsity tennis team. The future Secretary of State was not only a steady player but an innate competitor and he invariably beat me soundly. He and I, remarkably enough, looked so similar that people tended to get

transplantation. I loved seeing my smiling, modest, soft-spoken father being received like a king among foreign cohorts, especially since he had had some rough years enduring professional brickbats for an undertaking that mandated that he take an aggressive position for it to survive.

Dad had founded the world's first eye bank at the Manhattan Eye and Ear Hospital four years earlier, in 1944.* At that time, he was one of only two ophthalmic surgeons doing any significant number of corneal graft procedures in the United States, limited in those operations by the scarcity of donor tissue. Corneal transplants had been tried, using corneas from various animal species grafted into other animals, and sometimes into humans, but none of those operations was successful—and that remains true today.

My father concluded that some system had to be devised to facilitate the procurement and delivery of human donor eye tissue so corneal transplant surgery—technically called "keratoplasty"—could be performed often to take care of the thousands of patients with otherwise incurable corneal blindness.

A precedent of considerable influence upon eye banking was blood banking, which had been developed for blood transfusions in the Spanish Civil War in 1936. Blood banking introduced to the public the concept of giving human tissue to benefit those in dire need. But it had a distinct advantage over a bank for a "formed" tissue in that it did not require either a dead donor or the removal of a vital organ. At the time Dad conceived of an eye bank, there were no other formed tissue banks in existence.

---

* Previously, I have written a more complete tribute to my father, referenced as the final listing on page 294.

Doctors in those days were not accustomed to lecturing the public about needs related to health care; traditionally, they were expected to be professionally discreet. Moreover, if an individual was asked by a corneal surgeon to permit the donation of a deceased relative's eyes, it was unlikely that the person's clergyman or rabbi would support "desecrating" the dead.

So my father came up with an ingenious plan. Thirty miles north of Manhattan was the notorious Sing-Sing prison, located just off the eastern shore of the Hudson River. From 1940 through 1944, the prison executed 77 inmates, all by electrocution in "the chair." During those years, my father arranged to have the superintendent's office notify him when an execution was scheduled, always at night. He would drive up-river to the prison and, with the assistance of clergy, get a signed consent from the condemned prisoner. Then, after the execution, he would perform the eye removals and temporarily store the eyeballs in our refrigerator overnight, once leading to a ghoulish household incident when the cook discovered two human eyes in a bottle alongside the cocktail olives.

While continuing to perform corneal transplants, my father was struggling to figure out how to augment donor sourcing, to work out a means of temporary storage and to systematize the distribution of the tissue. In the absence of any funding for staff salary, he began enlisting volunteers. However, not long after the eye-bank office was established but still struggling without sufficient administrative leadership, a Mrs. Aida Breckenridge entered Dad's life. While suffering from advanced glaucoma, she had been a patient of Dr. Wilmer's in Washington, D.C., and was credited with not only suggesting, but helping to raise the financing for The Wilmer Institute at Johns Hopkins. She was a widowed society woman in her sixties who became a patient of my father's upon moving to Manhattan. And when her dwindling fortune was in need of replenishment, she signed on as the employed work horse of the eye bank's development and promotion. She was intelligent, capable, energetic, demanding, outspoken--and very difficult to deal with for everyone except for my dad, whom she greatly admired. She deserves much credit for the early success of the bank.

as instructed) was an amusing and congenial person at that point in
her subsequently disappointing life, although her British accent was
so extreme that I could scarcely understand what she said. (My next
and only other meeting with the princess would be at the home of a
socialite in Houston thirty-three years later, at which time she was
showing serious signs of the alcoholism that grips some who are tor-
mented by the monitoring of public limelight and the proscriptions
imposed upon royal lives.)

From London we flew to Iran, arriving at the Teheran airport
where we were met by the ophthalmologist and close advisor to
the Shah who was to be our gracious host for our extended visit.
In later years he was considered for an appointment as Minister of
Health of Iran.   However, subsequent regime change would not
only put an end to his career but his life at risk. He and his family fled the country. I am going to give him a pseudonym, Ahmed
Masoor. The Masoors, when last heard from about a decade ago,
were living as immigrants in the United States, but Ahmed had
severed his connection with all who knew him as a high-ranking
medical doctor serving the Shah. Letters to his address are returned, rather than forwarded, and his phone number no longer ex-
ists. Some allies of the Shah still live in fear of reprisals, even in this
country.

Prior to our arrival, Prince Shams, a socially powerful Iranian
ophthalmologist with royal blood, had announced that he had discovered a cure for trachoma. Other ophthalmologists in Iran had taken
exception to his claim, while having to be careful about contradicting
a man of much power and governmental influence. My dad had been
sent to Iran to be The Decider as to whether or not the Prince's cure
was effective. We were never to meet Prince Shams, who was out of
the country while we were there, but we knew he had recommended
that medical offices and clinics across the country purchase an electrical instrument that his trachoma cure required. (Only later were we
told that he would receive a percentage of the price of each of these
instruments sold.)

We started our visit by watching a demonstration of how his machine worked in a Teheran clinic for children with trachoma. Prince

Shams' treatment consisted of turning over the upper eyelid and rub-
bing its undersurface with the ball tip of an electric cautery probe,
thereby breaking up the follicles (tiny clumps of inflammatory cells)
and allegedly killing the organism causing the disease. A drop of
topical anesthetic was ap-
plied to the lid but it did
not do much to reduce
the pain of the treatment.
The children had to be
restrained by the clinic's
assistants, although they
withstood the pain re-
markably well. After the
cauterization, their eyes
were dressed with a sulfa
ointment and both eyes
were covered by a head
bandage for no less than
an hour. During that time, the gauze bandage became blood-soaked
from the bleeding eyelids. When the bleeding ceased, the eyes were
uncovered and the children sent home with this instruction to the
parents: *If there is any further sign of trachoma, such as pain, redness, discharge or even itching, the child is to be returned for a second treatment.*

Needless to say, very few children were brought back to those
clinics. Prince Shams kept a record of the number of children treated,
and since hardly any returned, his data indicated a remarkable rate
of success. However, it was my father's finding that any benefit that
might have come from the painful Shams treatment was derived from
the use of the sulfa ointment that was applied after it was over. As
time passed, other surface-applied antibiotic ointments and eye drops
proved to be curative for trachoma when applied in the pre-scarring
stages of the disease. Shams was a sham in our report, and to my
knowledge my father never heard a peep from him in rebuttal or con-
cession.

The remainder of our visit was given over to recording an estimate of the prevalence of trachoma in all regions of the country,

except across the wide desert to the East, which we did not cross. In some locations, such as the city of Dezful in the southwest corner of the country, people of all ages suffered from the discomfort and ultimately blinding effects of trachoma. For several decades, that city was referred to as "the city of the blind."

Our itinerary took us north to the Caspian, where we each consumed what today would be $500 worth of gray caviar as breakfast snacks eaten by the spoonful, and to Tabriz, where some of the great rugs of Persia have been woven. In the South, we saw the oil storage tanks and docks of Kermanshah, and in the more central regions, we visited many small villages and even tented clans of migratory people. For ten days I was laid up in the Park Hotel in Teheran with dengue fever—a viral infection also called "breakbone fever" because of its painfulness in the acute phase--but my recovery was uneventful. Then back to the ancient cities of Abadan, Isfahan, and Shiraz, taking time to visit King Darius' tomb, walk around the first known polo field, and photograph some of the beautiful mosques, with their blue-tiled domes and lofty minarets.

At the end of the summer, Dr. Masoor arranged for my father to submit a verbal report directly to the Shah. Word came from the palace that the Shah would meet us at a particular time in a palace where he received visitors from the world over. We were to appear in morning coats, which meant long black formal coats, striped trousers and an appropriate shirt and tie, not to mention black shoes. Dad had been annoyed enough by our having to take tuxedos to London (which we sent home as soon as we left London), and he was not willing to rent fancy suits in Iran for a quick visit with the sovereign. I myself would have rented an ermine cape and a cavalry sword had it been necessary. Happily, a compromise was reached by Dr. Masoor. We met the Shah informally in his office in a different palace, which to us looked grand enough for a coronation. He was only twenty-nine years of age, straight and erect, warm and welcoming. He was wearing a rust-colored, double-breasted business suit, and we were in our seersucker finery. After shaking hands, my father began his oral report. Evidently the bad news about Prince Sham's "medical misconception" was taken in diplomatic stride, without any fuss raised that we heard about. It was a relaxed, almost cozy conversation, and the Shah's polished manners and thoughtful compliments of my father's work led me to believe he was truly a King of Kings; but we were to learn that life for kings is often not a walk in the park.

While in Iran we had seen no signs of secret police, nor had we heard about imprisoned patriots or mob violence. There was certainly no indication then that the Shah would one day be overthrown, that he would contract a deadly blood disease, that his health would be further endangered by lack a of cooperation between French and American physicians, that renowned heart surgeon Dr. Michael De-Bakey would operate upon him in Cairo, and that he would die at sixty years of age —by then a broken and disillusioned man whose country would become an arch enemy of our country.

There is a postscript to our visit to Iran. When the Shah came to the United States on several occasions in the 1950s, he stayed at the Waldorf Astoria Hotel in New York. He had various eye complaints that led to perhaps ten, even as many as fifteen, visits with my dad. His chief of household would telephone my father's office for an appointment. Always the Shah was seen promptly, no matter what the patient schedule was, and the examinations and treatments were pro bono. There was even a Thanksgiving Day when his aide called from Hyde Park, where the Shah was visiting Mrs. Roosevelt, to say that he wished to be seen and he would be arriving in an hour. I remember how that annoyed my mother, who was always huffy about any perceived acquiescence to special privilege, especially on major holidays.

One day the Shah's aide asked my father what the Shah owed him for his services. My father said he would have to give that some thought, punting until he could talk to my mother, for he knew she would get a kick out of helping him decide what to charge. My mother reminded him of a story that had come down in Wilmer Institute lore back in Baltimore.

When the King of Siam (later Thailand) was operated on by Dr. Wilmer, Wilmer sent no bills for his services. Eventually, after many days of care, the King's chief of affairs asked Dr. Wilmer how much was owed. "Nothing! The King can do no wrong," proclaimed Dr. Wilmer, with a grand sweep of his arm. The man bowed and departed.

was generous in allowing other players and would-be players to try out boogie-woogie or popular tunes on his precious piano. One night while he was away and we were sleeping very soundly, a couple of loud, over-served pals arrived to use Dets's piano. One played as the other danced the Charleston in golf spikes on top of the piano. Dets never quite forgave us for sleeping through the mayhem. He went on to become a computer genius who, with his wife, Lynne, eventually turned into a homebody and happy grandfather.

W. Barnabas McHenry—who later became a noted patron and owner of museum-worthy art as a result of his earnings from his legal work for the *Readers' Digest*—was a man of acerbic wit, a fount of attack words designed to humble even the most accommodating of friends. But under that formidable armament lurked a pussy cat. He and Dets shared one of the two bedrooms, each just large enough to hold a double-decker bed and two small chests of drawers, plus a bedside desk and a clothes closet. They survived that arrangement for all four years. Barney married his college sweetheart, Bannie. And despite his terrible tongue, they managed to have three sons, a passel of grandchildren and a marriage that has lasted for well over fifty years. He is a dedicated, award-winning "green" lawyer and still a cherished friend.

My roommate was my friend from The Hill School, James A. Baker, III. He chose the lower bunk on Day One, maybe because he had an aversion to heights; but from that first day in our freshman year, as at The Hill, neither of us questioned who belonged where. Jim was the son of a Princeton graduate who was a crack Houston lawyer and an uncompromising disciplinarian. No one could have suspected that Jim was headed for national acclaim, but anyone could have predicted that he had the makings of a successful dynamo. Well before law school, he had a lawyer's certainty, a businessman's ability to bargain, and a statesman's persuasiveness.

Jim was an honors-level history major and an notable college athlete. He and I played on the undefeated Princeton freshman tennis team but, as in previous years, he consistently beat me—not only with stronger and better-placed shots but by using his inherent power of intimidation. We may have divided up a double-decker without argument, but we tended to be unobtrusively competitive. I was elected Vice President of the Senior Class. Jim could not have cared less about such a position but I cared: it gave me a notch he did not have—just as it had at The Hill. At the end of our second year, all four of us roommates were invited to join The Ivy Club—an undergraduate eating and social club—where I later served as Undergraduate Governor, while Jim served in the slightly lesser office of Undergraduate Treasurer. (There were two higher ranks that eluded both of us.) Ivy was once described by F. Scott Fitzgerald as "detached and breathlessly aristocratic," but by the time we got there it was in transit toward gaining a more egalitarian reputation, despite the air of sophistication provided by its silver candelabra and its multiple tables for billiards.

When we were at Princeton, as at The Hill, students were not allowed to have cars and television sets were not yet available. More significantly, females were not allowed in our rooms after a certain evening hour. Barney exempted himself from that rule from time to time, much to the inconvenience of his roommate, Dets, and to the consternation of the campus proctors who were guardians of the rules by night and day. Barney also did not see himself as subject to the regulation that forbade student cars on campus, and he occasionally drove us in the black Chevy he hid by parking it off-campus to New York's Greenwich Village, where at Eddie Condon's and similar dives the music was easy on the ears and bar girls easy on the eyes.

We were seventeen years too early for Princeton's eventual decision to admit females. In fact, even after women did become Princeton students in 1969, it was twenty-two years before the Ivy Club included them as eligible appointees—one of the last of the club holdouts. That unfairness to female students so distressed me that in 1970 I stopped paying graduate dues to the club. I felt that once women were accepted by the college, they most certainly were not second-class members of the student body and should have been eligible for admission to all of the eating clubs. In fact, I have never resumed paying graduate dues. Despite retaining great affection for the club, I'm too cheap to pay for a membership I never use, and so the history of the club's former rejection of female members became my excuse for the intentional inertia.

When in Bermuda with a Princeton rugby team he played on, Jim met his future wife, Mary Stuart McHenry (no relation to Barney), at a match with players from Yale. Years later, in 1970, with their four sons in school, Mary Stuart tragically died of cancer. Jim remarried and with his second wife, Susan, had a daughter who became a Princeton student and eventually a member of The Ivy Club.

Well before Jim became famous, he was unofficially my best friend, always in that non-political, non-religious, non-intellectual, even non-athletic, category of Top Dog. Decades ago, any remnant of competition with his career was torn to shreds as he began to be the power behind presidential thrones and was eventually recognized as one of the best minds in public service. Beyond what the public may know about him as a statesman of great integrity and obvious intelligence, he is trustworthy, loyal and quick-witted. His oldest son, James A. Baker IV, is my godson, one who realizes that "godchild" to me does not carry the connotation it might to a better observer of "churchiness." As I have progressively set aside basic religious conventions, Jim has become a devout Christian and thanks his wife for that awakening. I don't think he is the slightest bit disturbed by that gap between our spiritual convictions; it is just an esthetic variant between friends in a free-thinking country.

Of course I would like to believe that I was accepted to Princeton University entirely on my own merits. But I must admit that there might have been a few other factors involved, such as the fact that I was not in need of a scholarship; my father, grandfather and great-uncle were Princeton graduates; and there was even a plaque dedicated to my great-uncle David Paton in one of the arches on campus. That David Paton had been an Egyptologist, who willed his collection of books on hieroglyphics to the Princeton library. As for his brother, Stewart Paton, my psychiatrist grandfather "Popsie"—he served for approximately a decade as a member of the Princeton faculty and was well acquainted with President Woodrow Wilson (then president of Princeton). In addition, a close friend of Popsie's who was one of the greats of Hopkins medical history wrote this note to him: "Dear Paton, I thought I would not embarrass you, but I am quite sincere in saying that I am of the opinion that you would make an excellent president of Princeton, and if I were writing to anybody else I should say more on the subject. Very sincerely yours, (signed) William H. Welch. November 14, 1910."

Anyone with such university connections would have to wonder at times whether he might have been accepted as a legacy instead of a fully qualified applicant, which is not the reason one wants to be chosen. There was also the fact that--legacy or not--I needed to try harder than the average student, owing to my undiagnosed learning disability that made studying certain subjects especially difficult. In those days, dyslexia (when it was recognized) was viewed as a fixed disability without much remedy. I had only tested in the 23rd percentile in the SAT spelling test as applied to college applicants across the country. I still read words as if they were individually "spoken" in my head rather than just being absorbed into comprehension. That remains true to this day. Multiple choice examinations were difficult because I could not finish them in the time allotted for reading the problem and selecting the answer. Being a slow reader is like driving an old car; nothing makes it go faster and, if pushed to the limit, it becomes even more unreliable. Math, including algebra, was also uncommonly difficult. In fact, at Princeton, I required extended private tutoring in Basic Calculus, which was a medical school requirement.

What I have said thus far about having a moderate dyslexia may sound like a person resigned to his handicap and willing to make the best of it. But I had no idea what "the best of it" truly entailed. Eventually, long after my college years, I came to view my reading and math limitations not as a barely tolerable learning deficiency but as the primary mechanism I had for channeling ambition, leading to a form of creativity that comes from deductive reasoning. Today, a third or more of prominent, creative achievers acknowledge having dyslexia. For me, that brain-adjusted creativity was to become the most useful factor in propelling my career and, without it, I believe that my entire life's work would have attained less than half its value.

Without getting too technical, these are the basics: A brain is capable of making cerebral adjustments to develop strengths that compensate for flaws that can be circumvented. It is well-known that the left and right sides of a person's brain have different functions. A person with left brain dominance is likely to benefit from a sense of order, logical thinking and inductive reasoning—meaning the ability to assemble answers formed from a basis of information--producing, for example, accountants and engineers. Those with right brain dominance are more likely to be artists, musicians, or simply people having a fertile imagination combined with an understanding of the big picture. They are facile in deductive reasoning, in that they start by visualizing the goal and their brains work backward to identify whatever ingredients are needed to attain it. Since dyslexics are impaired in functions identified with the left brain, they are likely to favor the right brain. If someone like me, with a left brain moderately impaired by dyslexia, is determined not to rely on legacy for achievement, then his right brain's autopilot will maximize whatever potential it can uncover. The more ambition, the more creativity is likely to surface. What seems lacking in the literature about dyslexia is an explanation of its spectrum for, as with autism or with cerebral palsy, there can be a number of variables as to what brain functions are affected and to what degree they are impaired.*

Consciously developing creative achievement in a brain befuddled by dyslexia might enable others like me to take delight in what once might have seemed a frustrating impediment in their lives. Even if I did not understand what was occurring, it worked for me, so much so that by the end of freshman year, I was awarded the Class of 1883 English Prize related to creative writing. I wrote better than I could spell. But I continued to struggle with mathematics, eventually making just enough progress to keep my overall grade point average acceptable for entrance to medical school.

Albert Einstein was a distinguished scholar-in-residence at Princeton when I was a freshman student. I recall vividly his unprepossessing appearance as he sat in a chair in front of a student conference: the wild hair, shoes without socks and overgrown mustache accompanied by a gentle smile and kindly eyes. Einstein, creator of symbolic formulas and mind pictures, had done poorly in mathematics in school and later in life was determined to have been dyslexic. The power of his right brain was obviously ideally calibrated for the creativity that led to his world-shaking discoveries.

In my senior year, my most decisive creative endeavor up to that time may very well have been what got me into medical school. Princeton required all students to submit a senior thesis as a requirement for graduation. I had selected biology as a major because it sounded achievable and pre-medical. When it came time to write a thesis, my thesis professor, the eminent Dr. John Bonner, wanted his thesis students to write papers that could be considered for publication as a valid scientific contribution. That meant he would be looking for well-documented experimentation, preferably within his own field of special interest which was, unaccountably, slime molds, a subject in which he became the world's expert; in fact, in later years, he became affectionately known at Princeton as the Sultan of Slime.

---

* Thanks to functional cerebral imagining research, new information about dyslexia and its spectrum is being collected almost daily. Authorities may consider the explanation I have given to be over-simplified but what matters is the now rather widely accepted relationship dyslexia has to creativity in certain persons.

I had no idea how to go about writing a thesis about slime mold, or any other topic that would necessitate a facility in mathematics, combined with creative experimentation. Nothing came to mind that would fulfill the graduation requirement. Then, luckily, a brilliant, presumably left-brained, classmate and good friend, Paul Koontz, asked if I would collaborate with him in writing a joint thesis. He thought I might be able to figure out how to measure the meandering, brainless paths of slime mold slugs (collections of unicellular amoebas clumped together without any form of command center) as they traveled aimlessly around on the surface of agar in Petri dishes. We could photograph the tiny slugs and, by enlarging the pictures, obtain an accurate reading of their changes in size over a period of mindless migration across a path of agar, nutrition-free so that they would not be tempted to stop and graze. But how, Paul asked, could we measure those wiggly paths that were created during a precisely timed period of wandering?

My only contribution to the thesis was figuring out the answer to that question. I mounted the Petri dishes in front of an old-fashioned slide projector, so that the images of the slugs' paths appeared hugely enlarged on a screen some dozen feet away from the projector. These paths were then measured by a small, hand-held map mileage indicator used in those days for measuring distances on car maps, on sale for a buck at most filling stations. The little wheel at the base that was guided along the slug's path turned a larger wheel just above it, where there were units marked on a dial. I counted the number of wheel revolutions (and fractions thereof) for each slug's journey, and this information was matched to the size of the slug early and late, in its trek across the agar. It may not sound like rocket science, but it turned out that the speed of migration of each slug was in direct proportion to its size (determined by the number of constituent amoebas), and the speed diminished over time, as some of the amoebas were left behind in the slimy pathways. Our discovery, simple as it may sound, can be distilled to the statement that the speed of the slugs was dependent upon the number of constituent amoebas and not upon any possible surface layer of specialized amoebas. Therefore, all slug cells are created equal, just as Lincoln observed about people a good many years earlier without having to deal with hypotheses and mathematical formulas.

The guts of the paper is the mathematical discussion by my partner Paul Koontz regarding the "principle of similitude" and the fact that our slimy slugs' volume increased according to the cube of their linear dimensions, while their surfaces varied as the square. I had nothing to do with the interpretation of the data. Our professor was delighted; the thesis was given a high mark and eventually published. What's more, both of its contributing authors were accepted to the medical schools of their choice which, in my case, was Johns Hopkins.

Mathematics aside, years later, in 1985, I received an honorary degree from Princeton and, in 2005, I was given the Princeton Class of 1952 Distinguished Classmate Award, further proof that a so-called "handicap" such as dyslexia affecting words and numbers does not have to limit one's aspirations and achievements, especially if the proper collaboration is procured.

CHAPTER SIX

In June, 1952, after graduating from Princeton and before plunging into medical school at Johns Hopkins, I had a job driving two teenage boys, ages 15 and 16, all around the country to introduce them as thoroughly as possible to the physical wonders of the United States—the mountains, the seas, the great lakes, the forests, the deserts—plus the towns and cities, with their characteristic appearances and their contrasting populations. Thanks to their parents, it was an all-expense-paid trip lasting three months during which we drove 6,550 miles and for which I received a fee of $500. Neither of the boys was given to feasting his eyes on natural beauty, nor particularly enamored of guide books or talks by rangers and tour directors about points of interest. For me, those three months called for equanimity and vigilance, for each day involved chauffeuring, controlling, chaperoning and just plain withstanding two unrelated teenagers who were both traveling under duress. They had been classmates at one of Manhattan's well-known private schools and, owing to parents with summer agendas that did not include their boys, our America-First tour had been cooked up to keep them busy – and presumably happy.

Hardly had we driven through the Holland Tunnel en route to Chicago from Manhattan than Ethan, 16, and Jeff, 15 (pseudonyms), decided they not only disliked each other intensely but that their parents—one set Jewish, the other WASP--would also never dream of associating with one another. From Jeff's description, his Jewish parents sounded like country club habitués, addicted to sports and social boozing. They were in the process of getting a divorce and wanted their only child out of the way while the fur was flying at home and lawyers were preparing to do battle over the spoils of a considerable fortune. Their son was a short, pugnacious, athletic kid who was in the early throes of female fascination and had recently been kicked out of school for smoking.

When fall came, it was at last time to start learning my chosen profession. The prospect of stepping into human science was exhilarating, and the thought of returning to the city of my birth was another pleasant prospect. I had been invited to set up home life in Towson, a 15-minute drive from the medical school and hospital, with my widowed and almost stone-deaf great aunt, Mrs. Lewellys Barker, whose late husband had been Chairman of Medicine at Johns Hopkins after the departure of Sir William Osler. Eighty years old, Aunt Lilian needed someone to spend nights at her house and, for me, her copious memories, ongoing interest in medical affairs, and well-informed liberal opinions made her one of my favorite people from the start and to this day, long after her death. She was a heavy smoker, outraged that after it became acceptable for a woman to smoke on the streets of Moscow it was still not acceptable in Baltimore. She supported equal rights and the alternative lifestyle of gay men and women. She had severe arthritis yet rarely complained about anything. To follow her favorite baseball team, the Baltimore Orioles, she would turn up the volume on both the radio and the television. I could hear that cacophony of yelling broadcaster voices all too clearly while studying downstairs in Uncle Lewellys' office, surrounded by his books and his favorite pictures in the dim light of her economical 60-watt bulbs. When I could no longer stay awake, I climbed three floors to my assigned guestroom to lose consciousness until jarred awake by the alarm clock at a variable, but invariably early, hour.

The first day of medical school was spent largely in the anatomy lab, where there were a dozen narrow tables, each with a supine mummified body wrapped in cotton cloths. The room was filled with the penetrating, engulfing stench of formaldehyde. The students were divided alphabetically into groups of four, each team assigned to its own corpse. Dissecting gowns were distributed. Interestingly, we were not issued rubber gloves—despite the fact that Hopkins was the place where the use of surgical gloves was instituted. Barehanded, we were instructed to remove the damp tan cotton wrappings that covered the stiff bodies and gingerly we did just that, thereby invading an anonymous privacy. We had become grave robbers, as generations of physicians before us had learned to be, for there is no adequate substitute for the value of that human dissection.

In the three months of half-days in the anatomy lab, the class became familiar with identifying and freeing up the body's muscles, tracing the paths of the major vessels, following the course of the tendons, opening the heart, exploring the size and substance of every organ, measuring the cavities, removing the eyes, isolating the pancreas, probing the ducts and ureters, sectioning the testes—and slicing the brain. If there was ever an initiation rite of passage more suited to test the mettle of its novitiates than the dissection laboratory, I don't know of it.

But there would be another test of our mettle in the spring term, in the animal neuro-physiology laboratory. There we were lectured on the anatomy and functions of the nervous system, as demonstrated by the abnormal physiology induced in cats by surgical intervention. Our professor, one of the department of surgery's most noted cardio-vascular surgeons, diagrammed on a blackboard how he penetrated the skull or, in other cases, the backbone, of anesthetized cats; how he was able to approach the area of the brain that accounted for specific motor or sensory functions; and how various irreversible injuries were created to demonstrate a broad spectrum of brain and spinal column malfunctions in a collection of scientifically maimed cats.

Then, in came the cat cages. In groups of four, we were given the cats to determine, by testing their abilities and disabilities, where the experimental lesion was located. Either they were placed, standing, on the table, or they were allowed to walk on the floor, if they were able. There were about a dozen of these cats, operated upon in prior weeks and now healed into a stable state and becoming "classical" for one or another kind of major neurological lesion. Some cats were unable to use one leg, or two, or had a weakness in one side of the body. Others had eyes that moved only slightly, or mouths that were not capable of chewing normally. Trained animal lab technicians cared for these caged animals between the demonstration classes. Sooner or later, as their general health failed, they were put down, to be succeeded by other "preparations."

As students, most of us found this course to be a difficult exercise for our own sense of equanimity; I certainly did. But I have to say that no one ever objected openly to the demonstrations nor spoke out on behalf of the crippled animals. It was just what was done as a teaching mechanism in those days. Such animal abuse was stopped entirely in the latter part of the twentieth century. What amazes me, however, is how such intentional destruction of animal abilities was, in my training days, considered normal procedure, possibly a remnant of the brutal days of surgical and medical managements that were the only means of treating disease before the progressive refinements of the last century.

Each morning, before rounds on the wards, we medical students would draw the patients' blood—sometimes as much as a pint—just for routine studies, and we tended to the intravenous drips that sustained the patients with fluid replacements and a few supplements, given mostly for urgent circumstances. We worked incessantly, on the wards and in the clinics, boning up on medical knowledge, attending lectures, participating in laboratory instructions, and occasionally witnessing surgery in the operating rooms. The Hopkins-identified iron-man principle held that if a student or resident can learn to work for many consecutive hours, despite exhaustion, he will master efficiency, hone his self-respect, and emerge as a fine doctor.

As medical instruction moved progressively from the primary lecture hall and dissection laboratory to the clinics and bedsides, clinical pathology became one of my favorite subjects. The chairman of that department was the highly acclaimed Dr. Arnold Rich. He was, Aunt Lilian told me, the first Jewish department chairman in Hopkins history. Among the earliest teachers and researchers at The Wilmer Institute were some of the most distinguished Jewish professors, whose reputations had much to do with the growing prominence of the Institute. Today, neither Wilmer nor the entire Johns Hopkins medical faculty would be worth much without the brilliance and leadership of the current greats, largely Jewish, who are following in the footsteps of the distinguished handful of Hopkins' medical founders—an opportunity that, unfortunately, was not available to their forebears.

CHAPTER SEVEN

My first wife waltzed into my life at an afternoon tea dance in New York City during a school break in December of 1944. After my four months of incarceration at The Hill School, being at the dance was like being granted an idyllic parole, with females galore and the Lester Lanin band playing pieces even the tone deaf knew by heart. The dance was in the ballroom of the elegant Cosmopolitan Club and was a fairly typical private party for adolescent Establishmentarians. There were sixty boys, intentionally out-numbering the girls because it was predictable that a high percentage of the boys would prefer horsing around to dancing. I was on the fence about dancing, liking it slow and easy but not with just any old partner.

My date was the daughter of friends of my parents. She was nice, probably bright, with a smile that revealed an iron mine of heavy metallic braces. Attached to her name was the "ie" suffix so favored by the young women of that slice of society, names such as Muffie, Pammie, Sharmie, Connie, and so forth. Suddenly I spied *her*—totally blonde, laughing blue eyes, slim, gracefully rhythmic as she danced—and I gulped. I heard her unique voice—part speeded up Victrola, part Bermudan lilt, another part nobody else. I asked her to dance. Flirtatiously, she lied that I danced beautifully—and furthermore, could I believe that it was snowing outside and wasn't the man playing the banjo out of this world and, guess what, that song came from the calypso Talbot Brothers band in Bermuda where my mother and stepfather live. As we circled to the one-size-fits-all-music in a two-step, I caught her looking over my shoulder, checking out other boys while pretending not to. Her name was Janie.

It seemed that every New York minute there was another lout cutting in, which was regrettably a common custom in that era. One floppy-haired, cocky, sweaty quarterback or lifeguard after another would tap me on the shoulder and dance away with her to the fox trot, the Charleston, the samba, lindy hop, Lambeth Walk, Viennese waltz or rumba. For the remainder of that event she somehow seemed to stay just out of reach. I didn't see her or even hear about her for another year, but I didn't forget her.

She remained out of reach after she entered Madeira, a boarding school for girls in McLean, Virginia—-but I began running into her in passing at various New York functions. The quintessential Madeira girl, she was the object of much attention everywhere she went, and there always seemed to be boys around who could barely keep from drooling over her. She remembered me, probably because I watched her so intently, and we often exchanged smiles. Then, during our boarding school years, she began inviting me, along with one besotted swain or another, to escort her to the New York black-tie dinner dances held during school vacations—the Holidays (for the younger teenagers), the Metropolitans, or the Assemblies (for the debutantes who were coming out): white gowns for the girls, white tie and tails for the escorting boys. At those subscription dances, the girls had to be "qualified" to attend—Social Register-pedigreed—before their families were permitted the privilege of footing the considerable bill.

It was customary for girls to ask two escorts to these dinner dances. In the afternoon of the day of the event, each escort would send a corsage from a neighborhood florist. Both boys, rarely close friends, would arrive on time and sometimes bump into each other in the elevator riding up to, in her case, the family's 8th floor apartment at 117 East 72nd Street. Her mother and devoted stepfather would have about forty-five awkward minutes to vet her dates before she joined us. Suddenly she would burst into the drawing room in a swish-swash of taffeta or sizzle of crinoline—all smiles and fragrances, vivacious and apologetic, coy and provocative.

Over time, she became engaged to a sequence of Yalies—John, Danny, Walker. I gave up. She was out of sight but still not out of mind. So in 1953, when I was a second-year medical student and she asked me to join her and another boy, presumably a current boyfriend, whose family had a home in the horse country of Virginia, I accepted before wishing I hadn't. The circumstances were not exactly to my liking. Driving all the way from Baltimore on a Saturday, my only day off, I was wondering what it would be like after not having seen her for so long when suddenly there she was, in jeans and boots, messy shirt and a mane of blond hair—with him, Steadman the Studman, by her side. Was I ever overdressed in my grey city suit! She was as giggly and gorgeous as I remembered and still had a habit of patting and pushing and pinching when greeting someone—touching was part of the dynamic of her seductiveness.

We went out to look at Steadman's horses and observe how high the fences were for the foxhunt to follow the next day. I was asked to stay for dinner, for what I assumed would be hamburgers from the grill out by the horse barn. Maybe we could chat about killing foxes. Oh, and by the way, others would be coming for dinner. Would I wait downstairs while they changed? Sure. When she finally came down, she was wearing something slim and slinky, almost to the floor. Steadman was in the full formal regalia of foxhunting evening clothes: red (they called it pink) cutaway jacket, green velvet collar, white tuxedo vest, black trousers, velvet slippers appliquéd with fox heads. Suddenly I was grossly underdressed. Guests kept arriving, all clad in formal foxhunting ensembles. It turned out to be a private dance for local horse lovers, accompanied by hunting music (French horns, violins, tuba) and overlaid with the ever-so-slight aroma of their mounts.

By the end of the evening, my old fevered yearning for her had returned, intensified by years of pining and perseverance. Then, a few weeks later, out of the blue she called me and we began seeing each other in earnest. Why she called, I still don't know. My best guess is that she had grown tired of so many flirtations and flings and was won over by my longstanding, steadfast obsession with her when it was time to settle down. However it came about, on June 4, 1953, Jane Sterling Treman—then known to one and all as Janie--and I were married in a beautiful church ceremony in New York, she in a dazzling, full-length white gown, I in a rented cutaway and an ear-to-ear grin—Q.E.D., as it were.

That was a year of enormous emotional challenges in my family. First, in May, shortly before my marriage to Janie, came the sudden death of my sister Joan's husband, twenty-five-year-old artist and writer Bernard Peyton, Jr., in a private plane crash when she was pregnant with their third child. And then, in July, when my nearly fifteen-year-old sister Pam was cavorting with friends at a summer camp in the Adirondacks, unaware that the brook they were splashing in led to a small waterfall, she was swept over the falls, her head was crushed on stones at its base and she drowned.

After getting the news, I accompanied my alarmingly self-contained father on a frenzied two-hour drive to La Guardia to catch the next available plane to Troy, New York. We were met there and driven to the funeral home, where my father made the necessary official identification of her body, his face expressionless throughout the ordeal. When it was time to leave, we traveled home in dead silence. My sister Joan and our mother and our grandmother got very busy with the myriad arrangements that a death requires – where would the funeral be held, who would officiate, how could the funeral home be visited and what about the body itself? I was not a part of that side of things, and neither was my dad. The only way he could cope with Pam's death was by forcibly putting it out of his mind, avoiding every reminder or mention of her and of how much she was loved and now how dreadfully she was missed. He sought no counsel, nor was it offered to him. After all, he was a doctor! Doctors tell others how to cope. They don't need anyone to help them cope. For the remaining thirty-one years of his life, he continued to be unwilling to talk about Pam and would make some excuse to leave the room if her name came up.

At sixty, he retired from his New York practice, earlier than one might have anticipated in view of his great success as an outstanding eye surgeon with a large referral practice. He and my mother moved to Southampton, New York, where the small community hospital was eager to have him, as the only ophthalmologist in the area.

Again, he became very busy and soon took on two young associates. He enjoyed his life in Southampton and he played tennis vigorously and regularly when he could spare the time from his office and hospital work. He planned and led an annual meeting of corneal specialists at the hospital, and he continued to take an active role in his surgical specialties, corneal transplants and cataract surgery.

Dad was my first and most important mentor, a terrific father and a sensational doctor, but there came a time when we all had to watch his life gradually fade and his mind lose its luster. He probably had a series of small strokes, limiting him to such degree that by the time of his death at eighty-three he had become incapable of anything more than basic communications, but he took an apparent comfort in being at home and well-loved. My mother and sister Joan, in going through his office and home effects, found, to their enormous surprise, small bottles of liquor hidden in various spots and theorized that he might have become a secret drinker.

Whether alcohol became a crutch or not, one incontrovertible fact remains: For decades, he fought a lonely battle against a secret sorrow, secret because he was determined to keep it that way so he could maintain the show of strength that he felt befit the head of a family. Although his father had been a psychiatrist, I feel certain that Dad had no insight into the debilitating intensity of his personal war with that ever-present tragedy. I am convinced that the loss of his Pam was like a poison that spread through his system and that his refusal to speak about her was his iron defense against a sad preoccupation. His unwillingness to release his emotions eventually became the trigger for age to close in on almost all his thoughts and might even have hastened his death. He could not bring himself to give permission for Pam's eyes to be used for his cherished eye-bank, but well before he died in Southampton Hospital he had the presence to remind his office partner, Dr. Nathaniel Bronson, to see that his eyes were used by the eye bank. And they were.

Pam's death hit us all very hard, but Joan helped salve our grief by naming her third child, who was born after her husband's death, Pamela. We called her Pam, like the aunt she would never know; or, more often, Pammie. If ever there was a godsend, it has been Pammie.

In her we found the joy and the spirit of her namesake. Pammie was born with cystic fibrosis (CF) and, just to give an inkling about her specialness, she consistently maintained that CF was her best friend, for over her fifty-seven years of struggle with its manifestations, including the need for a double lung transplant that served her for a decade and the need for colon surgery for cancer with subsequent liver metastases (probably induced by the medications needed to manage her primary disorder). Her very life constantly reminded her of the privilege she felt in being alive and the joy she found in its most simple pleasures. Joan and her siblings were always available to lend a hand, to be there for Pammie when her husband's employment in a nonprofit agency kept him away. Pammie she giggled and teased her way into every heart, managing to take photographs like a professional and gasping for breath in a way to make it seem only from excitement.

In her twenties, Pammie married Bill Post at a time in his young life when he, too, had a disorder thought at the time to be fatal, Hodgkins Disease. Bill not only survived that lymphoma but, with Pammie, fought as a team the many threats to Pammie's life, an incessant series of setbacks and improvements made possible by scores of hospitalizations. Neither she nor Bill ever gave the slightest sign of surrender, but on July 13, 2010, her death could no longer be postponed. She died quietly at home, one of the oldest survivors of cystic fibrosis. More than any person I have ever known, she epitomized the supremacy of attitude in averting disease and of the effectiveness of using humor as a replacement for despair. Why else would three hundred and fifty people of all ages and occupations attend a memorial church service in her memory on October 5, 2010? Both of the Pamelas in our family's lives are unforgettable.

Returning to 1953, I went back to Johns Hopkins, and, with a new wife in tow, it was time to leave Aunt Lilian's home. Janie and I rented one of the narrow houses with white steps across Wolfe Street from the hospital compound in East Baltimore, just a few doors away from where my parents lived when I was born. Life just couldn't have been more satisfactory in almost every way, especially since Janie, fresh from her job at CIA headquarters in Washington, adapted surprisingly well to life as an impoverished homemaker in a Baltimore slum.

Would-be doctors yearn for the day when their professional usefulness can begin. That transition from student to doctor usually comes with the start of an internship immediately after graduation from medical school. But I didn't want to wait that long. Although I found medical training to be demanding and engaging, there was too little hands-on patient care and too much record-keeping and case-reporting for my taste. I needed more action, more blood and guts, more do-gooding than medical school had to offer.

Between their third and fourth years, there was a three-and-a-half month elective period when medical students could chose to do more or less whatever they wanted, provided it was "medical" in essence. I was overstuffed with student idealism, impatience, ignorance and expectation. All of that went into trying to determine how those months would be utilized, while also considering Janie's desire for something that would offer some excitement or entertainment—and, most particularly, a change of scene.

A name, Dr. John Olds, was mentioned by a faculty member at Hopkins. For all thirty-five years of his professional life he had worked on an out-island hospital off Newfoundland, but at the time he was on leave of absence for treatment of tuberculosis and alcoholism at an American sanatorium. He was a Hopkins-trained, reputably irritable, reticent but greatly admired physician-surgeon--not a missionary but, by description, a sort of irreligious, profane Albert Schweitzer with an incurable medical calling. His remote hospital sounded like just the place for a gung-ho medical student, a cinder block structure where marvels were being accomplished. I sent an inquiry for a short-term job and was accepted--Hopkins was sufficient reference.

Notre Dame Bay Memorial Hospital was on a distant island in an iceberg-laden sea off the northern coast of Newfoundland, situated on the south twin of a pair of islands called Twillingate. There would be limitless opportunities for rendering patient care, medically and surgically. Beyond that, there was nothing much else to do. Nothing, in fact. I failed to paint that part of the picture in describing this exciting opportunity to Janie.

In early August of 1954 we flew from Baltimore to Gander, arriving in the early evening. By contrast to sweltering Baltimore, it was cold when we got off the plane—in the low 40s. We took a night train to a nameless town (no signs in the station) near the northern coast of Newfoundland, where we sat with our suitcases in the station until 4 in the morning, when I managed to find a man whose car was used as a taxi (the first car we had seen) who drove us to Lewisporte. There we loaded onto the coastal ferry that went by a circuitous route to Twillingate.

The boat was about thirty feet long and was frustratingly lethargic in wending its way through the waves, turning the few sea miles to our destination into a three-hour trip. As a saved letter to my parents explains, the boat "had a cabin heated to 90 degrees by a kerosene stove, and there were a handful of locals staring at it with us." In the days ahead, Janie and I would become accustomed to the staring; it was a notable avocation of the Newfoundlanders. As strangers, they were unlikely to speak, but they stared intently, unblinkingly, and unceasingly. Not with a smile, mind you. This was serious, inquisitor business. In the margin of the same letter are notes added by Janie about the passengers, but they deal so graphically with group seasickness that they need not be quoted here.

We had barely eaten since leaving Baltimore and had only dozed off-and-on since arriving in Gander. Doubt was rising in the expressive eyes of my partner. Her chin was quivering, which I recognized as a sign of discontent. She had not been the one envisioning a summer of medical heroics. What she wanted was native beauty. Peace and quiet. Rest and relaxation. Maybe even a husband on "time out." Instead we were about to disembark on a treeless, rocky island where the only noteworthy feature of the landscape was the occasional iceberg floating by ever so slowly in the near distance.

When the ferry reached the Twillingate wharf, a gangplank was shoved to the dock and as it rested on the gunnels we walked the plank to the dock, carrying our bags. There we stood on the squeaking, empty boards of the pier with water lapping on the piles, inhaling an horrendous smell. We looked at the shoreline to the right and to the left. Most of the island that was visible was barren, except for scattered wooden houses with very small windows. Straight ahead, up the dirt road from the pier, was a grey, cement block building that was surely our hospital. A tiny school house with a tattered flag was off to the right. There were clumps of bushes here and there but only a few small trees. The landscape also contained numerous platforms elevated a few feet from the ground and constructed of criss-crossed, narrow pieces of lumber with small, flat, light brown objects covering their surface. We were to learn that those were the "flakes" which constituted the ubiquitous, defining identity of this remote land. Flakes were used for the process of salting and drying codfish— the livelihood and lifeline of these out-island Newfoundlanders---but what a foul-smelling home industry it was to unaccustomed noses!

Someone evidently noticed that two strangers remained on the dock after the ferry left. A man came with a two-wheeled hospital cart to take our things to the staff's quarters. He was a nice fellow and spoke in friendly enough tones but in a jargon that defied easy understanding. Still, all we needed was "friendly." Looking back at the harbor, we saw that it was quite beautiful in its quaintness, with dark blue water and small fishing dories both at anchor and lined up on the beaches. Other islands could be seen in the distance. There were several coves along the coasts, with tiny wharfs and splayed nets strung up to be dried in the sun. An occasional man with high rubber boots was tinkering with fishing gear or working on his boat. A clump of houses and several small steeples indicated a village about a mile away.

The only road was the dirt one we were on, leading toward the school, with a branch leading to the hospital. It came from what we were soon to call "the village"---a few white houses, a church and a general store. There were some tire tracks on the road, meaning that there was at least one motor vehicle on the island. Our ferry was now a dot on the horizon. We had arrived—and would be confined to Twillingate for the next fourteen weeks. It turned out that, having gotten the dates confused, no one had been expecting us on the day we arrived, which explained the absence of a reception.

The hospital staff consisted of an Acting Superintendent who was a Canadian doctor with a non-superintending disposition, meaning he was anything but officious. Locked within himself, he was not a born teacher but he was friendly and capable. This was a doing hospital, not a teaching hospital. There were two Irish doctors and an English surgeon who, with their wives, were immigrants to Newfoundland. And--great news!--there were two Harvard medical students invited by the hospital for the same reason I was there, to be an extra pair of cheap hands, willing to take on any job we were given. All in all, the medical staff proved to be made up of a bunch of excellent people. Fun-loving, relaxed, happy—and remarkably competent. Except for the students, each had been at the hospital for several years and knew the locals well. They were familiar with the "going" diseases and how to treat them.

One of the assignments to be taken in rotation by me and the two Harvard students was boat duty twice a week. Decaying fishing dories with inboard engines and identical specifications would come from other islands or distant coves to take a "doctor" to see a sick person unable to come to the hospital. From the pharmacy, we would get the hospital's black bag that contained a stethoscope, blood pressure cuff, ophthalmoscope, hand light, ace bandages, gauze in various sizes, and an assortment of about twenty kinds of pills. There was one other essential piece of equipment, a *Merck Manual.* Its pages were Bible-thin and its print was very small. There were no pictures or diagrams, just text, and it contained as much information on diagnosis and treatment of disease as any volume available anywhere.

Often, when brought to a far-off island as "the doctor," I would examine the patient as carefully as possible and then ask to be excused to visit the outhouse. There, sitting out of sight inside the tiny structure, I would open the *Manual* to confirm my diagnosis and select the best choice of pills from the black bag left at bedside. Returning to the patient, I would wash in the hand basin, thump the patient's chest again or perhaps feel the abdomen, then dispense the pills, providing enough of them for the illness--say ten days' worth--and always extra pills because I soon learned that every patient squirreled away a portion of the allotment to keep for winter, when there was no access to medical care until the boats could again be launched.

The medical island-hopping brought independence, adventure, challenge, uncertainty, and some exciting successes. I might treat a patient almost on death's door with a problem such as pneumonia or heart failure and return in two weeks to find that person in the full force of life and contentedness. It was a time and place where there was no resistance to the standard antibiotics and where acute illness could be effectively treated with the basics, such as digitalis for the failing hearts and penicillin for most acute lung infections. Obstetrics was another big activity and obviously one that kept going day and night. I delivered upwards of thirty babies in the three months I worked in Twillingate, one from a young woman who evidently didn't know she was pregnant and was admitted in eclampsia—a severe hypertension that can come with a neglected pregnancy.

Newfie language was amusing at times. A patient might say, "Aye finds me stum," meaning, "I find my stomach," another way of saying he has a stomach ache. Or, "Me bowels is stuck somethin' wonderful." "Wonderful" was used to mean "severe" or "very much." Twillingate had a population of European stock with an accent modified by grammatical disregard, and a way of life that was a backward slide from whatever were the United Kingdom origins of these fisher folk's forebears. I remember them as docile, counter-evolutionary Europeans.

The island was "dry" and strictly overseen by what the local staff referred to as "the Harmy." To my amazement, the Harmy turned out to be a local, pseudo-Cockney word for "the Army," meaning the Salvation Army. The islanders had to be self-governed when the harbors froze over for very long winters, making the people dependent for guidance upon the wisdom and discipline of the Army members among them. The Harmy wore hats and jackets exactly like those worn by the men and women who jangled for contributions by shaking little hand bells near dangling pots on Fifth Avenue in Manhattan at Christmastime. The local people considered the Harmy their civic, as well as their religious, authority.

When the X-ray technician/pharmacist wanted a vacation, he taught Janie how to measure body dimensions for X-ray calculations, how to operate the one-machine-does-all device with its frame-mounted films, then how to develop the films in a dark closet with a red light as its only illumination. Janie took all the hospital's X-rays for a number of weeks and then moved on to the pharmacy, where she reorganized an inventory of boxes and bottles that had become disorganized over the years. It was a pharmaceutical education in labels. I teased her by saying that with only a bit more experience she would be qualified to work in a drugstore when she got home, but she was not amused.

The hospital was in dire need of nurses. None of the willing but slow-moving women who worked on the wards had any training other than that given them by the medical staff and the women who had preceded them. The open male and female wards were served by an assortment of young and old women, whose responsibilities were not apparent from just seeing them, for their uniforms consisted of somber house dresses selected to suit the weather, not the work. One day, word came by letter that a real nurse was to arrive. She was coming from a government hospital in St. Johns, Newfoundland's capital. The Superintendent was as pleased as I ever saw him at the news.

A day or two later the ferry let off a single passenger. A tall woman of about thirty, she was a sight for sore (or deprived) eyes. She wore a black velvet dress that was at least a size or two too small, which provided an appealing definition of her body, fore and aft. Her shoes were high-heeled and black patent leather, and her luxuriant blonde hair was swept up in a bun and partially covered by some sort of hat. Her most noteworthy feature was her bright red lips, which had been generously covered with lipstick that somewhat exceeded the outlines of her own naturally voluptuous mouth. She was like a glamour photo torn from a tawdry movie magazine as she stood there in those high heels waiting with her two suitcases to be picked up. Along came the Acting Superintendent to "shake hands hello," as we Newfies stared and stared.

I can't remember her name but she proved to be surprisingly pleasant, her warm friendliness belying her Belle Watling exterior. The Acting Superintendent showed her to her accommodations, and soon she reappeared in a clean white nurse's uniform with a graduation pin, a small handkerchief in her left breast pocket, and a crisp nurse's cap on her head. Now we were a hospital with a real nurse! The doctors were exuberantly grateful that she had come.

Two days later, the effective Newfoundlander grapevine shed further light on her arrival. Our warm and friendly nurse had been sent to us by the veterans' hospital in St. Johns to do penitence of sorts. She had allegedly climbed into the bed of an irresistible soldier on the open ward, where beds were only separated by drawn curtains. Over "home brewed" beers in the weeks to come, we doctors shared fantasies about just how that encounter came about and precisely what the scenario had been that led to her banishment. Beyond patient care, there were few distractions to turn conversations to fresh topics so this was a welcome diversion. (It's fair to say our wives were less intrigued.) The lady worked hard and for all I know served out her penitence dutifully and not too unhappily in a no-touch locale where any male in our hospital beds was likely to smell like dried codfish.

Every five or ten years, Canada celebrates its relationship with the United Kingdom by declaring a Queen's Day in honor of the monarch in England. It so happened that while we were in Twillingate, the Queen's representative, Governor General Vincent Massey (incidentally, the brother of actor Raymond Massey), came bearing the Queen's respects to the citizens of the town. The school children were lined up along the road to the one-room school house. The townsfolk also lined the sides of the road from the pier, and the schoolmaster distributed tiny Canadian flags to wave as an alternative to clapping, which Newfoundlanders– as far as I could observe—preferred not to do. To describe them as undemonstrative would be an understatement.

A Royal Navy frigate hove to in the harbor and a tender brought the Governor ashore – all decked out in uniform, complete with medals and an ornate cap and a sword at his side. He smiled broadly and shook hands with the dignitaries before the schoolmaster ushered him up the road to the school. Naturally, everyone stared, silently. On the steps of the school's porch, the Governor turned and addressed the gathering, paying special attention to the children, their flags held motionlessly. He extended the Queen's greeting, spoke about the beauty of Twillingate, mentioned how privileged he was to be there, and so forth. It was a very nice speech, a gracious expression of magisterial affection for distant subjects.

"And now," he said in conclusion, "I have the pleasure of granting a day of holiday on behalf of Her Majesty. It is a day on which you all you children may be absent from your school. Select when you wish that day to take place, chose it so that it will be a remembrance for years to come. Please think about your Queen and have a day of much happiness in so doing." His news was greeted by the usual Newfie response, namely none. Not even smiles or exchanged glances. The Governor was clearly nonplussed. But he rallied quickly and offered, "I take your silence to mean approval." (Often when teaching in later years I would quote Governor General Massey's face-saving comment when encountering lack of feedback from a lethargic audience.)

The silence was one Newfie characteristic and another was to come. Twillingate's crop of wild blueberries is picked by the women and children and made into jams and jellies to help feed the population in the winter months. One might argue that Queen's Day should have been designated to take place at some point during the winter, when it would provide an appreciated break from school routine that would definitely have reminded the kids of their benevolent Queen in a positive way. Instead, what was decided by the schoolmaster in consultation with the Harmy was that the children's summer vacation would be extended by an extra day, thereby adding one more day of fall berry picking but making Queen's Day no different from any other day.

That was Newfoundland. For all my joshing about their idiosyncrasies, I left with great affection for those simple, honest, quiet, isolated people. Janie felt the same.

Today, there is a causeway that connects Twillingate by bridge to another island, with further bridge linkage to the mainland. Until quite recently, over-fishing had led to a complete disappearance of codfish, followed by a too-late law that forbade cod fishing. Eventually the fish returned, but by then the population had become adapted to tourism. I hope "something wonderful " that they have not lost all of their inimitable lingo and contented lifestyle, but it is a safe guess that everything is different now. It has been more than half a century since I spent time on Twillingate, but its uncomplicated existence, its "reduced-European" culture, and its cinder block hospital are as fresh in my mind as are the prototypical incisions and knots of the surgical procedures I performed there, mostly for the first time. It would be fun to see faces I knew when we were all young, but it would be equally wonderful to be shown a few hernia and appendectomy scars I left with them in the course of learning to be a useful doctor.

Upon returning to Baltimore I had another full year of medical school before my medical services could be considered legitimate, but in Newfoundland I had begun to uncover a basic truth about giving care to those in need: It brings such gratification to the do'er that he may weigh his services as on the selfish side of kindness.

CHAPTER EIGHT

After the long haul of medical schooling, patient care of almost every conceivable kind, exhaustive and exhausting tests, and a new familiarity with working around the clock, graduation finally arrived. Hardly had my classmates and I ceased practicing writing our names with the finishing flourish of MD in capital letters than it was time for internship, starting over once again at dreg level in the hierarchy of medical standing. At twenty-six, some of my college classmates were already independent business people, mid-level military officers, published authors, or country club members with season tickets to football games and three kids in school. Me, I was about to become a ninety-dollar-a- month uniformed doctor in a starched white suit with a sous chef's white shirt buttoned at the neck.

My year of internship began at six a.m. on July 1, 1956, at Cornell Medical College in New York City. As always, the way the house doctors were dressed told their daily story. Starting out in pristine whiteness, uniforms would collect daubs of human excrescence, dust and dirt from meeting rooms and basement corridors, ink from leaking ballpoint pens, and stains and wrinkling from eighteen hours of hands-on services to infection, heart failure, liver disease, asthma or stroke. Mine was a straight medical internship, with disease de jour kind of experience—almost every day offering a new and engrossing experience in healthcare. By the time I walked through the door at night, I had become a microcosm of eclectic exposures and exciting experiences: "Hi, I'm famished. Wait 'til I tell you about a case of tertiary syphilis that I saw in the Accident Room. What's for dinner? Gotta get to sleep early tonight, I'm dead tired . . . What's the matter? "

For two people who had been brought up in Establishment comforts, we—in particular, Janie—adapted fairly well to a less decorous existence. We lived across from the hospital on York Avenue in a cramped, two-room walkup above a deli that had a few customer tables and chairs. The fare downstairs consisted of hot dogs, hamburgers and fried foods, and their aroma leaked under the door and through the pipes we shared from below.

For me, it was a particularly productive year of learning generic medicine from the top down, from tic douloureux to painful piles. But it was the major disorders that were most fascinating: heart failure, lung cancer, cirrhosis, diabetes, multiple sclerosis, strokes and tuberculosis. And New York, like Baltimore, had more than its share of violent injuries, not to mention other acute needs for immediate care, which made the nights on call as full as the days--with far more cases needing emergency care.

Still, one incident above all the others made the deepest impression on me because it was something that I could never quite digest. I was in the autopsy room to get information about a patient whose care I had assisted in before his death when I noticed a middle-aged man, properly dressed for visitors to autopsies in a scrub cap and white gown over his business suit. He had entered from the doctors' dressing room and had gone straight to a table where an autopsy was in progress. I heard him introduce himself to the pathologist as a fellow doctor. That all made sense. Masks were not required for routine autopsies when there was no suspicion of a contagion, so I had a good look at his face. He was closely shaven except for a waxed handlebar moustache sticking out horizontally about two inches beyond his cheek on each side. Even in those days, waxed moustaches were rare enough in themselves, but even more striking was the fact that the doctor had a second pair of straight handlebar "mustaches" coming from the region of each ear canal—ear mustaches—and extending parallel to the ones below. These were almost as long and almost as thick at their roots as the mustaches from under his nose. Thus, he had four neatly waxed, parallel, tapering antlers. It must have taken him years to grow such a pair of ear beards. While I tried not to stare, he spoke softly and minimally, maintaining a hushed voice in deference to the dead.

The autopsy this doctor had come to observe was approaching its final phase. The autopsy room technician, a so-called diener, applied the usual electric saw to encircle and remove the cap of the skull.

He removed the covering membranes from the brain and cut it free by severing it from the spinal chord. Then, as the diener was handing the brain to the pathologist for dissection, the mustachioed doctor stepped forward and took the brain from his hands, too quickly for an "if you please" or "may I?"

The doctor cradled the brain lovingly in both hands, keeping his gaze fixed on the evidently seductive sulci and gyri of gray matter as he explained, "This is my mother. Her brain." Long pause, as the pathologist, the diener, myself and the team at another autopsy table, froze. "It is beautiful even in death." He kept turning his clasped hands in one direction, then another, to get as complete a view of the brain as possible. After an undeclared moment of silence, when we all must have experienced the same impulse to be respectful of whatever the visitor had found to be sacred, he carefully handed the brain to the pathologist and slowly made his way to the doctors' dressing room.

What I had been missing in my medical adaptation to scientific reality was the impact upon all physicians of a human death—and, similarly, of incurable blindness. Those are dreaded end points in a healing profession. The behavior of that mustachioed physician, an outlier of sorts, exemplified the awe of the human body that grips caregivers most profoundly once the body is lifeless--or the human eye sightless. Once the animating spark of life is lost, the miracle of anatomy and physiology rekindles the fascination that defies definition but underlies the spell medicine has for its acolytes.

After I finished my internship in 1957, Janie and I moved to Bethesda, Maryland, where I had been accepted for a two-year appointment as a senior assistant surgeon at the National Institute of Health (NIH) in the U.S. Public Health Service. We took up residence on a little street not far from NIH named Pooks Hill Road. In that neighborhood in the shadow of the many buildings filled with Nobel-level researchers, I would have expected something more along the lines of Pasteur Lane or Darwin Circle. I thought it unimaginable that a Michael DeBakey, for example, would have Pooks Hill on his stationery. But there we were, for the two-year duration.

At NIH, I became involved in investigative work with sickle cell disease and its eye manifestations. Using the clinical microscope, one of my NIH colleagues, Dr. George Goodman, observed and reported in a published paper a tiny but seemingly characteristic capillary dilatation on the surface of the eyes of patients suffering from sickle cell disease. Fascinated by his observation, I called in as many sickle cell patients as possible and, after giving them careful eye examinations, noted that the abnormal configuration of the capillaries on the whites of the patients' eyes was a means of differentiating a form of sickle cell disease disorder that was severe (likely to affect the eyes and other parts of the body) in contrast to a milder form that only showed up in special laboratory testing. Goodman's capillary curlicue was, I believed at the time, an important diagnostic and prognostic sign of a serious disorder.

Someone much senior to me at another eye department in another state, to whom I had written about this clinical finding, was alleged by his former laboratory assistant to have gone to his laboratory staff with my letter and asked, "Why haven't *we* made this observation?" He called in some of his sickle cell patients, confirmed my finding and proceeded to publish the finding *as his* before my first paper on the subject appeared in the literature. To me, it was a devastating revelation about the pressures, frustrations and risks of scientific research in the academic environment of "publish or perish." This man was an influential and socially popular individual, with a lovely wife and adoring children. He was also a close friend of my new mentor at NIH, Dr. Ludwig von Sallmann, who shook his head when I told him what had happened and advised me to let it go. I did. But it remained in memory as an indelible warning about the risk to intellectual property when shared in trust across institutional boundaries.

From the spring of 1957 until the spring of 1959—my two NIH years in the Public Heatlh Service—eye research was lumped in with neurological diseases, the parent organization being the National Institute of Neurological Diseases and Blindness (NINDB). There I was once again at the bottom of the doctor heap. The chief of ophthalmology, von Sallmann, had a distinguished international reputation as clinician and researcher. He was 68 years old—a tall, slightly hunched, strikingly pale gentleman with all-white hair, caring eyes and a shy smile that projected the antithesis of professional

aggression. I came to admire that man as much for his polite and genial presence as for the voluminous knowledge stored in ready access
in his head. Originally from Vienna, he spoke an Austrian-accented
English that belied the vastness of his vocabulary, which encompassed
the Latin or Greek of medical verbiage, along with the French or German of medical syndromes affecting the eye. He often spoke so softly
that you wanted to pull yourself closer into his private space to catch
the wisdom being dispensed before it dissolved into thin air. He had
taught in Austria, China and, more recently, at Columbia University
in New York. He was well-rounded in the arts and the classics, and
his gentle, kindly nature had no cutting edge. His life seemed to
have brought him all that he ever desired, and his ability to diagnose
eye disease was often an exemplary exercise in combining thorough
knowledge of the literature with acute clinical perceptions.

One of the most memorable times I spent with Dr. von Sallmann
was on a trip we made by car to Halifax County in North Carolina, to
examine the eyes of the Halowar Indians. They were a tri-racial group
of impoverished individuals whose genetic origins included Native
American, African-American and Caucasian ancestry. They had an eye
disorder never previously studied or reported, locally called "Red Eye."

We found that there were 350 persons identifiable within the lineage of those affected with the lesions that caused their eyes to be as
red as if they had been drinking or crying for several days. We examined them, adults and children alike, in a room of the only school
in that area. Each case had a variably shaped, wart-like elevation of
tissue over the white part of the eye which was richly supplied with
blood vessels, hence the striking redness. We biopsied those lesions;
they proved to be a mole-like genetic growth that, along with the
contribution of the dermatopathologist, Dr. Carl Whitkop, we published as a newly reported entity. As with the work with sickle cell
patients, becoming a part of a medical discovery (even if no specific
therapy was called for) constituted a second time within the same
year that I experienced the thrill of being on the ground floor of productive clinical research.

While I was working for Dr. von Sallmann, a middle-aged Caucasian woman was referred to our clinic with the complaint of an uncomfortable, red and oozing eye, certainly an infection of some kind. The worst part of her history was that a similar problem in her other eye had turned into an uncontrollable inflammation that had resulted in the total loss of the eye, whose remnants had been surgically removed, leaving only an empty socket which was still plagued by chronic discharge. By the time she came under Dr. von Sallmann's care, a brownish ulcer on the lower part of her remaining eye's cornea had progressed about an eighth of an inch toward the center of her vision.

Eye examinations by all of the eye doctors, smears for microscopic study, cultures, and everyone's individual effort to reach a diagnosis by questioning the patient left us without any diagnostic clues. She appeared to be a healthy woman in other respects, 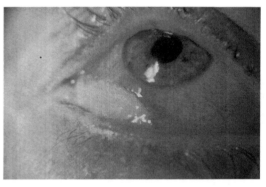 fully cooperative, resigned to the danger now confronting her only eye, and always willing to answer anyone's list of obvious and not-so-obvious questions when she was "presented" at patient rounds. She remained our out-patient for several weeks. Dr. von Sallmann concluded that she must be damaging her own eye, which she denied in such a pitiful rebuttal that tears of sympathy welled in the eyes of several of the doctors. Nonetheless, he held to his assumption. The patient had a session with an NIH psychiatrist. No dice. Next, Dr. von Sallmann requested that another interview be conducted under sodium pentothal, "truth serum." This examination of the still cooperative lady was conducted by a doctor very familiar with how to get the truth out of someone in the twilight of consciousness. He came back with the verdict: "Negative."

We kept the patient hospitalized and continued treating her worsening eye. She became my assigned responsibility. I was instructed to look for suspicious behavior. Following Dr. von Sallmann's instructions, one morning at about five a.m. I woke her for a surprise peek at her eye with a portable microscope we used for bedside eye exams. For the first time, I saw white deposits in a slime of discharge on the inner surface of the lower eyelid and on the cornea itself. I took a few swipes of these with a wire loop and transferred the gunk to a slide, then sent it out for pathological examination.

The diagnosis was acetyl salicylic acid—aspirin. It turned out that she was putting a portion of a crushed aspirin under her lower eyelid; the powdered medication embedded in the tissue with which it came in contact; the acid solution created by that soaked into the lower part of her eyeball and, as its damage progressed, left a festering brown burn of increasing size on the lower part of her eyeball. This was the first time we had examined her at a time when the aspirin's foreign body granules had not yet dissolved, thus betraying her secret commitment to inflict upon herself a gradual, painful blindness.

The woman was confronted with the diagnosis. She seemed distressed but, oddly, more disturbed by having to leave our care to transfer to another venue, the psychiatry service. We ophthalmologists now knew *what* was causing the trouble but the shrinks would have to cope with *why*.

CHAPTER NINE

One day at lunch in the cafeteria of the Clinical Center Building of the NIH, I overheard from the next table that an ophthalmologist was needed for a month's assignment in Ethiopia. I moved closer to join the conversation. It was a nutrition project. The investigators were looking for an expert on eye indications of nutritional deficiencies, of which several types exist. The job would require special knowledge of so-called tropical eye diseases and the skillful use of ophthalmic instruments. Government ophthalmologists, if any were available, would be given preference.

Although there was no extra pay for such work, it offered an entirely expense-paid experience in a distant, mysterious land. Abyssinia--more recently called Ethiopia--was the land of Emperor Haile Salassie, possible descendent of Solomon and the Queen of Sheba and at that time the only black monarch in all of Africa. The immediate lure of Ethiopia and the possibility of assuming the role of a real ophthalmologist suddenly became an irresistible yearning. I saw it as a step in a natural progression: from my simple work as a scribe in Iran, to the role of general doctor in Newfoundland, then to studying genetic disease among the Halowar Indians in North Carolina and now to investigating why a nutritional disease was causing blindness in a remote part of Africa.

A few months earlier, on June 5, 1958, our son, David Townley Paton—named for both his father and his grandfather--had been born, a child who was in a constant state of motion from the very beginning. I was delighted with him. Not for me the silent, compliant infant gazing contentedly at the ceiling above his crib, only to become the serious, boring, laid back adult of tomorrow. But Janie had him well in hand so, I reasoned, it would be okay if I were to slip away for a few weeks, right? Yes, have fun!

That night I studied all I could find about nutritional eye disease in the NIH medical library. The next morning I was as familiar with the subject as with the recitation of "Paul Revere's Ride," a poem I had once learned entirely by heart. The only minor detail was that I had never actually seen any of the disorders that I now could discuss in detail. Fortunately, I'd come across some useful photographs that gave me a pretty good idea of what those abnormalities looked like.

With just one phone call, I arranged to meet the physician in charge of assembling the team that would go to Ethiopia. He asked me if I knew about Bitot spots, keratomalacia, nyctylopia, conjunctival xerosis, and eyelid changes found in vitamin deficiencies. I certainly did! I also knew how to use the major instruments, such as the ophthalmoscope and the slit lamp and, with some cramming at night, I found it was easy enough to become an "authority" on the indications of vitamin deficiency that eyes could convey. Testing for night blindness—as happens with Vitamin A deficiency—would require totally dark rooms for testing purposes, but all we would need for that was some material to cover windows and doors and stuff into cracks. I managed to persuade the project director that I could do the job so off I went to Addis Ababa.

Under the auspices of the International Committee for Nutrition for National Defense (ICNND), a governmental project had been

funded to determine what supplements were needed by Ethiopian school children to reverse strongly suspected vitamin deficiency.

A team of U.S. public health experts had been sent to Addis Ababa six months earlier to survey four typical schools. The head teacher in each school was given bottles of capsules, half of which contained placebos and the other half, various combinations of vitamins. Each child received one capsule daily and the teachers only had to keep track of which students got which color of capsule. In that manner, bias on the part of the teachers as well as the subsequent examiners would be avoided when we performed our examinations to identify differences in the student groups.

The time had come for the important follow-up intended to demonstrate the value of vitamin therapy for the school children. As the only so-called ophthalmologist, I had stepped into the project as a Johnny-come-lately. Upon arrival in Addis, I looked up and later moved in with a Princeton classmate, Edward Streator, and his wife, Priscilla, who lived in the comfort of ample quarters owned by the American Embassy, where Ed was a junior member of the staff. During the day I worked diligently at the schools and in the evenings, the Streators and I would use car lights to chase hyenas--fierce-looking animals with strong teeth and a pack mentality--in the hills above the city. To get to the hills, our route took us through Addis's red light district.

The only red light district I had previously seen was when I was a seventeen-year-old student working for a summer as a tutor for a family vacationing in Claix, France, after which I toured Amsterdam. There, along the notorious Rosse Buurt, beautiful young women sat outfitted in elegant flimsiness framed by first-story windows, tapping the glass invitingly at passersby. They seemed very refined and were thoroughly legal "operatives"—the euphemism for women of the night. In Addis, sadly, the district was worse than just a residential slum. It was a series of shacks amid garbage, puddles, wandering mongrels and offensive aromas. Disinterested women lurked in the shadows of their poorly lit hovels, with but a few scattered red light bulbs hanging from wires within the shacks to signal the occupants' willingness. The poverty in that region of the city was so desperate that one could not help hoping that these women would receive a knock on the door. Actually, I saw no doors, only dangling, tattered cloths suspended from doorframes, with kids running in and out. Maybe I was just growing up, but whatever fascination I might once have had with whorehouses and prostitutes was dealt a serious blow in those Ethiopian evenings.

As for the project I had come to participate in, the head teacher of each school would line up the children, and I, wearing loupes (eyeglass frames with an extension of magnifying lenses), would go down the line looking at every pair of eyes after the general physicians examined them for skin problems or other indications of nutritional deficiencies. The kids looked pretty undernourished but there were no specific signs of vitamin deficiency, none whatsoever, whether or not they had received vitamins instead of placebos. I was particularly looking for Bitot spots, for children with them would be tested for night blindness. In the course of four days, I examined 1,790 pairs of eyes and discovered only fifty-one Bitot spots; in each case, they tested negative for night blindness.

Suspicious, I selected several children at random and asked for a demonstration of how they swallowed the fairly large capsules each day. A few of them managed to choke down the capsule; others were not able to. How could that be, after six months of supposedly swallowing them daily? The other doctors agreed there might be something fishy about the pill distribution. They, too, had been unable to find any differences in the physical examinations in any of the school groups. Blood samples were drawn to be sent to an American laboratory.

Meanwhile, it became apparent that the Ethiopian school teachers were unable to lie effectively. Guilty looks soon gave way to a full explanation. It had been a tough six months. Money was in very short supply so the teachers had sold the unlabeled bottles of capsules as "American Medicine" to be used by the purchasers for any cure they might wish. The children had not taken either the placebos or the vitamin capsules after the first day or two of the six months' trial.

Scientifically speaking, the research trip to Ethiopia was a total bust, a waste of taxpayers' money, but for me it was a lesson in how precise one must be in conducting clinical research, where monitoring is just as important as the framework of the project itself. That was the science lesson; and the Ethiopian adventure became my first trip abroad as an "ophthalmologist"—well, at least a doctor beginning to consider himself an ophthalmologist.

Toward the end of my first of two years at NIH, I received a letter from Professor A. Edward Maumenee, Director of the The Wilmer

Institute. He wrote that, knowing my father and being acquainted with me as a Hopkins med student, he was extending an early acceptance to the Johns Hopkins Wilmer Institute residency. On the one hand, thank heavens for Dad. But on the other hand, why was he always there when what I really wanted was to win on my own?

CHAPTER TEN

In June of 1959 I started the Wilmer residency, the first offspring of a former Wilmer resident ever accepted to that program. As a Hopkins medical student, I had taken an elective course in ophthalmology, which is where I had met Dr. Maumenee. By the time I became a resident, he had replaced the much celebrated, now elder statesman, Sir Stewart Duke-Elder, as the key man on almost every roster of national and international leaders in the field. Over his career, at least a dozen of his trainees were to become departmental chairpersons in major academic institutions across the country. No other eye department chairman anywhere in the world, before or since, can claim such a record of personal influence. In fact, today the Wilmer residency program has been the source of primary training for one hundred ophthalmology chairpersons worldwide.

Dr. Maumenee was not just the top professor in a large, full-time faculty but an ally and promoter of each trainee in his department. He loved to play tennis, and that sport brought me into more frequent social contact with him than most any of my peers or even faculty members at the Institute. I was often his doubles partner, and we won more often than we lost—which was very important to him. But early in my first year of residency, Dr. Maumenee let me know in a tactful manner that I had better stretch hard if I intended to keep up, which I took as an indicator that he didn't want his "legacy kid" to be an embarrassment to the Institute.

Ophthalmologists remember their first major eye operation as vividly as they recall the first girl they kissed or the other firsts less often made conversational. If that sounds old-fashioned, so was the surgical technique of my first cataract operation, performed in June, 1960, with the Chief Resident, Dr. J. Lawton Smith assisting me. I can recall each moment of it with the clarity of perfect vision, along with the animus and apprehension all newcomers experience as they assume that rite of passage on the way to becoming The Surgeon.

It was a laborious process that required almost an hour of operating time and it employed the then traditional large incision (almost half of the eye's circumference) that was mandated by the techniques available in those days. The cataract was removed in one piece and the incision was then closed with numerous silk sutures. The patient was kept as an in-patient for ten days, later returning for suture removal a month later. Finally, glasses were prescribed somewhere between six and eight weeks following the operation. My first cataract operation was not only successful for the patient but it was like a post-doctoral baptism or bar mitzvah for me.

Over the three years of a standard residency appointment, I worked as hard as I knew how. Initially, I was toying with the idea of joining my father in his practice, although I did not want to tell him that until I was certain. My dilemma was that I knew that if I were to become a full-time academic on a medical school faculty, it would mean far less income. But I also knew that it would give me a great deal more professional leeway and a better opportunity to shape the kind of medical career that would fit with my pluses and minuses. However, there was now another issue to be confronted.

At home, Janie was doing her best to be a medical wife, with patience and tolerance. Our son, whom we called by his middle name, Townley, never ceased to be our most precious possession. But his mother and I were slowly growing apart. I had medicine as the proverbial mistress. She had nothing comparable to keep her feeling fulfilled. We were to continue living with that realization for several more years, as a medical life became, for me, ever more absorbing. I knew what was happening but couldn't, or maybe wouldn't, let go of an ambition so mixed with fascination that any career alternative seemed like a surrender to mediocrity. Wilmer under Professor Maumenee made academic ophthalmology endlessly intriguing.

The succinct way to describe the Wilmer general eye clinic is to say that it was a potpourri of eye disorders with a cornucopian harvest of instruction. We residents called the clinic "the Pit" because it was located in the basement of the Institute, was invariably jammed with patients, and was hot as Hades in the warm months when the doctors were sweating through their shirts, and their jackets as well. Air conditioning was non-existent. There were high-standing fans that moved the air around, but it was still the same hot air. The clinic was the size of a basketball court. Patients and family members sat waiting on rows of hard wooden benches that lined the back of the room, the remainder being divided into five parallel examination lanes so that residents could work independently within the open structure of the high-ceilinged clinic. There were two adjacent dark rooms to which patients were taken for various examinations requiring a dark environment.

That clinic brings back many early memories of both common and rare eye disorders. One of the statements most often made by adults when coming in for a change of glasses was that they no longer needed their old glasses for reading. "These days I can even read the telephone book without glasses. I must be getting younger, Doctor!" The fact is they were experiencing so-called "second sight," which comes from a change in the refraction of the eye owing to the hardening of its lens. Paradoxically, therefore, second sight is not good news in the usual sense, for it is a harbinger of cataracts. Today, that surgery can be performed as soon a person wishes and invariably with excellent visual results. Second sight has become little more than a signal that cataract surgery sooner or later will be a helpful cure. But in those days it usually meant a prolonged period of gradual sight reduction to the point of obvious functional impairment, at which time a cataract extraction became an appropriate surgical risk. About one out of five cases had some form of surgical complication following cataract surgery in the 1960s—definitely an operation not to be taken lightly.

I remember a man of about 40, I'll call him Mr. Love, who came to the eye clinic for a change of glasses. He mentioned he had neighbors whose son was ten and did errands for him and now was having trouble seeing the blackboard in school. Would I see the child? Of course. Would I take care of the kid personally? Of course. Would I be sure glasses were ordered if they were needed? I would try to impress upon the parents any need for glasses, yes.

The child—I'll call him Johnny Jones—came by appointment, accompanied by both of his parents. A routine, dilated eye exam revealed minute spherical spots in the center of the child's crystalline lenses. They were too tiny to affect vision but were distinctive congenital markers that would be with him throughout life—like hidden tattoos. I called in several of the other residents, who enjoyed seeing these rather rare and actually quite beautiful microscopic lesions. I explained to Mr. and Mrs. Jones that we were merely observing tiny spots of no medical significance whatsoever. He did need glasses, however, and I provided the prescription.

A week later, Mr. Love returned for his follow-up appointment, including an examination of his retinas, which I had not been able to do during the first visit because he hadn't wanted his pupils dilated that day. As he sat in the examining chair and I wrote on his chart, Mr. Love told me that Johnny's mother was kind and thoughtful but Mr. Jones was an angry person and might well be beating the child. Mr. Love could hear the child's screams through the walls in the evenings. Did I have any advice about interfering with the Joneses for suspected child abuse? We talked about that for a while, agreeing that it was a situation that might require tactful handling.

When I dilated Mr. Love's pupils, I saw that the lenses of his eyes had the identical central, spherical spots that I had found in the neighbor's child, Johnny. The kid may have had problems in his home, but he also had a paternity situation that only I, and perhaps his mother and real father, knew the truth about. I wonder even today if Johnny Jones ever found out who his real father was. Not telling Mr. Love about what I had learned was a judgment call, but I suspected he knew.

Another memory of mine--etched in detail--is of a patient whose photograph appears in a book that I and another resident, Morton F. Goldberg, authored on injuries of the eye. One very late night when I was on call, the Emergency Room operator phoned me to come over as quickly as possible to the E.R. I got dressed in a matter of seconds and ran to the hospital. The patient I was to see was a thirty-two-year-old man who was exceedingly, combatively, drunk. He was being restrained on a gurney by several orderlies and a nurse or two. I was summoned because the handle of a large jackknife was sticking out from alongside his right eye. I snapped a photograph of the man's predicament—as real academics do when an instructive case is anticipated--and set about seeking its solution.

The bartender who had called the ambulance reported that the patient had been in an argument with another man at the bar. They reached a point of mutual disrespect, and the other man took out his knife, opened the blade and jabbed it at the eye of my patient—then promptly made his exit. The bartender knew one thing about such an injury: Like the Dutch boy with his finger in the dike, if he pulled out the knife, a flood of bleeding might ensue. So he left the knife in place and called an ambulance to come quickly.

The first order of business was to get the patient sufficiently calmed down to permit an accurate examination and to have a portable X-ray machine positioned for a view of whether the tip of the knife was reaching into the man's brain. In fact, the X-ray did show that the knife tip was at, or very near, the carotid sinus (just like a large vein) right behind the orbit. The consensus was that the knife's removal should not wait until the patient could be brought to a fully equipped operating room in the department of surgery.

Okay, my turn. With a full team of other medical people hushed and standing in readiness, I gently grasped the handle of the knife and ever so carefully, ever so slowly, pulled the blade out of the man's head--slowly, slowly, no evident bleeding, slowly and finally completely. Nothing happened. Monitoring the blood pressure and the man's neurological status indicated no adverse effect. The Dutch Boy Syndrome was not in play. To everyone's surprise, including my own, it was the easiest procedure imaginable. He was given an antibiotic to help prevent infection. None occurred. The vision in the eye did not return to normal because the optic nerve had been damaged by the blade, but it was nonetheless a favorable outcome in view of the nature of his injury. The man was kept in the hospital overnight to sober up and get his instructions for follow-up when he would be able to remember them.

The 1960s were at the tail end of a scourge of one of East Baltimore's most notorious and most dreaded methods of meting revenge with a weapon anyone could get his hands on—intentional lye burns of the eyes. This was soon to become a crime punished by imprisonment, and only then would the epidemic of lye burns diminish. Generally, the people injured with lye were a tough lot, accustomed to domestic violence that almost always could be traced to sexual indiscretions. My most memorable of perhaps ten such victims over the years was a woman in her thirties who was brought by ambulance to the Wilmer Accident Room. Maryjo arrived with her face reddened and blotchy, both eyes clamped shut, and tears streaming from under her eyelids. She explained amid sobs that, suspecting infidelity, her husband had thrown toilet bowl cleaner at her face.

First aid for ocular lye burns is sustained irrigation of the eyes and removal of any particulate lye-containing substances or clumped denuded surface cells. I irrigated her eyes for more than half an hour. Afterward, I examined her corneas with the biomicroscope—the slit lamp. It revealed seriously injured eye tissue, leaving only the ability to detect hand movements. She became a long-term patient treated symptomatically, but after two years with her eyes then quite comfortable, her vision was still limited to perceiving a moving hand in front of her face. Surgery was indicated and I was the man for the job, feeling confident that by then I had become a pretty good corneal surgery.

Fortunately for me, the transition to microsurgery was just beginning as I began my residency. Within two years I was permitted to perform a few corneal transplants with the assistance of the senior resident or a member of the faculty. My first such operation was on a young woman, Maryjo, three years after having had lye thrown into her eye by an angry husband. Transplants after lye burns were not usually successful in those days but that has since changed for the better, as improved means of preventing corneal rejection are discovered. After a second graft was performed, her vision was at least enough to enable her to get around by herself. About that time her husband "up and died," to use her expression, but she did not want to tell me about it. Maryjo was a woman in great emotional distress—who but the law could blame her? Every case of serious visual loss becomes a social as well as a medical concern, and the neophyte surgeon is likely not to have mastered the objectivity that is sometimes necessary for effective coping with his patients' personal issues.

Then there was the 45-year-old visually disabled, retired schoolteacher who came to me to be considered for a corneal transplant. He had sustained a chemical injury to both eyes twenty-five years previously, with loss of the right eye and only the barest perception of hand motions at close range in the left eye. This gentleman had long ago accepted blindness as his fate, and for the intervening two-and-a-half decades he had become fully adapted to life as a blind man. His wife told me he hardly ever asked for her help except for activities that were not a part of his routine. He used a cane and had no interest in getting a guide dog, believing he did well enough by himself. After several tests, I concluded that his remaining eye might be much improved by surgery. I recommended a corneal transplant, and he eventually accepted the proposal but with more misgivings than the typical patient hoping for restored eyesight usually had.

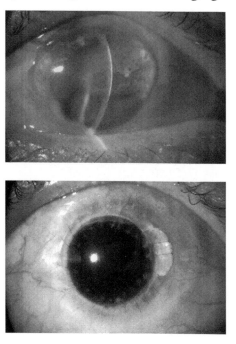

The operation was a combined corneal transplant and cataract extraction and it went very well, even though it was the first such combined operation I had ever performed.

However, on the initial post-op day, when his eye was unpatched and I examined it with a small flashlight, he was very uncomfortable, even though he could already see my hand moving in front of his face more clearly than before. I was surprised—and, I have to admit, a little disappointed—that he remained so peculiarly quiet, certainly not a happy celebrant of regained sight. For the first few weeks, his vision did not improve much more and he seemed to be almost sulking, making little effort to get around by himself. But gradually, very gradually, he regained more vision and his mood finally brightened. Two years after the operation, he brought me a present, a watercolor of a sailboat coming into harbor that he had painted. I have had the painting behind my desk ever since, next to photos of his eye pre-operatively and post-operatively.

In a letter written in 1749 by the French critic, Denis Diderot, he asks a blind man (and here I am paraphrasing): "Don't you wish you could see the moon again?" To which the blind man answers, "That could be very nice indeed, but if I had arms long enough, I would rather feel it than see it." Restoring sight to a person who, like my patient, has become thoroughly accustomed to blindness and life in a tactile world, may present him with a difficult return to the sighted world. I was just glad that my patient eventually was able to counter-rehabilitate to the visual orientation of a sighted person.

I have noticed that eye doctors tend to keep those who are blind at a distance, something that did not make sense until I thought it out. Blindness haunts us, unwittingly. It is not that we are unmoved by the plight of those individuals but, rather, that our inability to be of service to them makes them a frustrating presence. How many ophthalmologists' offices are there with blind receptionists? We may employ amputees, dowagers, dwarfs, or retired belly dancers, but you won't find a blind person working in an ophthalmologist's office. I think it is because we are intolerant of failures to cure.

As a medical student taking a course at The Wilmer Institute in 1955, I watched cataract surgeons stand as they operated, routinely making the then-conventional half-eye circumferential incision but also cutting away a segment of the iris so that the eye, after cataract extraction, would have a keyhole-shaped pupil. This standard procedure was not only cosmetically unappealing, but it caused the eye to be sensitive to light.

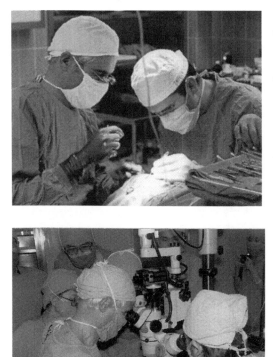

When I started as a resident in 1959, the common loupe had become more powerful—four to five times magnification--and by then surgeons were sitting, not standing, at the head of the patient, with their arms supported by armrests that extended from their chairs. Some of the older surgeons were still making the cataract incision with an extremely sharp sliver of a knife blade known by its designer's name, the von Graefe knife; but no matter how the incision was made, all were the traditionally large ones that required extensive suturing and at least a week of hospitalization.

There were many new ideas and instruments coming from other countries and the American ability to adapt and perfect them helped change the landscape of modern eye surgery into being largely dependent upon the use of a microscope for increasingly precise eye operations. The microscope began to be popular in the1960s, becoming commonly used in the 70s. Much earlier, in 1949, Harold Ridley, a British ophthalmologist, had been the first to demonstrate that the vision of patients having cataract extractions could be improved by the implantation of a plastic lens to be permanently retained within the eye that had been operated on after the cataract had been removed. This was an exciting advance. To avoid thick, heavy, image-distorting spectacle lenses was a blessing, especially for the elderly. The same could be said about the use of contact lenses by persons who have had cataract surgery; while greatly improving the post-operative vision, inserting and removing them daily was a major inconvenience for the patients. Ridley circumvented that difficulty by placing an inert, transparent plastic lens in such a way as to have it permanently retained within the eye. Not all cases were successful, but the precedent had been set, "catching the eye," if not the approval, of the profession.

Ridley's daring surgery prompted outcries of horrified objection from medical contemporaries. During a film shown of the surgery at one of his lectures, Sir Stewart Duke-Elder was so disgusted by seeing Ridley place a plastic "foreign body" within an eye that he stormed out of the hall. Ridley's highly criticized operation was to be likened by his colleague-critics to planting a "time bomb." In fact, it was true that many eyes with the early intraocular lenses did eventually develop serious late complications, but Ridley's work constituted a major breakthrough by a much respected, articulate and pleasingly modest clinician. Despite ophthalmologist-to-the-Queen Duke-Elder's condemnation of the intraocular lens, Ridley was eventually knighted by her in 2000, but only well after Duke-Elder's demise and just one year before his own death.

As it turned out, Ridley's intraocular lens (IOL) became the inspiration for many increasingly improved IOL's that followed, as microsurgery came into common practice. In the 1960s, a controversial American ophthalmologist-inventor, Charles D. Kelman MD[*], was working on a way to remove cataracts through a very small incision, only three millimeters to be exact, less than a third of the traditional incision size. When I was at Johns Hopkins, it was too early to know if the Kelman operation was going to be beneficial or just a flash in the pan, but at the very least it was an example of changes in surgical technique the challenges of learning new skills that were affecting the practice of ophthalmology across the country and throughout the world.

The three years of residency at Wilmer went by in a happy blur for me. If I could set aside almost anything that required mathematical facility (which was not all that hard to do), I found the rest of

---

[*] For further description of this most unusual individual, please find my essay about him in the book's postscript, entitled Trouble With An Upstart.

ophthalmology to be engrossing, emotionally rewarding and addict-
ing – every day, in just about every way. I do not think I was different
from my peers at Wilmer in that enthusiasm, for we all caught the
contagion of, in particular, Dr, Maumenee's curiosity, surgical excellence, vast knowledge of research and clinical advances, and had a
cheerful respect for his entire team of faculty and trainees. I was to become increasingly aware during my Wilmer years that ophthalmology, possibly above all other medical fields, brings an extraordinary
reciprocity of satisfaction to the doctor from what we are taught to
provide to our patients.

One day in the middle of my third year of residency, Dr. Maumenee and I happened to meet in the corridor. He called me into
his office and, after some preliminary small talk, said, "Dave, the faculty has decided you should be the Chief Resident from the present
third-year group." Just like that, I was being asked to be "on deck"
for the appointment of a fifth-training year in the capacity of Chief
Resident. At that time, the Wilmer Institute was the only residency
program in the country that had a fifth-year resident position. This
was comparable to a junior faculty appointment, and it meant being
in full charge of the residency's clinical program on a day-in, day-out,
basis. It also meant I could have my choice of any kind of eye surgery
and that I would be responsible for the program's didactic schedule
and for advice and guidance regarding every non-routine admission
to the Institute for medical or surgical management. And further, it
meant that I would have a close working relationship with Professor Maumenee, whenever he was in town. And—I say this for its
smoldering social consequences at home---it meant I was to become
even more of a total medical workaholic, for that was the way it was
expected to be and it would never be otherwise: Johns Hopkins.

I did not presume that I was the first one to be asked. Others of
the six of us who were third-year residents might have turned it down,
choosing instead to go immediately into practice. But it really did
not matter. What I considered to be the job of a lifetime was being
offered to me. I didn't ask for time to talk to my wife or to discuss it
with my father, or even to think it over. I accepted it on the spot.

CHAPTER ELEVEN

The fourth year of a Wilmer residency was always spent by the appointed Chief Resident at some other institution, as a means of broadening his experience on his way to assuming the leadership of the residency the following year. Most of my predecessors had spent a year of basic or clinical research at another American institution, or in some developed country such as England or Sweden—wherever the work best suited the interest of the individual. Because of my two previous years at the NIH, my third year at Wilmer was really my fifth year of training in ophthalmology. I needed a change of scenery and a change of culture.

The year away required developing a project of some kind. I turned to Dr. Miguel Martinez, my laboratory colleague who had been collaborating with me from his lab in Manhattan. A bio-engineer instrument inventor who had been fully trained in Mexico as an ophthalmologist, he preferred to confine his work to the laboratory. We had numerous clinical interests in common that lent themselves to the gadgets and instruments he created and to my clinical application of the new devices, so we were a good match, professionally. He was making progress with his variant of an artificial cornea (keratoprosthesis) that was working well in the eyes of rabbits and was deemed ready for clinical trials. We decided that it would make the most sense to carry out such trials in a place where corneal transplants were not feasible, due specifically to a lack of donor corneas—meaning no eye bank work had been undertaken. That would be my part of the project. To fulfill it, I sought a year's job in Jordan, where trachomatous blindness was rampant, and with some luck I found just the right opportunity at the St. John Ophthalmic Hospital in Jerusalem, Jordan. Janie was quite agreeable to this venture—feeling, as I did, that a change of scenery might also do our marriage some good—and Townley was too young to express any objection.

I was looking forward to a year in a new environment with less intense pressure and with a great deal of eye surgery and basic clinical eye care mixed in with the research project. My grandfather once wrote, "We need to cultivate leisure if we care to develop not only a sane outlook on life, but sufficient opportunity for the functioning of the subconscious processes essential for original thinking."' That is the other side of the "iron-man" doctrine of work, with its advocacy of near exhaustion as a way to make a better man and a better doctor.

I was fortunate to obtain an NIH grant of $11,000 to cover the cost of the clinical research and travel expenses, paid by the International Eye Foundation in Washington, D.C., and its co-sponsor, CARE-Medico. As a fourth-year resident, I would also receive half-pay while out of town, about $6,000--so we had enough income if we were careful with our spending.

In the 1960s, all foreign aircraft arrived in Jordan at Amman, the only civilian airport in the country. When we deplaned, the heat of the desert was immediately oppressive, almost enough to send us back on board. A CARE representative was there to meet us in a company van and drive us to Jerusalem. From Amman, it was more than a two-hour drive down to Jordan River Rift at the river's entrance to the Dead Sea--at which point we were 1,300 feet below sea level. The road crossed the Jordan at the later-named Allenby Bridge, skirted the town of Jericho and climbed the steep hills of Judea, the West Bank. The winding road in its ascent through desolate, undeveloped rocky land provided a glimpse of the empty Qumran caves, and finally reached the elevated central plain upon which Jerusalem had been built many centuries ago.

There, a transformation occurred. Leaving the stony desert, our van quickly brought us into a crowd of quaintly costumed persons of every age filling the street as if cars were invaders into their lives. It was a cast of hundreds, awash in the sounds of a culture entirely foreign to our ears. The CARE driver had to honk and pause, swerve and sometimes stop—as the road was taken over by the hosts of people who lived on the outskirts of Jerusalem. We rolled down the dust-coated windows to take it all in.

There were high-piled donkey carts with impatient owners; men wearing red-checkered *kaffiyehs* held on their heads by a black band; women in embroidered black dresses and white head scarves; dogs belonging to no one; boys in school uniforms scuffing carelessly, kicking balls or throwing stones while happily mingling in small groups; girls holding hands with each other or with their mothers, the older ones wearing longer and darker skirts; tourists defined by their cameras, their comfortable shoes, and their hesitant curiosity as they alone seemed to notice our vehicle; and several small black cars and one or two narrow trucks. The daily structure of our life-to-be unfolded when the mullah called his people to prayer, broadcast over a loudspeaker mounted at the top of the distant mosque's minaret.

The kingdom of Jordan in the early 1960s included the Old City of Jerusalem and numerous other cities and towns such as Bethlehem on the so-called West Bank of the Jordan River that remained Jordan's share of Palestine after the Arab-Israeli war of 1948-9, in accordance with United Nations mandates. Half a million Palestinian refugees were given Jordanian citizenship, having been uprooted from their homes in territory granted to Israel, and therefore there were refugee camps and extensive poverty and anger among the residents of Jerusalem during the year we spent there. That anger, however, did not extend to us as Americans working at a beloved and highly respected British hospital dedicated exclusively to the Arab population and underwritten by philanthropy for most of its carrying costs. The hospital was located only about a stone's throw from Israel's eastern border, defined by a no-man's land with barbed wiring on both sides. There was a guarded gate through which we could enter Israel; but if we chose to do so, we would not be allowed to return to Jordan with an Israeli stamp in our passports so, in effect, we couldn't. Thus, we were to be living in a war-torn land but within the influence of a respected institution.

The Order of St. John of Jerusalem had once led crusaders to this biblical region, where they established a hospice near the Via Dolorosa for their own needs, and thereafter maintained the structure as a charitable hospital for Palestine. Ninety years before our arrival in

1962, the hospital had become an eye hospital and was relocated not far from the Mount of Olives, within easy walking distance from ancient Jerusalem.

The eye hospital, still owned and operated by the Order, was overseen from afar by none other than the commanding, multidimensional, sharp-witted Sir Stewart Duke-Elder.

Our first view of the hospital compound was of an almost storybook settlement of small buildings made of mortared stone blocks that matched the walls of the simulated castle, the hospital. A Jordanian flag flew from the hospital's turret and a pennant of the Order waved just below. The compound was encircled by a stone wall, with iron entrance gates bearing the coat of arms of the Order. The other buildings in the compound were the "flats" occupied by the medical and nursing staffs. There was another separate stone building that I would soon find out was the VIP Bungalow.

The official language of the St. John Ophthalmic Hospital (SJOH) was English, and just about everything about the hospital was British, from the many decorative touches reflecting the influence of the chivalric tradition to the grey bedspread on every one of the fifty-five beds in the open male and female wards, each with a large, embroidered blue felt crest of the Order.

The medical staff was under the command of the head doctor, called the Warden, a position assumed at that time by Arthur Boase. In England, surgically-oriented medical doctors were called "Mister" but in foreign lands the British surgeons called themselves "Doctor," like the rest of us. Dr. Bose was a delightful, reticent, modest Englishman who was curious about, and somewhat skeptical of, my Wilmer-based advocacy of an operating microscope for intraocular surgery. Small wonder, for without a microscope but with many years of surgical experience, Dr. Boase did fast and uncomplicated procedures with the traditional large incision far better than I could do at four times his magnification.

The British nurses were addressed as "Sister" and it was not long before I recognized they were the backbone of the hospital's discipline, its precise routine and its overall cleanliness in a land where everything else looked unwashed and dusty. The head nurse, Ms. Anne Blewitt, was addressed as "Matron." She had a commanding authority second only to that of Dr. Boase.

Sir Stewart ruled iron-handedly from London. He made at least one annual visit to the hospital, and in 1962 it came in the latter part of the summer. Wreathed in smiles, Sir Stewart emerged from the VIP bungalow, nodding to the full Jordanian serving staff arranged as first greeters along the path to the hospital. The Warden stood at the great door awaiting his distinguished visitor. Someone clapped and, after a moment's pause, all joined in for what became a spirited ovation. Duke-Elder made no acknowledgment of it as he shook hands with Dr. Boase before they entered together but it made quite an impression on me.

Beside myself and Dr. Boase, there were four other ophthalmologists at the hospital: two from England, one from Ireland and another from Scotland. In all the years of the Eye Hospital's existence, there had never before been an American doctor on staff. We doctors stood in the foyer as observers, wearing our scrubs and apart from the reception line of nurses that now greeted "His Excellency." The six young British sisters were uniformed in dark blue blouses and matching full skirts reaching to well below the knee, starched white nurse's caps with small protruding wings, and white, starched pinafore aprons that featured the crest of the Order of St. John. At the end of the line stood Matron, also uniformed but in a more reserved blue dress, upon which she wore a medal of the Order pinned over her heart. The glowing Duke-Elder shook each nurse's hand and--I pledge the truth--reached around behind every single one of the six young nurses to deliver his hallmark pinch. They later complained about the presumptuousness of his Victorian grope but I must say, at the risk of sounding chauvinistic, they appeared to appreciate the pinches at the time. (Matron received just the handshake.)

Others on the hospital team were young Jordanian men and women serving as aides and interpreters for the English-speakers, each dressed in predominantly white uniforms with a white skull cap. The fifty-five beds were divided into large open male and female wards, plus a few private rooms for special cases and VIPs. Patients having cataract operations were held in the hospital for seven-to-ten days of post-operative care. The majority of routine cases were operated under local anesthesia, and only I was persistent in trying to do the intraocular surgery with an available floor-standing microscope customarily used by the doctors for a variety of other purposes. In retrospect, I do not recall any arrangements for prayer for the Muslin patients, not that they would have been allowed out of bed to touch their heads to the floor.

I found it amusing that the great Sir Stewart—still the most well-known ophthalmologist in the world—was now my boss, in absentia except for his annual visit to Jordan but nonetheless exerting tightly-held authority. The hospital could not requisition eye patches or even rearrange an examination unit without first obtaining his signature. Sir Stewart was the hospital's benevolent despot, revered by his minions even though they were intimidated by his importance. I was not appropriately intimidated, being an outsider and possibly somewhat brash by British standards. I admired him, even wrote him personal letters about life in Jordan, to which he responded promptly in extended long hand, which was not easy reading but always worth the effort.

Since there was no available space for us on the compound, I found living quarters for Janie, Townley and me near the hospital in an old two-room structure clinging to the side of a steep hill. But it occurred to me that the VIP bungalow was not only on the grounds of the hospital, but was a showpiece-like architectural structure having all of the comforts of home. It was used by Sir Stewart during his annual week's visit, but sat empty for the rest of the year. I would gladly have paid our current rent to the charitable Order of St. John if we could live in the VIP bungalow except when it was required for official purposes for that one week each year, at which time we would go elsewhere until it was again empty. I tried out my proposal on the warden, and he blanched at the audacity. No. No, NO! When I brought it up again a few days later, he suggested I write directly to Sir Stewart with my proposal, which I did.

Sir Stewart answered like a shot. He said, as closely as I can recall, as follows: "My dear David, I must respond with my regret not to be able to accommodate you and your family. You know, of course, that the answer deserves no explanation. Your invitation to live in the bungalow awaits the time when you shall return in splendid seniority, at which time I shall no longer be its doorkeeper, I expect that will come in a matter of a few decades. Yours. . ."

He signed it "Stewart" but that was not the way I was ever to address him, nor was anyone else at the hospital, except possibly Dr. Boase, who, however, was too tactful to refer to him by his first name in front of others.

So Janie and I settled into our adobe hut just a goat's path away from the hospital compound. At least it had the advantages of being private, costing us only the equivalent of a couple of dollars a day, and allowing us to live among indigenous people instead of being isolated in a British compound.

I had set my sights at SJOH on identifying patients who had two blind eyes from corneal blindness and who might have their vision restored by the surgical insertion of a corneal prosthesis, since there was no eye bank and thus no source of donor corneal tissue. It was not difficult to find such patients and in the course of three months, I performed approximately ten keratoprosthesis operations, using the plastic device that my partner on the project, Dr. Martinez, had designed and manufactured in his Manhattan laboratory.

The surgery itself always went well enough, and the immediate post-operative care was generally uneventful; however, within weeks, or sometimes months, various troubles began to occur that had not occurred in our rabbit experiments: Either corneal tissue grew over the prosthesis's front surface, or membranes formed on the back surface or on the corneal substance itself, permitting fluid from within the eye to leak, soften the eye and potentially allow infection to enter at the point of leakage. Using dead, glycerine-preserved corneal tissue obtained from eye banks in the United States, the blind corneas were restored by patching, thus allowing whatever light perception the eye may have had pre-operatively to be preserved but not enhanced. In short, the keratoprosthesis project was a bust.

I either had to mount a worthwhile project or return to Baltimore with the taint of failure just before assuming the role of Chief Resident and leader of the remaining twenty-three residents in training at Wilmer. Changing course, I received permission from NIH and IEF-CARE-Medico to use the remainder of the year's funding to establish an eye bank in Jordan. But none of my English colleagues was interested in campaigning for eye banking in a Muslim country, although they would be very pleased to help do the surgery. The challenge of successfully advocating local sources for donor eye material was obviously not their cup of tea. They would leave that delicate matter entirely to me.

Only eighteen years after the world's first eye bank had been founded by my dad in New York, I was about to give eye-banking a try in Jordan. I explained my plan, along with my predicament, in a letter to Dr. Maumenee. Remarkably enough, he received the letter while attending an ophthalmological conference in nearby Beirut and said he would like to visit us at SJOH. Excited at the prospect, we looked about for a knowledgeable guide for his visit to Jerusalem.

Janie and I had become friends with a Franciscan monk, an American by the name of Father Brian. He wore the brown robe, white rope belting and sandals of the Franciscans, but he was American at heart, having once been a substitute team player for the Pittsburgh Steelers. Father Brian was about my age. He was an amusing and invariably happy man with a single known failing, the Irish virus of alcoholism. He had been assigned to the Church of the Holy Sepulcher, the holiest site of Christian faith where Christ had been buried. The building is always guarded, in distinctly separate areas, by four

Christian orders, the Franciscans being one of them. The church is opened at four a.m. and is securely locked for the night at seven p.m. Always! On several occasions, another friend or two joined me in carrying the hopelessly inebriated Father Brian on our shoulders to "get him to the church on time" before it was locked for the night. From his commanding position, he would sing out instructions to his bearers along the lines of "Take me to the Latin Quarter!" Once, when we were too late getting him to the church, he had to spend the night outside. We loved that man.

We decided that he would be a superb choice as Dr. Maumenee's tour guide. Janie and I came along, thereby seeing the famed sights of Jerusalem led by one of the most engaging fellow countrymen one might imagine--stone cold sober. He took us to most of the public sites of religious importance in the city, flavoring our three-hour romp with chants, jokes, and abbreviated devotionals. We were even shown the Al-Aqsa Mosque in the Dome of the Rock compound, which is the third most sacred shrine of Islam, and were taken to the Wailing Wall, which at that time was covered and inaccessible to visitors.

Dr. Maumenee was pleased with the tour, as well as with his visit to the Eye Hospital, where he met Dr. Boase and others on the medical staff and some of the nurses--whom he made no move to pinch. He was easily convinced that the Patons were in a stimulating environment acquiring incomparable experiences of ophthalmological and sociological importance so he approved my experiment to develop an eye-banking project, but warned it would undoubtedly be as futile as the keratoprosthesis project had been. Dr. Boase had done a number of corneal transplants over the years, using the rare donor material he could obtain from eyes that had to be removed for whatever reason. Unfortunately, the procedures were infrequent, despite the thousands of men, women and children whose sight could have been restored had donor corneas been abundantly available from Jordanian donors.

The strategy for initiating a system of eye banking that was intended to correct this situation had to begin with eyes imported from donors in the United States. There, eye-banking in one city or another often had more fresh donor eyes than could be used within the

short period of time from a donor's death to about one week thereafter. In those days, the entire eye was delivered to the surgeon even
though it was only the cornea that could be used for transplantation. The available donor eyes were flown to Amman, and from there
were transported by the CARE van to Jerusalem. The corneas were
expeditiously scheduled for corneal transplants, often within a few
hours of their arrival at the hospital. Within a few weeks of starting
this importation of donor eyes, several dozen corneal transplants were
performed. The outcomes of these operations proved gratifyingly successful, which impressed all who met or heard about these patients,
so I naturally assumed that the eye-banking pump was being successfully primed and soon would run on a local supply of eyes from the
Jordanian dead.

But there was no immediate action in that direction, so my next
assumption was that a further key to successful eye banking would be
to get to know the local Jordanian movers and shakers, and to con-
vince them to promise their eyes for use after death-- thereby giving
sight to the blind with Muslim eyes. I met with as many educated,
involved citizens as possible, but I found that asking my Muslim
friends to pledge their eyes was like suggesting they agree to a Christian crucifixion. They were not persuaded by the story of the biblical
blind man of Jericho, which the Pope had cited in 1956 as his justifi-
cation for approving eye banks. Instead, one Muslim friend explained
to me with much tact and concern that the Koran states it is a sin to
break the bones of the dead, therefore it is a safe assumption that it
is also a sin to take the eyes of the dead. No Muslim--to my knowl-
edge--ever refused a corneal transplant to restore his vision, but in
1962-1963, no Muslim in Jordan pledged his own eyes for future use
by fellow countrymen. There is no reason to be judgmental of that
reluctance, however, for it took a long time for eye banking to flourish
in the United States, too.

During this period of awakening interest in corneal transplantation, I was asked by one of my Bedouin patients to attend a Jordanian
feast, a *mansef*. Janie was not invited to the all-male event. We met
near the hospital toward evening, when the sun was no longer hot.
My host, a middle-aged unsmiling man with tented eyes and a strik-

ingly crooked aquiline nose, drove me in his Range Rover to a desert location, where we met ten other tribesmen, mostly bearded and wearing checkered *kaffiyehs*, white robes and sandals. One of the men explained in faltering English that our host's nose had been broken by a kick from a camel, evidently a local joke told a thousand times. However, it lessened the formality even though we had almost no communication except through the translation of the host. We sat on Bedouin carpets at the mouth of a black tent. It was picturesque but to me it felt staged, somewhat forced—-like a display of tribal hospitality put on for my benefit.

The conversation, if it could be called that, became animated, including what I presumed were tributes to me because one or another of them would say something in a friendly tone, put his right hand over his heart and smile graciously at me sitting uncomfortably on a lumpy rug with my legs crossed.

Next, a tribesman brought glasses of tea and a huge tray of food heaped up like a pyramid, with a single sheep's eye placed on top. It was shriveled, like a large overripe grape. My host reached for the eye with his right thumb and forefinger and offered it to me. I hesitantly accepted it with my left hand, which I learned later was a faux pas of major proportions since the left hand is only for cleaning oneself and is never to be used for eating.

Switching the soggy, dark-colored glob of "sheep sight" mixed with a viscous "ocular" sauce to my right hand, I contemplated it with what I hoped was hidden horror. I had heard that it was the custom for the guest at a *mansef* to eat the eye of the sheep but I had thought it was just a rumor to titillate tourists. The solemn expressions of the assembled group suggested otherwise. All my professional life I had trained to preserve eyes, to restore them, to respect them for the great organ that they are. I felt like gagging just in anticipation of what had to be done. But, honored guest that I was, I ate the damn thing: chewy, salty, sticky, emitting its own uniquely unpleasant odor. In short, it was awful. I do not know how they might have reacted had I refused to eat the eye, but I felt I had to do my best to assimilate into the Arab culture, even in this trying instance.

Word got around that an American doctor was going to cure blindness in Jordan and patients flocked to me for whatever miracles I had to offer. Largely on false hopes, sad to say. I gave talks and met with hospital staffs throughout the western portion of Jordan. It was a blitz approach, carried out in my so-called spare time, but the real solution to what was needed lay in finding pledges that eyes could be removed for corneal transplants at the time of deaths.

One incident almost put a halt to any further importation of donor eyes from the United States. An eye bank in Rochester, N.Y. sent me two eyes that I used immediately for corneal transplants, the recipients being two blind Palestinian Arabs. The deceased donor of the eyes had been a wealthy Jewish woman, who had given lavishly to the needs of Israel throughout her life. Prior to her death, she had her family promise to arrange for her eyes to be sent to Israel—the ultimate act of her lifelong devotion to the land of Zion.

Although the Rochester and New York City eye banks' staffs knew that I was performing corneal transplants in Jerusalem, on that occasion they failed to recall that my work was limited to the Arab sector of the city. Nothing would have come of the mistaken delivery had it not been for the adult children of the deceased. They asked the Rochester eye bank to check on the recipients of the gift of their mother's eyes, for the satisfaction of knowing that her final magnanimous gift to Israel had been successfully accomplished. Since the donor had been an enormously generous and prominent individual, the eye bank people compromised a strict policy of never revealing what becomes of the donor material and let the family know who had performed the surgery.

That is how it was discovered that the eyes from the Jewish woman had been mistakenly sent to me, for the benefit of Arabs in Jerusalem. Their mother's eyes had been given to the enemy! Soon those precious pieces of eyes would be allowing their new owners to look down gun barrels or to aim stones across the barbed wire that divided the two nations. The bereaved relatives were furious.

Profuse apologies were made. The eye bank staff was cautioned against carelessness, and I was exonerated on the basis of "abject ignorance." I was amused that my ignorance should be called "abject' by someone at the New York eye bank, less amused when I heard the whole episode had been recounted to Sir Stewart. But it blew over and in subsequent months, additional donor eyes were received from the United States and England. However, the supply remained limited, the shipments few and far between.

Things move slowly in Jordan, and I was becoming discouraged about finding enough donors to establish an eye bank when late one evening, Dr. Boase called me to say that Sister Claire, a European nun from the Children's Hospital in the Old City, was trying to reach me. She wanted to let me know that there were two eyes I could use for my surgery but that I must fetch them very quickly.

I had met Sister Claire only a few days earlier when she brought several children for eye examinations to the Eye Hospital. As I examined the children's eyes, I gave her my usual impassioned speech about Jordan's need for corneal transplants to establish eye banking. As she listened to me, she offered special loving help and encouragement to one of the children who clung closely--afraid to have her eyes examined. She was a young Arab girl with long black hair, tiny gold earrings, a mole on one cheek that was like a beauty spot, and a beguiling smile.

Observing Sister Claire's interaction with that child made me feel I knew all the good in her. Now, having had her admonition to rush, I pulled on my white doctor's coat, ran from my bungalow along the goat path to the hospital, located the Eye Donor Kit, and drove with it in the hospital van to the so-called New Gate of the Old City. The Old City was a maze of winding, cobbled passageways--too narrow for cars. At night the City was in blackness. I picked my way uncertainly through the unmarked streets, which I knew fairly well by day but not when distorted by darkness. Luckily I managed to find the Children's Hospital. The entrance was sealed by paired wooden doors, one of which had a central window crossed by thin iron bars. I thumped on the door and pressed my face to the window. A scragglyfaced man made Arabic barking sounds at me through the bars. Then the door opened. The guard didn't speak English, but he must have figured out by my white coat that I was a doctor.

In a moment, Sister Clare arrived. She beckoned me up a stairway and, with the help of her flashlight, into an empty clinic. From there, we made our way up another stairway and past a ward of sleeping children, curled in their cots, often with a parent or older sibling asleep nearby on the floor. Sister Claire urged me to move faster, explaining that the dead child's family was on its way to the hospital and would soon be told of their child's death.

We hurried through a corridor and came to a door which the Sister unlocked, hustling me into a small treatment room lighted by a bulb dangling from a wire over a table. There was a tiny crucifix on the wall, and a stench of vomit and feces. On the table was a body covered by a sheet. The Sister peeled back the sheet as carefully as one might turn down a bed. The deceased was a child of perhaps five, with frothy mucus surrounding her mouth and matted dark hair. Then I saw the mole on the child's left cheek.

"You saw her before. You remember?" The Sister's voice was steady, matter-of-fact.

"Yes, Sister. I remember."

I had never before removed eyes from a person whom I had known, even so briefly. As with many other times in my professional life, the nurse became the guide for the doctor. Sister Claire began emptying my kit of instruments and laying them neatly on the table beside the child's head. She held a flashlight to improve the scant illumination from the dangling bulb as I removed the first eye and placed it in moist cotton within a small jar in preparation for the return trip to the hospital.

Sister Claire never lost concentration. We packed the orbit with gauze sponges and went on to surgically remove the second eye, securing it in a second jar. Then I pulled the eyelids closed over the rolls of gauze that I placed in the orbits, so that no one could detect that the eyes were missing unless, of course, someone opened the lids. The eye removals had taken ten minutes, possibly less.

The Sister wanted me to leave as quickly as possible. She knew that by now the parents would have been informed of the death. I put the jars with the donor eyes and the instruments back in the kit and was leaving the room when a wailing, veiled woman rushed in, her husband following quietly behind her.

The parents must have assumed that my role was that of the doctor who had cared for their child in the final moments of her life. They kissed my hands and murmured prayers. As I left the room, the mother went to the child's body, grasped one of the little hands and held it to her face, kissed it and then, sobbing, flung herself upon the body.

That was the first of many similar visits to the Children's Hospital, each successive one making me tougher, more professional. Sister Claire and the other sisters became strong allies of eye banking in Jordan, and essentially the only ones. The transplants either took place the same night the corneas were obtained, or early the next morning. All the staff doctors took turns at the surgery.

Then one day an ominous phone call came to Dr. Boase. A Muslim cleric in Jerusalem had heard from the family of a child who died at the Children's Hospital that there was a young American doctor "stealing" eyes from the Arab dead––and with the knowledge and help of the Catholic nursing staff. The infuriated mullah had poured out his rage to Muslim authorities in Amman. My stomach lurched.

As reserved and polite as Dr. Boase was while telling me this news, it was implicit that deporting me to the United States might be necessary; religious infractions were taken very seriously. My crusade was on hold, on religious grounds––the worst of all reasons because I guessed there would be no forgiveness for infidel transgressions. First the plastic corneas had failed, then I had used eyes intended for Israel, now there was a jihad with my name on it. Something had to be done to correct matters––as soon as possible.

Just by chance, the turmoil in Amman over my use of corneas from Muslim children came at a time of great political unrest in Jordan. Street riots between Palestinians and Hashemites broke out, resulting in the closing of the St. John Hospital for a few days, which gave me time to worry and think.

A remote memory somehow surfaced of a Princeton classmate in the United States, Robert Doherty, who had casually, even teasingly, offered to help me if I ever got into trouble in Jordan. This was no joke. I contacted him and, after listening to my tale of woe, he called an acquaintance, a journalist in Beirut. The journalist called someone he knew in Amman. Finally, a call went to the palace. King Hussein was informed that an American doctor was in trouble for having tried to start an eye bank and to use eyes from dead Jordanians.

Whatever else was said to King Hussein, I will never know. But there is one indisputable fact about the chain of events: His Royal Highness, King Hussein of Jordan, descendent of the Prophet Mohammad, would personally come to the St. John Ophthalmic Hospital to officially inaugurate the eye bank being started by the American doctor. Allah be praised!

A week later, on January 16, 1963, after security agents had spent the night checking out every conceivable source of potential danger, the King arrived with a large entourage. The Greek archbishop, various mullahs, the Prime Minister, members of the press and their photographers--in all, about fifty people--followed the King into the hospital where Dr. Boase and I greeted them at the door and led them to a reception room prepared with chairs, a podium and a microphone. Hot tea in little glasses was served, always the kickoff to any formal gathering.

Dr. Boase welcomed His Majesty on behalf of the Order and the hospital staff. He then introduced me to say a few words about the newly formed, barely functioning eye bank. Of course, I emphasized the need to get pledges for the use of eyes after people died. When His Majesty expressed interest, I took him to an adjacent room where we had lined up five young men who had recently had their sight restored as a result of corneal transplants. (The fact that there were no female patients was merely coincidence, for the corneas had been distributed without regard to the gender of the recipients.) Enlarged photographs of the pre-operative eyes-- showing dead white corneas--were pasted on the wall behind each patient. The patients stood, stamped their feet like soldiers presenting arms on a parade ground, and in unison gave a cheer for their king.

The King seemed to love it. He asked me questions about each case, shook hands with the grateful patients, and then requested a pledge form for his own eyes. Allah be praised even more abundantly!

The press took pictures of his signing, which appeared in local newspapers within the next few days.

I never again stole eyes, not in any country, although my itinerant life would lead me to many other lands in need of eye banks. Fortunately, an important stride was made in eye-banking in the years that were immediately to follow, so that only the removal of the donor cornea was required, rather than removal of the entire eye. Even today, eye-banking in Muslim countries remains more dependent upon the importation of donor material than on local sources, although other religions also tend to reject the use of human tissue for transplantation; but as the surgery itself has become increasingly common and overwhelming successful, I feel sure that sooner or later the fear of breaking the bones of the dead will no longer be an impediment to corneal transplantation by Jordan's skillful eye surgeons.

Despite the difficulties I had in soliciting local donor eyes when I was working at SJOH, the lessons from my experiences in Jordan regarding the impact of cultural differences, the variability of practical ethics and the influence of power were to remain with me forever.

CHAPTER TWELVE

In July of 1963, a few weeks after returning from Jordan to The Wilmer Institute to start my year as Chief Resident, Janie and I were invited to a Saturday evening dinner by our friends Joe and Ginny Tydings. It was to be held at Joe's family's country estate, about ten miles beyond Baltimore's city limits. Joe Tydings, a Democrat from Maryland, was the youngest United States senator. Having previously served as the U.S. Attorney General for Maryland, he was a hot prospect for a brilliant future career in politics. Ginny was fun and gorgeous, able to hold her own even with the most imposing career–conscious politicos.

The dinner was held on a near-perfect summer evening on their remote property in one of Maryland's charming, turn-of-the-century farmhouses surrounded by rolling fields, with no neighbors in sight. We knew something was up. We had been asked to arrive promptly, and had received several unusual advance calls from the Tydings to reconfirm our attendance. As we entered the landscaped areas around the house, we noticed there were Secret Service agents spread around. As if they had waited for us to arrive, two large helicopters thundered out of nowhere, circled the field and landed an easy forward pass from the terrace, where we were headed for cocktails. Down the steps of one aircraft scurried more agents and, from the other, stepped the President of the United States, the U.S. Attorney General, and the Assistant Secretary of the Navy. At the same time, a black Chevrolet came bumping down the long dirt driveway with Teddy Kennedy, the junior Senator from Massachusetts, at the wheel. The Kennedys had stopped in for dinner.

In a few minutes, our host introduced me—the only registered Republican in the room—to the President, who had already picked up that I was a Johns Hopkins doctor who had spent a year in Jordan at a British eye hospital. He began asking questions about the Jordanian people: Were the Hashemites distinguishable from the

Palestinians in appearance or attitude? What did I think about King Hussein—was he popular with the Palestinians? Had I visited Israel? Had I ever heard of a Mrs. Vester, who had founded the American Colony hostel in Jerusalem? That last question was most unexpected but indeed, I knew a good deal about that much-loved woman and had visited the house where she had entertained many distinguished visitors. President Kennedy knew far more about the spirit and the wounds of the Middle East than I could have expected of a man who had to be knowledgeable about the entire world. He was not only focused but intellectually involved in everything we discussed. I was frankly amazed and pleased, Republican though I was—having expected him to be far more interested in the two engaging women in our small group.

Following the Tydings' example, we all called Bobby and Teddy by their first names and the President, "Mr. President." Bobby would circle the group, picking off hors d'oeuvres from the trays being passed, saying a word or two to the non-Kennedys. He was functioning as a presidential outlier, touching base with his senior brother regularly, as a scout might report to a general about sightings in the field. The Assistant Secretary of the Navy, Paul "Red" Fay, was constantly smiling as he told a succession of stories—jokes, mostly— laughing loudly with the Kennedy brothers at his own punch lines.

Once dinner was over, drinks continued to flow. Teddy suggested it was time for songs and offered a trial burst of a ballad. The others laughed and began singing songs of their own, much as orchestral musicians do when warming up individually before a concert. The chairs were being rearranged, the table abandoned. The Tydings knew some of the songs' words and joined in as the brothers' singing began to get organized. But as the selection of a cappella ballads became increasingly Irish, just Red and the Kennedys were left singing. The President was clearly enjoying himself immensely and so was Bobby, who had locked arms with his older brother, soon joined by Teddy, extending the link—a true band of brothers.

They hung together like that for at least an hour and a half—it seemed a short while at the time—gleefully mugging at some of the lyrics, alternately seizing chances to take the lead but always to the obvious enjoyment of the others, who would then follow suit. The ballads became increasingly sentimental. I had never heard any of them before but they were evidently as familiar as nursery rhymes to the Kennedys. Then, quite abruptly, as if there had been a silent signal, it was time for them to depart—which they did after extending appropriate thanks for the dinner, thoughtfully singling out the two ladies for courteous goodbyes.

Teddy left with the others by helicopter, having asked if I would drive his car to Washington the following day since I had a meeting in Bethesda. I drove the car to the Senators' parking lot and left the key in his office and never met either him or his brothers again. But they remain larger than life among my selective memories.

Within four months, forty-six-year-old President Kennedy would be assassinated in Dallas. Five years from that happy, relaxed dinner party, Bobby Kennedy, then forty-two, would be assassinated in Los Angeles. Six years from that night, Ted Kennedy, then thirty-seven, would escape an early death but would be forever marked by the tragedy of his car accident that drowned Mary Jo Kopechne at Chappaquiddick, Massachusetts. He would have thirty-five more distinguished years in the Senate before being felled by a malignant brain tumor at age seventy-seven.

The loyalty of those brothers, each to the other, was deep and evident. On that night in Maryland, they showed themselves not as womanizers—Janie and Ginny Tydings, as appealing as they were, were almost ignored by them—but as compelling examples of brotherly love.

My year as Chief Resident was not far along before Professor Maumenee invited me to call him Ed. I found it much harder to call him "Ed" than it had been to call the nation's Attorney General, "Bobby." It took some doing but soon "Ed" became second nature to me. I found my schedule filled to the brim with surgery, teaching, night reading, and the daily load of private patients from Ed's office. One day the Professor—Ed--called me in to meet Mrs. Agnes Meyer, the widow of the former owner of the *Washington Post,* Eugene Meyer, and mother of Katharine Graham, who had recently become the paper's owner and de facto publisher. Mrs. Meyer had invited

Dr. Maumenee to join her and a group of famous guests for a month's cruise in the Caribbean. She was eighty years of age, highly intelligent and weighed some 260 pounds. Her daughter insisted that Mrs. Meyer have a doctor accompanying her on the cruise so Ed, who was unable to go, asked if I would substitute for him and take my vacation that year as a guest of Mrs. Meyer on a 165-foot chartered schooner, the *Panda*. After I said I could not leave my wife for a month of light duty in the Caribbean, Janie was also invited on the cruise but Townley would have to stay with his Paton grandparents, the prospect of which delighted him immensely.

We joined the *Panda* in Barbados for four weeks of cruising the Windward Islands en route to the final destination, Antigua. We sailed during the day and spent the nights at anchor in the harbors of Grenada, St. Lucia, Martinique, Dominica, and Guadeloupe. There was a crew of ten, all from the islands except for the captain, who was a rather dashing young Englishman educated at Eton. It became apparent that the fundamental reason for the month's cruise was to provide rest and amusement for Adlai Stevenson, then U.S. Ambassador to the United Nations. As his shipmates, our hostess had invited Johnny Walker (Director of the National Gallery in Washington) and his wife, Lady Margaret; Drew Pearson (the controversial, acerbic, and extensively read columnist) and his wife Luvie; and Borden Stevenson, the younger of Stevenson's two sons.

Mrs. Meyer made the daily decisions about when and where we would weigh anchor, where we would go and when we would eat. She was in total command even though well before the sun would drop over the yardarm, she would begin swigging straight bourbon from a handy frosted plastic glass. By evening, she would be "four sheets to the wind, " but even tipsy, she was fun to be with.

One day Mrs. Meyer complained to me that she was becoming a bit short of breath while moving around the ship--something new to her. Would I please give her a medicine that would stop it right away! She was half-lying, half-sitting, on a cushion on one of the bulkheads, almost panting. No, she was not going to go below to have a physical examination. That was a ridiculous idea. I got out my black doctor's bag that contained a selection of emergency and routine medications from the Hopkins pharmacy, along with a few bandages, a blood pressure cuff, a stethoscope and other standard paraphernalia. I checked her lower legs and ankles for the possibility of edema. My blood pressure cuff barely fit around her large arm and even when it seemed to be ready for inflation, the background noise from the slapping waves against the hull and the flopping of the rigging made it impossible to hear the beats of her pulse. I thought her pressure was elevated but could not be certain. Percussion of the chest was absolutely useless, like thumping through a foot of cotton swabbing.

I reassured her that evening that I would be looking after her as closely as I could. But the next morning, when the shortness of breath had worsened, I became much concerned. "Look, I think you have a heart problem but I am not an internist, and this could be a serious matter. We could put in a call to a heart specialist at Johns Hopkins and ask him to come and check you over—-or we could call Dr. Paul Dudley White in Boston (then reputedly the leading American cardiologist) and see if he can come down." I wanted to let her know I was aware that she could command just about any service from any doctor and that her needs would be fully met.

"Absolutely not! I told Ed Maumenee that if he couldn't be here then he should get me someone else. Kay insisted there be a doctor on board. That's you. Do your job, now. I'll be fine." And then, the afterthought: "This is a vacation for Adlai, and I am not going to cancel out on him. No sir!"

In my bag I had digitalis, the basic medicine that could be administered according to a weight-based formula over a period of several days. I had not treated heart failure in the seven years since my internship, and before that time, only patients who were hospitalized and within steps of a cardiologist and all the accoutrement of proper care—with the exception of student work in Newfoundland.

Mrs. Meyer was one of the most influential and wealthiest women in America, and I was about to treat her for heart failure without being sure of the diagnosis, unable to weigh her for an accurate calculation of drug dosage, isolated from others in my profession who would be able to confirm my diagnosis, and using a medication that even in 1965 had been updated by faster-acting, and perhaps safer, agents.

I went over the situation very clearly with her and again urged that we put in a call for help from the experts. Again she refused, so I started the process of digitalization. It would take several days to have any effect, I warned her. She thought it was strange that I could not restore her to health more promptly, but she agreed to take the pills as I prescribed them.

That was a classic case of the shortcuts too often taken in VIP medicine, with its risks and compromised judgment stemming from the dominance of the famous patient. It was something I had been determined not to tolerate yet here I was, yielding to the powerful patient's demands and complying with her sense of acceptable health management over mine.

Luckily, the remainder of the vacation cruise was uneventful. Mrs. Meyer got along fairly well, despite—or, more accurately, because of---the bourbon and the heart pills. When we reached Antigua, she was met by a chartered jet sent by her daughter and taken directly to a Washington hospital, where she stayed under observation for a few days. Her cardiologist was kind enough to call me at Wilmer to say that he believed that in fact she had been in heart failure and that her health management on board the *Panda* had been correctly handled. I was very relieved. She was discharged feeling quite like her usual self, and she invited Janie and me to join her at President Lyndon Johnson's inaugural ball on January 20, 1965. We accepted and had a thrilling black-tie evening, awash in political celebrity-watching.

CHAPTER THIRTEEN

Late in that Chief Residency year, it became obvious to me that I was headed for a career in academia instead of joining my father in his practice, but at the age of thirty-six I had no academic job offers of any interest, and time was running out. Just then, Ed Maumenee put my worries to rest by offering me a full-time appointment as an assistant professor at Wilmer. My office would be almost directly across the hall from his. At $15,000 a year, albeit with a month's vacation, my salary was only slightly higher than my secretary's (far too early then for the desirable switch in terminology to "assistant,") but, once again, to me it was the sweetest deal ever offered.

In general, my faculty years at Wilmer proved to be delightful, marked by several highlights, one of which was becoming, in 1966, the Johns Hopkins nominee for a scholarship from the Markle Foundation. The purpose of the scholarship was to assist approximately ten young academicians to become good teachers and researchers in one of the medical fields. These medical doctors were to be chosen from a large group of candidates—each U.S. medical school was invited to nominate one doctor from any medical discipline. All of these candidates then met in Williamsburg, Virginia, where our expenses at a fine hotel were paid in full. The other guests of the foundation were the interviewers, among whom were a dozen prominent men and women—lawyers, clergy, medical deans, college professors, business people and some from other professions. They were our judges.

As candidates, we were "exposed" to the interviewers and some of their spouses at every meal and at all times of the day and evening. Whether we were visiting sites in Williamsburg, or together in heavily scheduled meeting rooms, one to three of these formidable judges grilled us in the most thorough but thoughtful way, squeezing from us—alone or in small groups—far more information about our philosophy and attitude than one might imagine possible. We were quizzed on current events, sports competitions, historical facts, and personal experiences. Medical matters were usually omitted from the questioning, except for a few stumpers from the deans. Day and night we spilled our individual guts, and by the end of the weekend I, for one, felt emptied. The Cornell Medical School's candidate and I were assigned to share a room. He was a very personable fellow who was starting his career in neurosurgery. We stayed in touch after the weekend. He was notified about a week later that he had won one of the Markle scholarships. I was happy for him but sad that no such call had come my way.

One week later, the call did come—and surely none other could have been more thrilled by the favorable notification. Analytically, I thought then—and I think now—that I was among the winners mostly due to my Eastern Establishment comfort level with the mixed bag of judges, whom I may have found less intimidating than other candidates, once again a result of having been brought up in advantaged circumstances in which I had become comfortable with a broader smorgasbord of small talk than had other candidates with more strictly scientific backgrounds. I could shoot the bull, if necessary, in situations when others might close up like a clam out of water.

The scholarship benefited me in two ways: first, for the prestige it added to my resume and second, for the monetary benefits it provided. For the next five years, wherever I might be located, I would receive funds sufficient to enable me to pay, for instance, the salary of my collaborator, Dr. Martinez, at his hospital's surgical research center in Manhattan.

Along with many of my colleagues, I began joining a number of departmental committees and eye-related national organizations, but the one that interested me the most was the Committee on Admissions for the Johns Hopkins School of Medicine. That was a committee which I was not only eager to join but also felt fortunate to have been invited to do so. It was becoming ever more obvious to me that my path was different from that of the usual achievers. I guessed that being a Hopkins Markle Scholar had been the ticket to my invitation, the committee's assumption presumably being that such a scholarship indicated intellectual superiority—for who knew how the candidates for the scholarship were chosen? I, who continued to feel that I had been admitted to college, NIH, medical school and Wilmer more on the basis of coattails and beneficence than on merit alone, found myself advancing toward higher reaches of academia than most of the other left-brained scientists bearing the credentials of hard-core science. I, who had tested relatively poorly on SAT's, MCAT's and was mathematically deprived, was now to sit in judgment of the hundreds of medical school applicants who sought a Hopkins medical education and possessed indicators of excellence that registered far higher than mine. All in all, it struck me as quite ironic that, despite having a brain that tested rather indifferently, I had become one of the "deciders" for the student body of what I, of course, considered the world's best medical school.

For much of the year, the fifteen faculty members of the admissions committee met weekly to review student applications and, later, to interview several hundred of the most appealing candidates based upon their college records and their written biographies. It was a heavy load of extra work, but choosing the minds that seemed the most suited for the school's faculty to work with in the years to come was also a core responsibility. In 1967 and over the following four years, I served as Dean of Admissions, meaning Chairman of the Admissions Committee. That appointment amazed and delighted me more than almost anything else I was ever to achieve. We admitted more women and minority candidates in my four years of chairing than had previously been admitted, but it was still not a record revolutionary enough to boast about, merely a move in the right direction.

Many years later, in 1979, when The Wilmer Institute began a search for a new Director to replace Dr. Maumenee, a five-member segment of the search committee that included Dean Emeritus Thomas Turner flew to Houston to determine if I would be a candidate for the directorship. Suffice it to say I was not competitive with the person eventually chosen, but when the committee was leaving for Baltimore I suggested to Dean Turner, for his possible interest, that he look up my test results just to see how "average" they were, despite my having been accepted to the medical school and then considered a possible candidate for the Wilmer directorship. He clearly thought I was just being modest, but he did look up my file and when I spoke to him by phone to thank him and his search committee for making the effort of visiting me in Houston, he acknowledged he was quite taken aback by what my student record revealed. Flaunting failings if they serve to magnify successes is admittedly a vanity, but I have to say I enjoyed doing it.

Meanwhile, at home Janie and I continued to enjoy our wonderful son but we were less than happy with each other, for which I take the lion's share of the blame. My life was as full as ever, and hers was not. Medical work kept me out of touch most of every day and much of the night. I was with patients, on the wards, or preparing for the responsibilities of the following day. For Janie, who was spending long hours alone, a growing discontent became a frustrating emptiness and, finally, an intolerable isolation from the kind of life that she wanted and needed, which was being with the right man in the right environment for her. After ten years together, we faced the kinds of incompatibilities that mollycoddled people do not have to endure if they choose not to. Janie was worn out and lonely and, circling like buzzards, the men began their approaches.

On my side of the equation, I was finding other women alluringly available and caring. They liked my white suits, even though they were so heavily starched that in them I couldn't have made a fast move if I wanted to—and eventually I wanted to. So in 1966, after twelve years of marriage, Janie and I were divorced. Townley was properly mandated to Jane's custody, with specified visiting privileges with me. It was a miserable time for all three of us. Even sooner than I guessed it might happen, Janie married Clinton Gilbert, whom I knew, for he had been a year ahead of me at Princeton, and they have had a long and happy marriage ever since.

That same year, an unusual opportunity came my way. Being the son of the first eye bank's founder brought me name identity and accompanying credibility, which was the logical reason I was often chosen as a respondent to eye bank inquiries from various other nations. In this circumstance, I was offered an expenses-paid tour of several countries to lecture about the techniques and practices of corneal surgery and eye banking. Algeria, Tunisia, Libya, Jordan, Lebanon, Thailand, Taiwan, South Korea were on the list and I added Vietnam so that I could spend Thanksgiving there with friends.

My visit to Taiwan would be less routine than the other visits. The country was new to me and I could think of no more pleasing way to be shown around than by the charming Alice Huang, PhD, in Taipei, where she, an American, was planning to visit her relatives at exactly the same time as my scheduled arrival. The International Eye Foundation, which was picking up my expenses, had been asked by the frustrated ophthalmologists in Taiwan to send someone to their country to persuade the most powerful person in Taiwan—the step-mother of its president---that eye banking and corneal transplants should be given legal status. (The use of human tissue for surgery was still distinctly illegal.) That person was Madame Chiang Kai-shek. Her stepson was acting President of Taiwan at the time. Thus she was the key to changing the government's recalcitrance with respect to using the eyes of the dead. She cared greatly for the Chinese people and was immersed in the promotion of their arts, health, culture and in backing the political leadership of those who had become op-posed to communism, as had the late Chiang Kai-shek himself. She was also notoriously ambitious, power-oriented, ruthless, and head-strong—and thirty years my senior. But before figuring out how to persuade her to change the government's policy, I had to find a way to meet her.

Because the ophthalmologists in Taiwan had been at odds with her for not condoning corneal transplants, they could not be of as-sistance in making the connection. After a few weeks of inquiries and networking calls and with a patient's help, I was able to get in touch with Lawrence E. Spivak, who had recently taken over hosting a new television show, *Meet the Press*. Mr. Spivak seemed intrigued, and no doubt amused, by the idea that a young American wanted to go to Taipei to change the mind of the powerful Mme. Chiang—no matter what the issue. He contacted her---I have no idea how, nor do I know what he told her. All I know is that a letter came from Spivak saying that she would receive me with pleasure, adding, "Please notify Mme. Chiang the date of your arrival in Taipei," which of course I did.

Before going to Taipei, I spent Thanksgiving having lunch in Saigon at the home of family friends, Ambassador and Mrs. Henry Cabot
Lodge, Jr.. The gracious Lodges were welcoming and their Thanksgiving luncheon was traditional and irresistibly delicious. Since my
trip through the countries of North Africa had proven grueling and
grungy, my baggage was filled with dirty laundry. Thanks to Mrs.
Lodge, the staff did the washing overnight, possibly an illegal use of
government employees but I was in serious need. I "forgot" to include
my collection of overused socks because I was hesitant to actually
hand over a pile of aromatic socks to the wife of the ambassador.

While I was in Saigon, there was a cable from Madame Chiang's
office. My visit to Taiwan was cancelled. The doctors were "not ready"
for their eye bank promotion. I thought it was a little strange to
hear of the cancellation from the source of the intended proselytizing,
speaking on behalf of the doctors, but I attributed it to just a different
way of doing things. Not having heard from the doctors themselves,
I assumed that no response from me was necessary.

However, the cancellation was unsettling because after Taiwan I
was to be a participant in a meeting in South Korea and that date
was fixed and several days off. I had a hankering to go to Taiwan even
if the visit were to be completely unofficial. Alice would be there
and we could tour the city together. Therefore, I kept my originally
scheduled Taiwan destination unchanged. The flight path had a three
hour stop-over in Manila, during which I checked into the Manila
Hotel. Once there, I took a very long shower – justifying my prolonged use of hot water by simultaneously washing the six pairs of
dirty socks that had escaped the washing machine at the embassy
in Viet Nam. An easy solution for managing to travel with the wet
socks came to mind: My carryon bag was a pouch of soft leather with
a drawstring that, when tightened, pulled it closed at the top. By
hooking the wet socks over the top of the bag and then tightening the
drawstring, I could let them dangle against the exterior surface of the
bag, avoiding dampening the clothes inside, and it now didn't matter
how informally I might arrive.

The flight to Taiwan was almost empty, and I was the only passenger who got off. The plane touched down on time at about nine

in the evening and came to a stop twenty yards from the passengers' entrance to the terminal. The exit door was cranked open, and I was just stepping from the cabin when a man rushed up the staircase that had been wheeled into position by the ground crew and said, "Professor Paton?"

It turned out that when the ophthalmologists did not hear confirmation from me that the cable from Madame Chiang's office had reached me in Viet Nam, they assumed that I would be arriving on schedule. This was explained to Madame's people and apparently they figured what the hell, let the guy make his plea. Thus, the man who greeted me at the aircraft door was Professor Chang, Chairman of the Department of Ophthalmology at the University in Taipei, National Medical Center---the most senior ophthalmologist in Taiwan.

We shook hands and descended the steps to join fourteen other individuals lined up on the tarmac at the foot of the staircase. They were all ophthalmologists except for one woman, a nurse who was representing Madame Chiang. We shook hands in a little impromptu ceremony of nods and smiles, each of them murmuring a word or two of welcome, then backing off to permit the next doctor to step forward.

Meanwhile, Professor Chang took it upon himself to grab my carryon bag and rush ahead of the group to get everything cleared through Immigration and Customs well ahead of the slower pace the rest of us would require as the words of welcome continued. To do so, Dr. Chang had to cover about twenty yards of tarmac, followed by an even greater distance within the empty terminal. As he jogged hurriedly ahead, my bag's drawstring failed to keep a grip on my wet socks, which began to fall from the bag, first to the tarmac and then, as he progressed, to the floor of the terminal, each several yards apart. If anyone wonders what it feels like to lose face among face-conscious colleagues, let the following set the bar.

Half the doctors were now lined up to my right and the others, including the nurse, were lined up to my left. We had formed a V, like the formation of a flock of migrating geese, with me in the middle, observed from both wings. When this flotilla of doctors approached a sock, the person closest, either to the right or to the left of me, would bend forward with a hand extended as if to pick up the sock, but I was always permitted to scurry over, stoop even lower, and grab the sock myself. Soon I had wet socks dangling from my flexed left arm while I continued to grab the remaining socks with my right hand. We moved as a single body of non-touching but linked physicians, swaying this way and that according to whatever displacement the next sock had from the plumb line to the formalities desk. No one cracked a smile throughout the whole maneuver, least of all me.

The Professor informed me that a room had been reserved for me at the Grand Hotel – owned by Madame Chiang. We loaded into three black limousines to head there for further welcoming. In 1966, there was a large foyer, and dead ahead was a false wall that could be circumvented by walking around it on either side, thereby reaching the bar along the back surface of that wall. The numerous tables and chairs were all empty at that time of the evening. The bar itself was typical of the best-stocked bars one might find in the West, displaying tiers of liquor bottles of every imaginable size and label.

A waitress seated all fourteen of us together at one huge circular table, too far apart for convenient conversation, but we continued to smile and nod at each other. Dr. Chang sat on my right and the nurse sat on my left. I was uncomfortably aware of my sloppy, informal travel togs, since everyone else was dressed in business suits. Although not a heavy drinker, I had been looking forward to some strong alcoholic sedation, and there was obviously a wide selection available. When the waitress came to take our order, Dr. Chang insisted that I order first.

"Whiskey, please, with a small amount of water. In a highball glass."

The other orders went around the table and every single one of them was for orange juice. When it was finally her turn to order, the nice old nurse on my left asked what it was that I had ordered. I told her, and she said she would have the same. I was grateful for her thoughtfulness and also grateful for the whiskey, when it came.

Next morning, Dr. Chang and Dr. Lin from the Veterans General Hospital came to the hotel to take their "persuader" to meet with Madame Chiang. I had been warned that Madame's power was not without its dangers. Few Americans knew then any of the details of her darker side: the almost sinister scope of her ambition, the disregard for the lives of her opponents, and the boundless appetite for personal publicity and power. Some people are all heart, others all power. How would she deal with a vagrant eye doctor seeking a change of her reputedly hard heart? I asked if Alice Huang could come with us, correctly guessing that the Generalissimo's wife would not object to an additional person in our entourage. So Alice joined Dr. Chang, Dr. Lin and me for the visit.

Mme. Chiang greeted us in her lavish reception room. She was shorter than the average American woman but well-proportioned, exuding a graceful willingness to be approached. We sat at a table and were served some kind of juice. Then, businesslike, she opened the eye surgery topic by saying she understood I favored corneal transplants and the means to gain a supply of corneas from the dead. I nodded, and knowing Madam was a Christian, I began my pitch to her with religion. "The Pope gave his approval for use of human eye tissue by recalling the blind man of Jericho and saying how wonderful it would have been if he could have had his vision restored." That was as folksy as I could make the Pope's encyclical sound. I forged ahead, bringing in my father's role in starting eye-banking. She listened to my enthusiastic recounting of the wonders of this means of restoring vision. Everyone knew she was a big believer in the United States as a source of important worldly contributions, so I played that tune also. Her affirmative nods seemed to indicate we were on a path to a successful conclusion when she asked, "How do I know that my (sic) doctors would know how to do corneal transplant surgery?"

I had done my homework. "Just a month or two ago," I replied, with a nod and a smile to the doctor, "Dr. Lin published a paper in a medical journal describing forty-three corneal transplants that he and his associates had successfully performed." I noticed that Dr. Lin looked surprised—even alarmed--that I knew of that paper.

"Dr. Paton, do you realize that corneal transplant surgery is not permitted in Taiwan? It is not an approved surgery. Our doctors could not have done such surgery." Madame Chiang was firm.

She turned to Dr. Lin with a scathing look. He paled as she spoke to him in Chinese, responding quietly. She spoke again—-at some length, her eyes burning into him. The doctor looked stricken. No words came out. I began to worry that not only was my cause lost, but that I had ruined Dr. Lin's professional prospects. She added another comment or two. There was a little period of silence on both sides.

Then Madame Chiang looked straight at me and said, "Doctor, I want to thank you for coming to Taipei to promote corneal transplants and to begin eye banking. I feel certain such work can have wide acceptance in this country, as it has in yours."

She smiled the famously fetching smile that had served her so well in winning millions of American dollars for her husband's regime. Here, it was the seal of her approval. A photographer appeared out of nowhere and we all formally shook hands while he took our picture.

Color was returning to Dr. Lin's face. Dr. Chang was smiling and even Dr. Lin eventually managed to muster a smile. But I didn't flatter myself that I had single-handedly turned things around. The photographer in the wings suggested Madame Chiang had anticipated the conclusion.

Alice Huang and I spent the afternoon touring the city and its environs, then meeting with her distinguished family at their home not far from my hotel. She was—as she is today-- a brilliant, as well as an unusually attractive, woman and within a few years she married Dr. David Baltimore, later to be a Nobel laureate.

That evening, I went back to my room in Madam Chiang's hotel, delighting in a feeling of global brotherhood, the sense of human oneness that comes when cross-cultural relationships seem to be holding strong. I had an early dinner and went to my room by about nine in the evening, looking forward to catching up on sleep for the first time since leaving home. Not five minutes later there was a knock on my door. I waited to see if it was a mistake, but it came again, so in my boxer shorts and T-shirt--ready for bed--I went to the door and opened it just a couple of inches. In pushed a bent older woman covered by a shawl and wearing a long wrinkled cotton skirt. She was holding the hand of a younger woman, trailing behind her. There was a musty stench of unwashed humanity. The old woman took the younger woman directly to my bed, left her there, then said to me, "She for you." With that, she left the room, closing the door behind her.

Holy smokes! A prostitute, brought for my entertainment. It was a situation unlike any I ever experienced, before or since. The young woman was sitting on the edge of the bed, dressed, silent-- motionless other than a faint swaying movement of her upper body. She started to undress. Intending to shoo her out, I stepped closer and saw that she was only a child, with a pale, sad face. And then I noticed that she had two grossly enlarged, white, wandering eyeballs, indicating total blindness—specifically the blindness of neglected congenital glaucoma.

A call to the desk brought the old lady back after fifteen minutes of a most uncomfortable waiting period during which neither of us, the girl nor I, communicated with one another. There was nothing to be said, even if we had had a common language. I pressed some money into her hand, which of course she accepted.

I was to learn later that in China and in Taiwan, blind girls were still being forced into prostitution and blind boys were taught to become beggars. This was being played out even in Madame Chiang's own hotel, with one of her guests. Who had sent her? I have often wondered how Madame Chiang would have reacted had she known that my morning visit with her was followed by an unsolicited, illicit night visit from a female at the opposite extreme of society---an incurably blind child prostitute.

My meeting with Madame Chiang and my previous exposure to the Shah of Iran and the King of Jordan underscored an incredibly important, if obvious, lesson. Go to the top whenever possible. If the rationale of whatever is being sought can be explained in a way that indicates a benefit for the country's people, then the chance of its acceptance increases a hundredfold---maybe even a thousand fold--- over having to take the arduous course of persuasion from ground level up.

Returning home to Baltimore, I moved to the suburbs, rented a condominium in Elkridge Estates, and in a surprisingly short time discovered that just a few condos away there lived a tall, blonde, gorgeous, recently divorced woman who was at least a decade younger than I but who had a daughter just Townley's age. We took to borrowing sugar over the backyard fence, so to speak, and soon we were seeing each other regularly. We were married in February, 1969. Unhappily, it turned out that we were not made for each other, and our marriage was to end after almost eleven years. She asked not to be included in this book, which is too bad because, despite our differences, we had many enjoyable times together. However, I have respected her request for privacy.

CHAPTER FOURTEEN

By early 1969, my ophthalmic wanderlust, combined with invitations under the auspices of the Pan American Association of Ophthalmology and several other sponsoring sources, had led to teaching visits in nine Central and South American countries and, more specifically, trips related to investigative aspects of corneal surgery in Russia, Thailand and South Africa. In the latter two countries there had been reports of successful corneal transplants to humans from gibbon apes in one series and from a baboon in the other. Those reports turned out to be either untrue or about experiments that ultimately proved to be unsuccessful. However, my growing international exposure to eye care in a wide variety of countries set me to thinking about how one thing or another could be improved, especially in the places where the need for eye care was greatest.

Most of the estimated forty million blind people in the world had cataracts--possibly thirty million of them--and more than 90 percent lived in the developing countries. But there were many millions of additional people whose lives were seriously limited by other eye disorders, people who could be cured if appropriate eye care could become available to them. More eye doctors were needed, but equally important was the need to beef up the existing doctors' medical education. Emphasis had to be put upon the surgical aspect, for that was where ophthalmology could make its most important and most immediate impact on the global need to reduce world blindness. That realization led me to focus on two matters: volunteer ophthalmologists from the West to teach their colleagues in developing nations the new techniques in the field of eye care; and the necessary instrumentation and facilities to accompany the teaching.

The enormity of that challenge was daunting, and seemingly impossible to address in anything more than a superficial and piecemeal fashion, with the hope that whatever was done would become an inspiration for similar efforts to be made by others. It was obvious, furthermore, that medical volunteers would have to be organized in a way that was effective, efficient and appealing to all participants, for do-good actions without the proper infrastructure and the ability to implement them are ineffectual or, worse, counter-productive.

Shortly after the first moon landing in 1969, thinking big was becoming a reality. But how could first-class instruction for colleagues throughout the world, using expert teachers of microsurgery and opportune teaching conditions, be made available? Owing to the difficulties of mastering the operating microscope and the other highly technical new machines such surgery entailed, for the first time in medical history, textbooks, films and lectures were no longer adequate to teach the newest methods of eye surgery. Only hands-on instruction by experts would accomplish what was required. I mulled over various possibilities, quite sure that something could be done that would capitalize on the multiplier effect, so that in-put by the few could bring new knowledge and skills to the many.

Since the teaching was clearly the key, I considered packing trunks of equipment to be shipped to a recipient city prior to a team of doctors and their staff assistants spending time there teaching microsurgery to the leading local ophthalmologists. But that would be cumbersome at best. Physicians in the same field are not always collaborative and the trunks would have to be transported from one hospital to another. There are thousands of cities and hundreds of countries that would need such individualized instruction. I was in a dream world and dreaming big, but the solution still eluded me.

In the 1960s, Dr. William B. Walsh had founded and assembled a medical service project for developing nations known as the Hope Ship. I called him in Bethesda, Maryland, and we had a long talk. The Hope Ship was a not-for-profit venture whose work took place within a former military craft converted into a hospital ship for volunteer surgeons providing care for needy persons in Latin America. It would remain at a single port for weeks, if not months, at a time. It was an inspiring organization, but it was not the answer for ophthalmology. For one thing, a big ship was not needed, and ships have to confine their usefulness to ports, excluding land-locked countries or even large cities remote from a sea port.

Could an aircraft be the answer? A large enough aircraft could be converted into an operating theater, a teaching classroom and all the necessary facilities that go along with sterile storage and patient preparation and discharge. Of course! I was so enthusiastic about the idea of getting a moth-balled military transport aircraft to be set up as a traveling teaching machine that I took a day off to visit a high-ranking general, a patient of Ed Maumenee's, in his office in the Pentagon. Could I obtain a used and moth-balled government aircraft for teaching ophthalmic microsurgery overseas? He was cordial in his reception and, above all, a good listener. He said that it was not unreasonable to expect that a retired, government–owned aircraft might be given to a not-for-profit private foundation if it were to have a special purpose. My heart was in my throat. He was supporting my idea!

Then the general pointed out what should have been obvious to me. If such an aircraft were, for example, to blow a tire in a foreign airport, it might take weeks, or even months, before a spare tire or any other part for an old military aircraft could be sent as a replacement. So the general's answer turned out to be a definite no.

I returned to Baltimore that night feeling deflated. If the imagined teaching venture were to be feasible, it would have to depend upon a commercially available, currently deployed aircraft that could be flown and serviced by people with the right expertise having throughout its years of operation. How much would that cost? Unimaginably much. I discussed the idea with my colleagues at Wilmer, but most of them did not share my enthusiasm for the challenge of international education and its solution involving the aircraft industry.

Only Ed Maumenee and one or two special pals of mine were at all encouraging, although for a long while no one offered to get involved. Among the majority of the academics at other institutions with whom I later met in various committee assignments for national organizations, the very idea of performing ophthalmic microsurgery on a converted aircraft in an extended sequence of foreign airports was dismissed out of hand. Impossible. Impractical. Unaffordable. Ineffective. The more senior, the more powerfully situated, the more likely they were to be unwavering skeptics.

"David, old boy, how's it going with your airplane for saving the world? You know, the other day someone said you were heading toward a collision with the American Ophthalmological Society, but I said no, you had too much sense to do that. You know, you could just drop that idea of yours overnight. Think about it. You're becoming a laughingstock." I heard but did not heed.

In all honesty, though, enthusiasm for a far-out concept had to be tempered by the very real logistical problems that would have to be confronted. Along with others in a growing group of interested non-medical people, I began to give serious thought to the issues of, for example, having sufficient electrical power and potable water for the needs of an aircraft stationed in a foreign airport. In addition, we would have to design a teaching cocoon with sterile areas for surgery, along with a classroom and an audiovisual system with miniature television cameras for through-the-microscope photography and demonstrations of the hands-on instruction that each principal host surgeon would experience in turn.

Today this all may seem the obvious solution for the challenge of global instruction in ophthalmic surgery, but that form of teaching methodology abroad was entirely new in the late 1960s and 1970s and never had it been assembled for total portability aboard an aircraft. As they say, a camel is a horse made by committee. An airplane suited for teaching ophthalmic microsurgery and the other ingenuities of modern ophthalmology had to be a camel with a lot of horse power.

In August, 1963, Martin Luther King, Jr. had given his forever memorable "I have a dream" speech alluding to inalienable human rights, which became the clarion call for the American civil rights movement. In it, Dr. King went straight to the ultimate goal, without chipping away at the intermediate stepping stones leading to its achievement. I was learning that one's dream world is an effective laboratory for ideas. It converts imaginings from reverie to reality. But the dream itself has to remain the ideal, the big picture from which one's hunches extend downward into the practical means of achieving it, with compromise as the last necessity.

CHAPTER FIFTEEN

In the early winter of 1969, a Christmas card came from Betsy Wainwright, a friend of longstanding. In it, she added a note asking, "What interests you beyond your work?" Her card got a full-fledged answer, in probably far more detail than she'd expected. First I explained that I loved my work but was under a lot of pressure in the hospital and at home. Although recently married, I had added more curricular and extra-curricular activities to an already heavy surgical practice. To underscore my point, I admitted to Betsy I had developed an X-ray-confirmed duodenal ulcer in 1968, attributable to unusual stresses. Fortunately, the ulcer responded well to antacid therapy, long before antibiotics were used for that problem.

Then I went on to outline my dream scenario. I told her I had appointed an executive director for my aircraft project, Niles Bond, who, being a diplomat between governmental opportunities, was working on a pro bono basis, treading water until another government assignment came his way. Niles lived in the District near Foggy Bottom, where he wrote poetry and dressed as nattily as Dean Acheson. Unfortunately, it was becoming clear that he had no demonstrable ability to raise money, so we were not getting anywhere with our need to establish a project with headquarters and the beginnings of a staff.

Further, I explained to Betsy why it was impractical for foreign eye doctors to come to the United States for hands-on training, even if it could be offered. In fact, it would be unlawful to have unlicensed trainee-doctors operating on American patients. Besides, where would those doctors be lodged and how could any significant number of them get entry visas to permit them to provide patient care? And how could standardized lectures and demonstrations be organized domestically? Mastering ophthalmic microsurgery was the most demanding of all requirements to be addressed.

I explained about the need for one-on-one, hands-on instruction which was why, I told her, it seemed necessary to convert a large air-

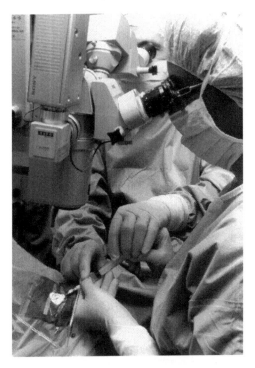

craft into a teaching mechanism for the improvement of ophthalmic care. Once the problems of teaching surgery were solved, then all other aspects of ophthalmic care could be worked in with lectures and demonstrations that would not require any particular structural considerations beyond audiovisual facilities.

She expressed interest in hearing more about my project. We exchanged more letters. Her enthusiasm for something that to her, a layperson, sounded both practical and exciting delighted me. She was optimistic—as I'd hoped she might be--that she could be helpful in gaining support for the teaching project. I knew that she had always had an interest in health-related matters, and had even worked with blind children at one point in her life.

Betsy's father, Juan Trippe, had been a founder and was the CEO of Pan American Airways. Trippe was a familiar name on Wall Street and in the extended field of commercial aviation. In fact, I knew both of Betsy's parents. Her mother was the sister of Edward R. Stettinius, Jr., U.S. Secretary of State for two years and later the first American ambassador to the United Nations. I had met all of her immediate family members at a weekend house party in East Hampton when I was 15, reaching the Trippe home by means of a 50-mile bicycle ride from our summer home in St. James, Long Island.

Betsy had always been the apple of her father's eye. No shrinking violet, she definitely had her father's genes and she used them effectively. What I needed most at this point was, paradoxically, the financial assistance and the networking of the Eastern Establishment that I had long been living without. I saw that Betsy could be the key to renewing such access, since she knew how to play the game of social bee and female arm-twister better than anyone I had ever met. Her belief in the project was fundamental; her skill in manipulating the affection and focus of the Establishment turned out to be indispensable. All I could eventually give her was a diagram I conceived for promotional work, drawn by a medical artist.

At this point, my idea had morphed into Project ORBIS. The word stood for "world" and also for "eyeball," the orb of Shakespeare and a host of other writers. The name was soon incorporated in the State of Delaware as a not-for-profit corporation with bylaws and a constitution. Betsy set about attending to the most immediate need: developing a board of directors. My first major task was to seek affirmation from leaders of the medical profession that Project ORBIS was a worthwhile undertaking. We needed a strong assertion from at least one highly credible voice in ophthalmology as to both the validity and the value of the project. Ed Maumenee was the most likely person to make such a statement, but he could not be considered an objective observer with me as his junior colleague.

Also, building the   project would theoretically be dependent upon volunteer participants from many disciplines—-medicine, aviation and international affairs—-which made it difficult to obtain an inclusive authoritative statement. In addition, there was no real evidence that any ophthalmologist from another country would want to be seen on a American teaching aircraft, let alone bring his patients for surgery performed by anonymous foreigners teaching new ideas. And some countries even then had more security at their airports than Brinks employed to protect its trucks from Chicago gangsters, making access difficult. I noticed as we continued to persevere, that there were always passive-aggressive naysayers around—people who had no vested interest in seeing ORBIS either succeed or fail but just enjoyed watching me get stuck deeper and deeper in a quagmire of complications and pooh-poohing every step we tried to take.

Fortunately, Betsy seemed quite immune to those negative vibes, particularly in the beginning when she had to deal with her own steep learning curve about ophthalmology and various aspects of the project itself. She convinced me that she could help put the corporate board together with a combination of her own confidence that ORBIS would be successful and her ability to persuade her father's powerful and wealthy friends that they must not let her (and him) down. My role in building the board would thus amount to little more than rubber stamping the nominees and adding a few favorite people of my own. Gradually, with a few donations to help keep the project afloat, a board was formed but it was unable to authorize a search for a suitable aircraft until late in 1974 because there were still too many loose ends—the most prominent of which was the question of the project's potential reception by the medical profession, both at home and abroad.

Time passed. Dr. Maumenee was often willing to have a helpful chat about ORBIS. Another friend, Dr. Bruce Spivey, made me feel sane when I talked about what I envisioned. Then a colleague I had known for a dozen years, Dr. Francis L'Esperance, who was a bioengineer as well as an ophthalmologist, joined in expressing his support for the basic idea. Soon, a few high-volume cataract surgeons heard about the aircraft project and became fascinated by its audiovisual concepts and its over-the-top, show-and-tell potential. Outriders of ophthalmic surgery, these surgeons were achieving independent power within the profession and considerable prestige with the public. A new breed of freewheeling, independent, entrepreneurial individuals, they were developing their own kingdoms of eye surgery in ambulatory surgical facilities which they personally owned. They usually stayed aloof from stodgy academics like me, yet they were to become extremely important to the promotion and implementation of ORBIS.

Some of the old guard in ophthalmology labeled them "buccaneers" because of what they presumed were their unmonitored and individually variable, high-volume, high-tech methods of ophthalmic surgery, and very few academic ophthalmic surgeons had much to do with them in the early days. But I visited as many of their surgical outpatient clinics as I could, up and down the East Coast. I needed these enthusiastic, young, and yes, sometimes all-too daring, surgeons to speak favorably to the ORBIS board and to anyone who needed to be reassured that the project was legitimately serious before contributing money. I imagined early on that eventually they might become some of the best ORBIS teachers of modern microsurgery of the eye, and so they did.

In contrast to its reception by the profession's academic leaders, the project invariably seemed fascinating and even feasible to potentially helpful wealthy laymen. But when these wealthy individuals were approached for any sizeable amount of funding, they were likely to check out the idea with their own respected community eye doctor, whose professional opinion was often expressed by a cocked eyebrow and a dubious expression accompanied by a turned-down thumb, even though rarely was any general practitioner in ophthalmology in possession of sufficient knowledge of the project's purpose and mechanics to have an informed opinion. Of course, those doctors had their own credibility to protect.

Never before had I been considered blatantly controversial. But in pursuing a project that was perceived as peripheral to ophthalmology in its infrastructure and unpredictable in its potential effectiveness, I had become an evangelical advocate of a vision that was gathering little intellectual traction. But I stuck to my vision and kept in mind my original commitment to think big, and in the end that made all the difference. As architect Daniel Burnham said about the challenges of constructing the buildings of the Chicago World's Fair in 1893, "Make no little plans, they hold no magic to stir man's blood."

CHAPTER SIXTEEN

It was about 7:30 on a rain-soaked evening in late June, 1970. Dog-tired from a long day in operating rooms and clinics, I had considered getting a quick snack for dinner in the hospital cafeteria before going home to sleep. The alarm would ring at 5:30 the next morning and the drive to the hospital would take 20 minutes—another early start. They all were. But instead I decided to go home and eat dinner with my new wife and her adorable 11-year-old daughter, Garrison.

We had just sat down for the meal when the wall phone in the kitchenette rang. Garrison sprang from the table to answer it, dutifully and eagerly. She enjoyed showing she could manage the phone calls that came at meal time, but it was a new talent still being developed and, after a series of miscommunications as our dinner cooled, I encouraged her to hang up on what appeared to be a salesman's call.

She did so and we returned to our meal. A few moments later, the phone rang again. This time I strode over to the telephone, grabbed the receiver and shouted brusquely, "Hello!"

It was the caller Garrison had hung up on, who turned out to be, not a salesman, but famous heart surgeon Dr. Michael E. DeBakey, president of Baylor College of Medicine in Houston, Texas. He was, arguably, the nation's most recognized surgeon and a leader of his profession. And he was calling to invite me—then 39 years of age--to become Chairman of the Department of Ophthalmology at his noted medical school in Houston. Holy Smokes!

Then, suddenly, an alarm bell clanged in my head. There had been a series of much-publicized problems the year before at that medical school, from which it had not yet recovered. In April of 1969, Dr. Conard D. Moore, a former evangelical preacher and, at the time, Professor of Ophthalmology at Baylor, had performed an operation about which details were either leaked or intentionally reported to the press. Miriam Kass, a medical reporter for the *Houston Post* who had at one time received special instruction in eye anatomy and physiology from Dr. Louis Girard, chairman of Baylor's Department of Ophthalmology, had gotten a tip from an anonymous caller stating that a complete eye transplant had just been performed at The Methodist Hospital. Aware of the fine reputation of the two medical institutions, she understood the importance of the story. As a result, the *Houston Post* headlined the scoop, opening its lead article with, "The world's first total eye transplant intended to provide vision to a human was performed Tuesday at The Methodist Hospital."

When that news was announced a day and a half later by Dr. Maumenee at a Wilmer Annual Meeting, the Hopkins audience jeered, bellowed, whistled and stamped its feet, thoroughly enjoying sending up the obvious farce represented by this supposed operation, news of which had somehow been taken seriously enough to be featured on various newscasts and in the *Baltimore Sun* that very morning. For the ophthalmologists assembled in Baltimore, there was never as much as a passing thought that such an operation could result in even the slightest ray of vision.

The outcry of disbelief was overwhelming and pervasive and indeed, several days later, the surgeon, Dr. Moore, rewrote his operative report by stating that the optic nerve had not, in fact, been spliced. He then denied that the intent of the operation had been to restore sight to the patient. This pronouncement was contrary to what the surgical assistant had observed, and then reiterated: that the optic nerve had been spliced and therefore the surgeon had clearly intended that the operation be considered as an effort to restore vision. But because the initially reported "achievement" had come from a major medical center known for pioneering heart transplants, the message that got out to the world was that donor eyes might very well be transplanted to restore sight to the blind and it took some time to correct that misinformation.

All in all, it was a messy business, and the Medical Center in Houston had already had its fill of scandalous news. Just one month earlier, the medical school had been wracked by the mysterious death after a short illness of a socially prominent, wealthy and beautiful doctor's wife, Joan Robinson Hill. Her husband, Dr. John R. Hill, was a native Texan and a Baylor graduate. He had trained under

Dr. DeBakey and elected to become a plastic surgeon. Dr. Hill was having an affair at the time of his wife's death, and was widely suspected of being her murderer. The press had a field day with the story, for it extended into the most elite medical and social circles of Houston and involved alluring women, a wealthy, possessive and powerful oil baron who was Joan Hill's adoptive father, famous lawyers such as Percy Foreman and Richard "Racehorse" Haynes, and a doctor described as obsessed by ambition, music and women. Dr. Hill was never barred from his medical society or hospital staff, since his guilt was never proven. Yet he was plagued by rumor and innuendo, rejected by partners and in-laws, and hounded by the press.

What Baylor College of Medicine's department of ophthalmology needed most was to get out from under the shadows of media scrutiny by turning the page with a new Chairman. Dr. Girard himself was entrenched in some other technical and personal skirmishes with the medical school and with its President, Dr. DeBakey. Dr. Moore was soon forced to resign from the school's faculty, the Houston Ophthalmological Society and several honorary medical organizations. And with the turmoil over poor judgment or unprofessional conduct by Dr. Moore, Dr. Girard himself was forced to fall upon his colleague's sword and to step down as Chairman of the Department of Ophthalmology.

Hence, Dr. DeBakey's phone call to me. But I feared I would be stepping into a hornet's nest were I to take what seemed at first glance to be a fantastic job. And there was also the instant heartache I felt at the prospect of leaving Johns Hopkins after so many happy years there. So, flattered as I was to have been asked, I told Dr. DeBakey that I was not interested. He countered by asking if I would be a consultant, to come up with recommendations of my own about who would be the best new chairman of the eye department. He went on to tell me that the medical school hoped to build a brand new eye institute and that they had enough funding to recruit numerous faculty members for it. As he talked, it began to sound like an interesting time for at least a visit to Houston, after all; if nothing else, I could spend some time with college friends there while checking out the medical school.

Within a week of Dr. DeBakey's call, I took the first of two trips to Houston, by then not just to consult but to assess, first-hand, the pros and cons of accepting the chairmanship myself. I had been in Houston three months earlier to attend the funeral of Jim Baker's wife, Mary Stuart, whom I had loved as a great friend, and I had witnessed and shared in the sorrow Jim was going through. Now, instead of sadness, my days of visiting there were filled with curiosity and an intriguing hope.

Dr. Girard was a handsome, well-mannered, athletic Texan who was twelve years my senior. We had enthusiasm and tennis in common, having played in various tennis matches on one or the other side of the net at medical meetings when the programs were over for the day. He was an excellent eye surgeon but his critics within the faculty found his surgical judgment to be too easily affected by the temptation to innovate, and his assertions about what he could accomplish too often over-blown. I had no personal experience with his role in ophthalmology so had no way of judging his reputation first-hand but when I was visiting with him in my scouting visits to BCM, he assured me that since it was inevitable that he had to resign, I was his first choice as his replacement.

In my conversations with Dr. DeBakey, he made it clear that he would be a strong advocate of the new chairman having sufficient assigned funding to hire new faculty expertise for the eye department, preparing it for later fundraising that would lead to the establishment of an eye institute of which I would become the director. I would have my own laboratory and could bring with me the staff of my lab in Baltimore. Surgery would be assisted by new O.R. equipment, as needed. The residency program would be increased in size, and research facilities would be expanded. We would soon be involved with planning a large eye institute in accordance with what I believed would meet the most advanced teaching, research and patient care standards of that era. Bench research and clinical research would be featured—I added "systems research" because that covered ORBIS as well as countless applications for improving care in developing nations. Dr. DeBakey waved his hand in a way that indicated, "of course." Finally, he said he would be referring all of his patients requiring eye care to me. Added to that feast of assurances, my base salary and related patient care income would jump to at least three times what I was earning at traditionally Spartan Johns Hopkins. There was to be an endowed chair for a tenured professorship—and, in short, it was all just too good to pass up. I especially liked the energy I sensed everywhere I turned, and from whomever I met. It wasn't long before I told Michael (already it was "Michael," not yet "Mike") that I would definitely accept the Baylor offer.

I certainly needed the increase in income that the job would entail. I had to borrow five thousand dollars from one of the medical school trustees who was a member of the search committee just to make a down payment on a house near the west loop of the Houston beltway, off Chimney Rock Road. I was right to dread leaving the Wilmer Institute—it was like cutting one's own umbilical cord--but it was time to move on, as was, in fact, expected of Wilmer faculty interested in leadership roles. Ed Maumenee was supportive, telling me, "You're going to have a big time down there in Texas!"

There were, nevertheless, some indications that I had better start presenting myself as a pragmatic and self-confident chairman rather than as a friend to everyone with a bit of advice and a list of complaints. I had heard that a faculty member at Wilmer, Dr. Howard Naquin, had predicted that I would never survive in the tough Houston environment, and I was determined to prove him wrong. The first day after arriving, I went directly to the Chairman's office in the Jewish Wing of the medical school building, where the Department of Ophthalmology was located, looking forward to taking my seat behind the Chairman's desk. However, I discovered that Dr. Girard was unwilling to vacate that seat while he was still tussling with the medical school over instruments and office furnishings he claimed were owned by his Eyes of Texas Foundation and were therefore to go with him to his new office across town. A settlement had not been reached in the two months between the announcement of my appointment and my arrival. Gracious though I knew him to be, Dr. Girard had not found it necessary to tell me about his decision to stay put.

As I was taken to a temporary office, a small desk-and-chair roomette adjacent to Dr. DeBakey's luxurious "Presidential Office,"

I began to wonder if Dr. Naquin was correct in his assessment of me. As it turned out, this arrangement lasted for six months, but the full force of the job started the moment I sat down in that roomette. Visitors to my temporary office had to wait in the hall, my secretary was located in the eye department, which seemed a mile away, and it was a long trek to get to the various departmental offices and labs where my responsibilities were concentrated. Dr. DeBakey was appropriately apologetic; he wasn't any more pleased by the arrangement than I was. Lou Girard, on the other hand, offered no apology. I was the younger man and it probably seemed right to him that I should be the one kept on the outside until his claims to departmental property were settled in his favor.

By the time I was finally settled in the Chairman's office, another shot came out of the blue, startling me by attacking what I thought was my best strength as Chairman. Typical of many of Dr. Maumenee's widespread acolytes, I often chose to personally cross-examine the residents presenting cases at weekly ground rounds, asking them increasingly difficult questions until they had to yield with a shrug or an apology for not having all the answers. It was a tried-and-true Hopkins-Wilmer teaching exercise and one that to this day seems to be the most effective means of motivating the trainees to study hard in preparation for oral recitals at weekly rounds. But one day I received the following anonymous typed letter that shows the cultural differences that can exist among American institutions. And among countries, the differences would be even greater.

May 28, 1971

Dear Dr. Paton: This note is merely to express the thoughts of a substantial number of ophthalmologists who attended the staff conference last evening. Your public ridicule of a resident before our entire group was an embarrassment for us all. Your lack of good taste and lack of common courtesy was appalling. In this part of the country we just don't treat a young physician like that, even though he is only a resident. A private conference with the resident (or intern or student) is the accepted and dignified practice.

I have kept that note over the years as a reminder that not all audiences think alike or are accustomed to the same kind of teaching methods. Insulting a resident or any other student has never, ever, been my intention, for I had struggled enough with my own slow learning to realize how unproductive it would be to feel badgered by the professor. Yet, the hostile letter was an indicator that my teaching could use some demographic adjustments.

CHAPTER SEVENTEEN

Houston was as different from Baltimore as any two large American cities could be. In my view, Houston's greatest asset was a dynamism that I figured came from the fact that, in the absence of snow-capped mountains, verdant forests, or pounding seas, the flat, sun-baked Texas land, with its own great gift of nature hidden underground, had to come up with a do-it-yourself creativity in order to achieve the international fame it aspired to. Compared to the cautiously expressed intellectualism that characterized Johns Hopkins, Houston's collective mindset was action-oriented, with a "get-up-and-go" spirit that defied the city's oppressive humidity. Everything was man-made, from the city's ship channel to the massive machinery powering its ubiquitous air conditioning. State-wide, there were pumping oil wells with myriads of buried pipe lines, like arterioles nourishing its industries and filling the coffers of its downtown banks. From those accumulations of wealth arose vivid displays of ostentatious imaginings: the unprecedented Astrodome, the extraordinary Space Center, and, remarkably, the vast Texas Medical Center, with its forty component medical institutions that were supported in no small measure by the benevolence of Houstonians.

The publicity related to the cardiovascular accomplishments of Dr. Michael DeBakey and the other star resident heart surgeon, Dr. Denton Cooley, was a key factor in drawing local, as well as national, attention to the mushrooming Center, with its modern and architecturally distinctive buildings crowded together on 675 acres where there were more than forty not-for-profit institutions either in place or on the drawing board. Its thirteen hospitals came under the aegis of one or the other of the two medical schools, Baylor College of Medicine and the University of Texas Medical System. To my knowledge it was the only medical center in the nation to be routinely included in the basic tourist bus tour of the city, and it was ballyhooed in the periodicals and brochures of Houston's hotels, restaurants and airports. All this was strikingly different from the Old World struc-tures in the crowded slum milieu of Johns Hopkins Hospital. Most Baltimoreans probably would have cringed at the city's manufac-tured charisma. I found it wonderfully bracing.

In moving to Houston in the early winter of 1971, I was entering an intellectual climate of optimism and expectation---"How much?" and "How soon is it needed?"

And an estimated $25 million in 1971 dollars is what the new institute to house BCM's Department of Ophthalmology—later to be named The Cullen Eye Institute--would need to complete the projected expansion of its existing full-time faculty and for bricks, mortar and equipment . The building was soon to become one of the three or four largest eye institutes in the United States, sharing its facilities with two other medical school departments, neurology and otolaryngology. All three academic departments would be closely linked within a single new building, The Neurosensory Center of Houston, to be jointly owned by BCM and TMH. The future looked very bright for this collaborative endeavor, especially since DeBakey and Bowen were close friends.

Meanwhile, I had a few projects waiting for development, starting with designing an eye care bus for five locations in Houston's inner city and a program for telemedicine consultations to be provided by our department's faculty, but the latter plan was never achieved.

The first of those plans came to fruition within two years and Dr. DeBakey himself helped celebrate its creation.

ORBIS would eventually require about the same amount of startup funding as the eye institute but for the aircraft project half might be sought as gifts in kind, such as the donation of an aircraft, generators, water purifiers, surgical instrumentation, audio-visual facilities, video cameras--essentially all the hardware aspects of the project's needs. It was far more dependent upon corporate sources than any other scientific project I had heard about.

Thus I, as the new Chairman of Ophthalmology and founder of ORBIS, would be seeking upwards of $45 million in charitable contributions. In those days, that was real money. Fundraising for the eye institute didn't begin in earnest until 1973, since it took some time for me to analyze our needs and set down the purposes of the department so that we could be vetted and then sponsored by a respected program called Research to Prevent Blindness (RPB), which gave us enormous credibility and fundraising appeal. The eye institute's campaign brought me face-to-face with the most prominent Houston philanthropists, many of whom were either BCM- or TMH-oriented in their primary allegiance as potential donors, even though all donations for ophthalmology went into a common fund for The Cullen Eye Institute. Several of these potential donors were Houstonians from the first generation of the Texas oil industry. I found them to be salt-of-the earth, wholesome and caring people . Many---perhaps most---were members of the Petroleum Club in downtown Houston, where they often lunched; they lived in River Oaks and socialized at the River Oaks Country Club, the Houston Country Club, and a few other elite watering holes. The majority of them had a ranch or two, usually for raising cattle and spending bucolic weekends amid the wild turkeys, deer and quail of the Texas countryside to the south and west. They worked hard, played hard, and enjoyed their families, their cars and their ranches.

Even the hospital administrators were power players to be reckoned with. One of these imperious men, Mr. Ted Bowen, Administrator of TMH, enjoyed the staunch support of Dr. DeBakey, whose patients the hospital managed with very careful attention to their needs and comforts. Ted was a cigar-chomping, authoritative, high-level wheeler-dealer who wasted little time on department chairpersons like me. He conveyed his hospital orders to all clinical services directly to Dr. DeBakey's desk for distribution from there-- or to his administrative minions. Nonetheless, I came to like Ted for his reg-

imental administrative ability and also because his tough-guy demeanor could easily dissolve into a sudden, full-faced laugh.

One day when I was making rounds on my patients at Methodist, a nurse called out that a doctor was urgently needed in a private
room close to where I was standing. The name on the door was, typically, a pseudonym. You really weren't a major VIP if your real name
appeared on the door's ID. I rushed into the room she indicated and
there was Ted, moribund, lying on the bed white as a sheet and without any evident sign of life. He had been admitted, the nurse told me,
for some complaint of no great moment, so this was an unexpected
turn of events.

Within moments I was giving Ted intermittent pressure on his
chest and providing him with mouth-to-mouth air--as was the first
procedure recommended in those days. The nurse secured tourniquets
on three extremities Several other members of the nursing staff arrived, and Code Blue was called on he hospital's speaker system.

Blowing air into whoever in that manner was not my favorite
maneuver, but that was then the first routine when no other source of
air was immediately available. The last time I had been involved in
cardiopulmonary resuscitation was in 1963 in the foyer of a hotel in
Cairo where an obese gentleman had had a severe heart attack. I could
find no pulse. I worked on chest massage with some diligence, alter-
nating with an effort to get air in his lungs. Not realizing that the air-
blowing should be done with restraint even for a victim grossly over-
weight, the poor fellow returned my air with a great heaving blow of
his own, sharing with me his copious breakfast. Gagging, massaging,
occasionally blowing more air, my efforts were working. He seemed
to be awakening from death. Then a local physician arrived, waved
me off, listened for heart sounds for at least a full minute, then announced simply, "Il est mort." The next day a Cairo newspaper said
that the Minister of Tourism had died and the article stated that an
American physician on the scene had been incapable of reviving him
when the attack occurred.

Despite that history—which I am certain was not my fault for its
failure—Ted soon had a pulse, regained some color and was moan-
ing and thrashing about when I left the room, replaced by a team of

resuscitation experts bringing a cart full of the right equipment. He recovered fully, but he was not the sort to make mention of having been saved by the new chairman of the eye department massaging his chest and blowing air in his mouth. I thought perhaps no one had told him what had happened so one evening, while having dinner with him and his wife, I told him, probably sounding boastful. His wife, June, was grateful; Ted chewed his after-dinner cigar and smiled dismissively and changed he subject.

Because I came from Johns Hopkins, where the Johns Hopkins Hospital was owned and operated by the university which was intrinsic to the medical school, I had some doubts about a private hospital's control of the lucrative patient care needed to support most private medical schools. I believe the dog should wag the tail, so to speak. Nevertheless, in Houston I felt fortunate to be in an environment of thriving institutions, with the best of Big Business's moguls as trustees of the medical school and our primary affiliated hospital. I could hardly wait to tap the generosity that I assumed would be made available to the doctor whom their hero DeBakey had recruited to Houston. But I was to learn that I was a complete greenhorn in the world of big-time money-grubbing.

In early 1971, prominent Houston businessman L. F. McCollum, former CEO of Conoco and Chairman of the Board of BCM and known as "Mr. Mac," had agreed to become the chairman of the board of ORBIS at the urging of his friend, Juan Trippe. How convenient for me! I suggested that he and I get together to plan our approach to fundraising with the various Houstonian and greater Texan philanthropic money sources to fit whichever of the two "causes"—eye institute or aircraft---was better suited to each of them. I was stunned when he announced to me in no uncertain terms that ORBIS would be off-base for all fundraising anywhere in Texas, and that it was my obligation to see that this rule—a rule of his making—was strictly observed, since his first priority was raising Texas money for the medical school. Evidently, a major reason why Mr. Mac had accepted the chairmanship of the ORBIS board was to be certain that Dr. Paton's sticky fundraising fingers would not wander from the medical school to the distracting airplane project.

Thus, Mr. Mac's dictum meant I was to be the principal spokesperson for two completely disparate money-raising campaigns, separately organized and separately operated but simultaneously conducted. Both would have national outreach, but for one of them—my baby!—Texas was out of bounds. There was reason for concern, as it began to dawn on me that the failure of either of these fundraising causes would result in a heavy cost to both my credibility and my professional standing.

Mr. Mac also informed me that no doctor would be permitted to serve on the ORBIS board, that the board agreed with him that it was not a doctor's business to be involved in the financial and legislative affairs of a nonprofit organization. I was taken aback by this decision—announced to me as a fait accompli—but not overly concerned since the board had its meetings at the ORBIS New York headquarters and Betsy Wainwright would be serving as the intermediary between me and them. This was to become a fatal flaw in the future.

There was one more disappointment. From the start of my Houston years to the day of his death in 2008, Michael DeBakey never once talked about ORBIS with me, the name never passing his lips in the hundreds of times we spoke together. And had I given him an opening to criticize the venture by bringing it up, it would surely have caused tension between us so it was better left ignored. ORBIS was apparently not something with which he could identify, or perhaps he just chose to direct all of his energies to his own projects. Reluctantly, I had to respect his disinterest.

CHAPTER EIGHTEEN

True to his word, Dr. DeBakey did refer his patients with eye trouble to me, the VIP's among them being ushered to my clinical office by his personal nurse in charge of monarchs and movie stars. I had a good many surgical referrals and was very busy as an eye surgeon, largely with cataract and corneal operations. Remarkably, when particularly high-strung patients like comedian Jerry Lewis or columnist Ann Landers (Eppie Lederer) or political leaders of any party were to be seen in my office, Dr. DeBakey himself would arrive with the patient and sit nearby throughout the examination. He was a man of incredible energy and endurance. He performed over sixty thousand major operations, many of them abroad in unfamiliar hospitals, invariably with a staff he brought with him. His younger former associate across the Medical Center, Dr. Denton Cooley—also a heart surgeon of rare skill and endurance---performed even more operations but was less academically involved than DeBakey. For me, these two extraordinary men were surgical giants looming like dissimilar but imposing towers marking Houston's medical identity.

One morning in 1975, Dr, DeBakey's nurse assigned to VIP patients called to say that "the Boss" wanted me to see a patient for him that afternoon, making it clear that this particular patient was so important to Dr. DeBakey that the visit was to take place in my laboratory, which offered more privacy than my office.

The patient turned out to be a blind, ill-tempered toy poodle that was being cuddled in the arms of her devoted owner, a gorgeous young German lady. The dog had a far advanced cataract in each eye, indicated by two large pupils filled with a dense white substance that obviously did not permit light to be projected though it. Whether or not the dog could see my flashlight was difficult to determine, because she was not eager to be looked at, and even less to be touched by a stranger.

There was no question about the diagnosis. The owner, who introduced herself as Katrin, asked pleadingly what I was going to do about the cataracts. I told her that although one could not see the retina, there was no reason to suppose that there was anything other than the cataract causing the dog's blindness. If there were additional causes obscured by the cataracts, it was still unlikely that anything other than cataract surgery could be done to try to restore vision. The usual disclaimer.

"But can you make my baby see again?" Her voice was pleading.

"I will gladly try. Can't promise, but I'll try." I smiled the sort of smile intended to reassure her that she was not to worry because she was in the best of hands.

Before coming to Baylor, I had done many of these operations on diabetic dogs at Wilmer so, as it happened, I was probably about as good a dog cataract surgeon as one might find anywhere in the country. Knowing that this lovely woman was a special friend of Dr. DeBakey, I was frankly delighted to have the opportunity to show off my surgical skill by transforming a yappy little bitch into a fluffy ball of happiness.

The following day, I was surprised to find that the Chairman of the Department of Anesthesiology had come to the lab with Katrin and the dog to take personal charge of the anesthesia. He got the dog asleep and well-secured on the table; the overhead operating light was adjusted and the microscope swung into place. I was in my element. The operation went perfectly. At the completion of the procedure, I sewed the dog's lids together with a few silk sutures and applied an antibiotic ointment over them. I instructed Katrin to keep applying the eye ointment to the surface of the sutured eyelids and to bring her precious pet back for lid suture removal in two days.

Back she came with the poodle, but not before some new information had leaked out: This beautiful woman was Dr. DeBakey's new wife. A German actress, Katrin explained as we were preparing the dog for suture removal on the laboratory's table that she had met Dr. DeBakey at Frank Sinatra's house in Los Angeles. At that meeting, she told the great surgeon what beautiful hands he had and asked if she could sculpt them. He agreed to her offer, she sculpted his hands, and soon after became his wife. It was a charming love story and it was good to know he had re-found happiness after the death of his first wife.

As Katrin whispered reassurances to her little dog, I easily cut the several silk sutures and to my delight the operated eye looked "perfect" with a clear cornea and a normal, round pupil, the white cataract now completely extracted. Katrin gently placed her pet on the floor of the lab. The dog's tiny stump of a tail began to wag and she took off. I was swelling with surgeon's pride--even a bit jaunty as I swung my arm as if introducing the next great dog act at the circus. Then, the most awful thing happened. The little beast ran smack into the laboratory wall, then crouched back on her haunches, hanging her head and whimpering. Katrin flew over to pick her up. Now that the cataract in her operated eye was gone, I could examine the dog's retina and optic nerve. The nerve was dead white. Optic atrophy! Meaning nothing could be done to restore vision, not even if the animal were human.

Explaining that to Katrin DeBakey, and later by telephone to a disgruntled but reluctantly understanding Michael DeBakey, resulted in a bad ending for what I had thought was going to be a very satisfying day. That operation on the DeBakey dog was never mentioned to me again, but although that was the only dog he referred he did continue to send me his patients with eye problems.

There was often a benefit-by-association effect that came to me from caring for DeBakey patients, who were so devoted to him that anyone to whom he referred them was assumed to be "top drawer" as well. For example, one such person was the dynamic and gracious Princess Lilian, wife of the exiled King Leopold III of Belgium. She was fascinated to hear about ORBIS, which she later visited, describing it as a "special visual experience," and she invited me to visit her at her home near Waterloo, not far from Brussels. When in Europe doing some scouting for ORBIS volunteers, I took her up on her invitation. Argenteuil, the chateau that she and the former king lived in, was an enormous structure surrounded by fields populated with stags, instead of sheep. The king told stories of the Congo, where he had lived and learned to appreciate nature—while raping the country, others would add. Life at Argenteuil was a far cry from the life he had led while a prisoner of the Germans, as an unsuccessful bargainer with Hitler on behalf of his country, and after being denounced by his people for marrying Lilian. She had been a glamorous commoner who visited him in prison, became pregnant, then married him. The king was allowed to return home but not as a hero to his countrymen. It is a long and complicated story but suffice it to say that his misadventures landed him on the cover of *Time* magazine in 1937. By the time I met him, he was living in quiet retreat as Lilian pursued her interest in cardiology and cardiac surgery---of course, worshipping my boss, Dr. DeBakey.

Some time later, when Betsy Wainwright and I were trying to stir up enthusiasm for ORBIS in Paris,

Princess Lilian showed up at the ophthalmology congress we were attending and asked the two of us to lunch with her at a favorite Parisian restaurant. She did the ordering, which included strawberries, wine and tiny sandwiches. When the meal was finished, the restaurant proprietor presented the Princess with a bill which she waved aside, telling him to take whatever money was needed from a roll of U.S. dollars that looked about three inches thick. She handed it to him, uncounted.

The man returned in a few minutes with his head hung in theatrically humble demeanor as he explained to her, in French, of course, that it distressed him to have to say that the money she had given him was not quite sufficient. The wine had been very special, he reminded us, switching to English. The Princess turned to me. "Doctor, can you help me out? Just a little bit more is needed, you see."

I gave him my credit card. The alleged shortfall for the bill was in excess of fifty U.S. dollars. In those days, that was a lot of money to add to the pile he had already received for a light lunch for only three people; but for an ORBIS fan, I considered it a small sum to pay.

Dr. Denton Cooley, a native Texan who had trained in surgery at Johns Hopkins, also referred some of his patients to me and both he and his wife Louise became friends over the years. One patient he sent me was a fetching socialite who had been in an automobile accident a few hours before I saw her. She was ensconced in a large private room, sitting in bed in a fashionable nightgown. Probably in her forties, she had cascading blonde hair and a lissome figure but her face and eyelids were swollen and a large patch covered her left eye.

Joy was an old college friend of Denton's. She oozed with admiration of him, despite the pain she was obviously feeling. After a brief examination, I re-patched her eye and wrote orders for her orbital surgery the following morning, when a plastic surgeon and I would be operating under Denton's unofficial surveillance. I prescribed two kinds of pain pills to be taken, the mild one every three hours and the stronger one twice during the night, if necessary.

Returning later that evening to see how Joy was doing, I found her to be much improved. "Denton was here," she told me. "He had the nurse put an anesthetic drop in my eye and he left orders for it if I need more. And tomorrow after my surgery, he said I can go upstairs in a wheelchair and watch him operate through the skylights in his operating room, if I feel up to it."

"I promise you, you are not going to feel well enough for that after surgery on your face, so put it off a day or two. And about using those eye drops: I have cancelled Dr. Cooley's order for them. It is a risk to your eye because anesthetic drops impair healing and can cause eye infection."

Later that same evening, Denton returned for a final, pre-operative visit during his evening rounds and re-ordered the anesthetic eye drop. Luckily nothing bad happened as a result. (He evidently didn't think eye doctors were credible as physicians, but without any influence on my part, his daughter, Louise, would later become an ophthalmologist.)

The next morning, Joy's operation was first on the OR schedule. The task of freeing up the inferior rectus muscle was easily accomplished and a left facial fracture was restored to its proper position. In the recovery room, I again cautioned her not to overdo for a day or more. But when I saw her later, she told me excitedly that, despite feeling sleepy and looking awful after the operation, she had accepted Denton's invitation and, sitting in a wheelchair propped up by pillows, had for two hours watched every move he made while operating. She was thrilled. "He even waved at me! It was an experience I'll never forget," she told me.

Neither would I. On the face of it, it was inappropriate to have let her even try to accomplish this feat, for it was likely to increase the orbital pain and add to the risk of gastrointestinal upset. But obviously, Denton Cooley knew Joy and was on target in thinking that his surgery would instead distract her from her post-operative pain.

Denton Cooley and Michael DeBakey were polar opposites from one another—except for the manual skills and extraordinary commitment to cardiovascular surgery that each displayed throughout his career. After his stint as DeBakey's associate, Cooley founded and ran the heart institute at St. Luke's Hospital, about 200 yards from The Methodist Hospital where DeBakey performed his surgery. The two heart surgeons had become bitterly estranged colleagues due to an infamous episode relating to Cooley's use of a mechanical heart developed in DeBakey's laboratory, to which DeBakey believed he had exclusive rights. It was not until shortly before DeBakey's death in 2008 at the age of 99 that he and Cooley, age 87, made up their differences.

CHAPTER NINETEEN

By the time I arrived in Houston, ORBIS was already ballooning into a medico-industrial miasma of necessities and uncertainties, with its fundraising always in arrears. Without guidelines or relevant histories to use as blueprints, everything had to be done in an ad hoc manner. There was no way to assess in advance the validity or popularity of this multi-million dollar gamble in advance, so any promotional efforts in fundraising for it had to be based upon the optimism and expertise of its founder coming from the medical world--namely, me.

Of course, I also had to represent the medical world when it came to raising money for the eye institute. It wasn't enough to have glossy brochures that described its attributes in well-turned phrases. Any big potential donor needed flesh-and-blood contact with the guy who had been selected to actually accomplish all the things the brochures and the administrative advocates were promising.

In addition, there were the many planning and fundraising duties involved with chairing the department. Those included beefing up and teaching the residency program, recruiting a dozen professors, enlarging the research department five-fold, and being extensively involved in patient care that involved a considerable amount of surgery and consulting on cases referred because they were particularly challenging, or, in some instances, involved patients with a history of litigiousness.

Still, I had no one to blame but myself for my over-commitment during those frenetic years—for indulging in what amounted to academic greed. I saw myself as a triathlon contender, confident enough to take it all on but having neither the ability nor the physique to sustain the pace indefinitely.

Although I was certainly one of the players in red-hot pursuit of other people's hard-earned money, I was not the campaign leader on any front. With the administrations of both BCM and TMH strongly behind the drive to create an institute, there was a great deal of support for my efforts. As for ORBIS, despite being a medical project, its board was comprised mostly of people from worlds of business, law and philanthropy. They tended to be born-and-bred Eastern Establishment, Wall Street-CEO types, or friends of friends of those people. If Betsy herself had not been familiar to them as Juan Trippe's daughter, and if I had not shared somewhat in that Eastern Establishment identity, I don't believe we would ever have managed to finance the project. In that culture, when aspirations seem too far out to gain a donor's support on their own merit, the impetus for participation may depend upon a clannish loyalty and the return of personal favors. Usually those are business favors.

We had started with a naïve goal of raising $6 million in cash, an estimate that varied depending on how much would come as gifts-in-kind. Betsy and I had to fly around the country on a shoestring budget for fundraising or technical discussions of existing or anticipated issues. For the personal "face time" necessary for landing major grants and gifts, Betsy, traveling from New York City, and I, traveling from Houston, met frequently in reception rooms in such places as Denver, Los Angeles, New York, Chicago, and Palm Beach.

Increasingly, Juan Trippe's designated hitter for ORBIS was Albert Ueltschi, his private pilot in years past. Ueltschi had started a company, FlightSafety International, whose purpose was to train airline pilots in the particulars they needed to know regarding foreign airports. As his company grew, it took on broader scope, with headquarters at LaGuardia airport and branch offices throughout the world. *Forbes* was reporting that Ueltschi was becoming one of America's wealthiest CEOs. However, despite his success, in those first years he was not a big donor to ORBIS, which I interpreted to mean that he had very real doubts about achieving our goal. He also frequently reminded me in the early years that he was helping out with ORBIS in deference to the wishes of Betsy's father, which I took to mean he wouldn't be there otherwise.

Everyone admired Al, but he was a man of few words, and often those words were irascible and impatient ones. As time passed, he took over as chairman from the elderly McCollum. Unfortunately,

Ueltschi totally supported McCollum's belief that doctors do not belong on corporate boards and that, even as founder, I was no exception. My contrary—but unpersuasive---view was that because this was a nonprofit organization, it should not have the business-only kind of board they were familiar with in the for-profit business world. But the only board meeting I ever attended was in the early 1970s, and that was as a guest.

The board began to include some appealing "fluffs" and dutiful "fillers." I suppose "filler" was the category in which the Trippe people may have lumped together several of my dear and capable non-medical friends whom I insisted receive board appointments. Not only did these friends care about the project's purposes, but I knew they would be my eyes and ears within the board should any issues not in the minutes of the meetings need clarification. One of the people I proposed, William Post, the husband of my niece Pammie, started in early 1982 as a volunteer finance manager and soon became salaried.

The participation of my friends and family notwithstanding, the power of the board was vested entirely within the tight core of its leadership, which boiled down to Ueltschi, McCollum (although eventually, as his health failed, in name only) and Peter Mullen, who was the senior partner of a vast legal firm known as Skadden, Arps, famed for its skill in hostile takeovers. Mullen was Secretary of the Board. He was also Ueltschi's personal lawyer. Charles E. Lord, a business executive and a dean from the Yale School of Management, later joined the Executive Committee and became its chairman by the early 1980s. Charlie had long been a close friend of Betsy's and soon became a friend of mine.

The work each week was generally laid out by Betsy and I admired how quickly she learned about the leadership and workings of ophthalmology--both domestic and foreign—and how familiar she became with the names of leading ophthalmologists across the world. She threw herself into the work of ORBIS with all of her energy, employing her considerable female persuasiveness on all fronts.

Generally speaking, we were able to hire excellent personnel who would have commanded salaries at least twice what they earned with this nonprofit venture--the kind of workers attracted to political campaigns

who, because of their devotion to the goal and their belief in the assertions of the candidate, are willing to work extra hard on pauper's
pay. That is, unless they are treated rudely or imperiously, in which
case they often, quite naturally, will quit. Betsy had never been an
employee of any other organization. Her function at ORBIS was remarkably similar to that of Mrs. Aida Breckenridge, the early essential
organization and promotion expert for my dad's eye bank. However,
like Mrs. Breckenridge, she was quite impervious to the consequences
of forceful command in a nonprofit environment. This caused serious
fallout from time to time, which it was my unique job to handle. I
did what I could in conversation but sometimes I found myself writing explanations and pleas for civility along the lines of these phrases
taken from my correspondence with her: "... *We all need kindness, never
arrogance or rudeness. . . . The tensions and criticisms and ego displays that
I know about and have heard about are not professional and not compatible
with the viability of relationships. . . The greatest reward and what can only
be considered a major contribution is in the accomplishment of tasks without
personality battles and with a great deal of selflessness.*" I leaned hard but
I had to do so or several good people would have quit our sensitive
nonprofit organization, where the glue was not financial, but spectral.

As a medical project with its predominant start-up need in the
aeronautical field, ORBIS was neither fish nor fowl in the eyes of
most foundation hierarchies, where guidelines to qualify applicants
for funding were often strictly observed. We were a skeletal crew
doing miscellaneous jobs to fulfill the growing requirements of an
elephantine undertaking. Betsy and I were the decoys out to attract
interest and dole out persuasiveness. The actual shots, more often
than not, were fired by the member of the board having the closest association to the organization or foundation we had approached. But it
was thanks to the persuasiveness of George Hambleton that US AID
became a lifesaver for our project, providing a grant of $250,000 early
on. In late 1981, when the organization was so financially strapped
that we feared we might have to close it down permanently, George
contacted the head of AID via Jim Baker and a grant arrived within a
week, salvaging us from total collapse. In all, AID contributed a total
of $1 million before ORBIS was launched.

Since ORBIS' greatest requirement in the early 1970s had continued to be obtaining an aircraft, the most important reason to be optimistic about the future of our project was an arrangement made by Ueltschi and Trippe with United Airlines' CEO, Edward Carlson. My longstanding colleague, Francis L'Esperance, made the trip to meet with Mr. Carlson in Chicago on a day when I was unavailable for travel. The deal was if we could raise enough money to have an old moth-balled DC-8 converted to the kind of flying teaching "hospital" we needed, then his company would contribute it.

The planning for how an aircraft could be adapted to its intended functions was assisted by funding from the Markle Scholarship money that I was permitted to transfer to BCM from Hopkins, which helped to establish a surgical research laboratory similar to the one I had founded at Wilmer. In Houston, Tom Decker, PhD, and Chris Kuether, soon to become a PhD, were the bioengineers who worked in the lab and willingly took on some of the challenges of fitting audiovisuals and ophthalmic instrumentation into the plans for the aircraft modifications in as effective an arrangement as both aeronautical and American Hospital Association standards would permit. Those men became the project's in-house saints as they worked for ORBIS in as much of their spare time as they could find.

The re-fitted aircraft would require large, fuel-driven generators for all on-board electricity once the engines were shut down. These would have to be stored within the aircraft when it was in flight and later lowered by an hydraulic lift to the tarmac from the baggage bins. The aircraft would also need many gallons of water for surgical scrubbing, air conditioning, heating, drinking, flushing, cleaning, and so forth. All airports have what I call "hose water" available to spray down machinery. Starting from that water, the mechanical systems for filtering and purifying the water were to be carried on board in the baggage bins and, like the generators, lowered to the tarmac when the aircraft was in its medical mode.

One of the areas on which I concentrated was to make sure that all foreign doctors expressing interest in ORBIS were welcomed, to help us internationalize the project. In the project's literature, we pointed out truthfully that the elements of ophthalmic microsurgery and

many related new scientific acquisitions were originally derived almost
entirely from foreign sources. Examples included the operating microscope, the just-developed tiny Sony television cameras for displaying the microsurgery, the virgin silk suture material, the intraocular
lenses, the best techniques for corneal transplantation, the binocular
indirect ophthalmoscope, and so forth.   I stressed that ORBIS would
include many non-American teachers and I persuaded selected foreign
colleagues to become identified as proponents of the undertaking by
serving on the Medical Advisory Board, after agreeing to volunteer to
teach on the aircraft. These admittedly tentative commitments were
then purposefully passed on to organizations that were potential sources of funding in the United States or, occasionally, in other countries.

Frankly, the early overseas acceptance of "hypothetical ORBIS"
went so well that it began to be something of a problem. As the years
of incubation dragged on, some foreign colleagues pointed out to me
that the way ORBIS had been presented to them abroad had suggested that it was already a fait accompli---while in the United States
it was, in fact, still considered a questionable pie-in-the-sky notion
by most American ophthalmologists in leadership positions.

But progress continued, however slowly. By 1979, approximately
fifty prominent American and foreign leaders in ophthalmology had
agreed to have their names on the ORBIS Medical Advisory Board
list and thus, by implication, declared themselves in favor of the project's development.   Still, I recall only a handful of colleagues who
actually committed to teach surgery on the aircraft, and volunteer
teachers were absolutely essential to the functioning of the mission.

In that regard, I remember all too well two American ophthalmologists who did come forward at different meetings to ask to be
listed as future volunteer teachers.   One had been barred from his
state ophthalmological society for unwarranted surgery, and the other
was a man I knew rather well who had been banned by his city's leading hospital from performing surgery at all, due to an outrageously
high incidence of operative complications. The O.R. nurses had finally refused to assist in his cases. Would these two be the kind of
volunteers the project would attract? And how would we know if our
volunteers were competent or not?

There was plenty to worry about. As we forged ahead on one front, there would be anxiety brewing on another, usually a portending financial collapse. Before we received the pledged plane, we could still have pushed back without much more than a loss of face. But once we got as far as refurbishing the aircraft, failure would call for nothing less than *seppuku*—dying with honor. It was, frankly, hell at times trying to keep hope alive.

At medical meetings, ophthalmologists would wander up to the ORBIS booth to inspect drawings of what the aircraft would look like and some would hang around, thumbing through the brochures and waiting to hear an explanation of its intended purpose. I would try to short-circuit their skepticism and criticism by giving them my well-practiced spiel, overlaid with friendly confidence. Some doctors would just wander off; others would try to bait me with questions they were sure I had never heard before, but which I invariably had answered many times: "Doctor, what if a patient needs to go to the bathroom? "What if the generator fails during the operation?" "How do you get patients to the aircraft when it is sitting on the runway and other aircraft are taking off and landing?"

Chairpersons for a number of scientific programs permitted me to speak briefly about Project ORBIS and yet, to the best of my recollection, there was never another ophthalmologist who presented or wrote a paper about the future possibilities of the project. My own talks were given a polite reception, but rarely did these presentations lead to anything concrete.

On the other hand, virtually everyone in ophthalmology was becoming intrigued by the pros and cons of a microsurgical cataract extraction, especially with the use of a highly controversial small surgical incision, as advocated by Dr. Charles Kelman in an operation he called "phacoemulsification"—often referred to as phaco. Virtually every surgically-oriented ophthalmologist wanted to see for himself how it was performed and to determine how difficult it might be to learn. Controversy in itself attracts attention, and for ORBIS we needed all the attention we could attract in persuading its validity to colleagues around the world who had the wherewithal to undertake microsurgery. In short, I began to preach that ORBIS would help to popularize phacoemulsification internationally and that phacoemul-sification would help to popularize ORBIS. This became a topic of such importance to me and to the aircraft project that I will include a post script to this memoir, page 259, dealing with it in more detail than seems justified here. I can't think of any other subject in this memoir that has afforded a more stimulating challenge to provide the description that it deserves.

The specifications for the ORBIS operating room were not easy to devise. First, we had to measure all existing medical and audiovisual equipment. Next, we had to make life-size models, then measure the space needed in their surround in order to figure out the most func-tional arrangements and also to calculate the volume and the weight of the materials that would have to be stored in the holds. For teach-ing, the aircraft needed a podium in the classroom, numerous fixed monitors for observing live demonstrations, and large mobile moni-tors and amplifiers to be carried in the holds that would be set up for use in a classroom in the nearby air terminal for overflow audiences.

The surgeons were to enter the operating room through a narrow scrub room, where there would be a trough with separate water taps to permit as many as five doctors and nurses to scrub simultaneously. The patients would be wheeled from the tarmac up a flight of aircraft stairs into a preparation area. From there, the patient would be taken on a gurney past the supply closets' semi-sterile environment into the operating room. There was a recovery room holding area for patients to rest for a short time after surgery.

ORBIS would have to be prepared for both cold host cities and ones that were intensely hot--since the interior temperature had to remain a constant 70° F in the operating room, with controlled, fil-tered air flow to limit the spread of germs and provide comfort to the patients. It was a matter of principle to us that ORBIS should be of-fered to other countries only in a manner that was fully acceptable to the American Hospital Association standards.

Television cameras would be fixed to walls and ceilings through-out the aircraft---six small television cameras in the operating room alone, plus one attached to the optics of the operating microscope to permit both the observers in the OR and those outside of it to see the enlarged surgical field exactly as viewed by the surgeon and the assistant. These cameras, along with amplification systems and recording devices, would be controlled by a single technician in the adjacent audiovisual compartment. Any surgery of particular interest, or even just routine cases that a student-doctor might want to have for his own purposes, would be provided to him on VHS tape when he stepped out of the aircraft.

In the front end of the plane, in what had once been the space for first-class passenger seats, a classroom capable of seating thirty doctors would be created. The doctors would wear headphones and listen to talks by the visiting teachers, either in English or from a translator speaking in their language. The classroom would have a large television monitor for teaching tapes of prior surgeries, lecture projections or a live surgical operation.

A full ORBIS crew would consist of a minimum of two visiting teachers, at least one of whom would be a specialist in ophthalmic microsurgery. There would be two to three young ophthalmologists serving on fellowships with ORBIS, plus a nursing staff of at least four full-time RN's. Two or more ophthalmic technicians were needed not only in the operating room to assist with the lasers and the phaco machine but also to be responsible for any adjustments needed in the audio-visual hardware during surgical sessions. The chief audio-visual technician was a key appointment, as was an overall handyman and jack-of-all-trades who could deal with aeronautical as well as electrical problems that might arise. Beyond those individuals, the project would need a director who would be in charge of all aspects of the deployment. The actual cost of the salaried staff was greatly reduced from the norms of income for such individuals, on the basis of the idealistic and venturesome opportunities ORBIS had to offer. The pilots were all to be volunteers and were highly experienced---usually retired airline pilots very familiar with DC-8's.

The conversion of our plane was a major undertaking. The fuselage of the aircraft had to be stripped and its interior completely remodeled to meet the sometimes conflicting medical, audiovisual and aeronautical functions that were basic to the project. Thanks to Anthony Zuma, a former pilot and aeronautical engineer, many of our difficulties in finding compromises and unforeseen alternatives were resolved. Our invaluable new ORBIS employee assumed the job of Executive Director during the aircraft conversion phase. He was a wrinkled-faced, chain-smoking, slow-talking, kindly Texan who was thoroughly familiar with the technical side of the aircraft industry. He had flown DC-8's and he knew about their servicing and also the companies that might want the job of converting our aircraft. After providing detailed specifications to five potential bidders, Tony orchestrated a bidding competition among several of those companies. The lowest bid came from the Flying Tiger airline in Los Angeles.

A deadline for completing the work was agreed upon, the contract was signed, and the donated aircraft was flown on its last trip as a United Airlines carrier to the hangar of the Flying Tiger Company in Los Angeles. Several of us flew out to L.A. to see the DC-8 arrive at its temporary home. Thanks to one of our Los Angeles donors, Bob Hope and other noted figures were also on hand to cheer its anticipated future.

On that day, we were very aware that we had reached the point of no return. Ahead would lie equipment intolerances, frustrating delays, and shortages of cash payments in the plane's challenging transition into its new incarnation. It took a year and a half to get the work done; but finally, like an elephantine butterfly from a cocoon, ORBIS emerged as a wondrous flying machine. Meanwhile, those of us playing the waiting game had continued the drum beat to excite the profession for so long and with such intensity that I had to wonder if the idea would be worn out before the actual plane arrived on the scene. There was no telling.

CHAPTER TWENTY

In February of 1982, the former commercial DC-8 aircraft, freshly painted and bearing on its tail the large ORBIS logo of two hands encompassing an orb, was flown from Burbank, California, to Ellington Field in Houston. There it was received with "whoops and hollers" from

the likes of me and my colleagues at Baylor, L.F. McCollum, Albert Ueltschi, Betsy Wainwright, ORBIS's ophthalmology fellow Dr. Robert Munsch and ORBIS's new Executive Director, George Hambleton, and actress Dina Merrill, to add a touch of glamour. Also present were many members of the support staff and the medical crew--nurses, bio-engineers, flight surgeons, and supplies managers.

First Lady Barbara Bush

Dina Merrill, Klaus Heilmann MD and DP

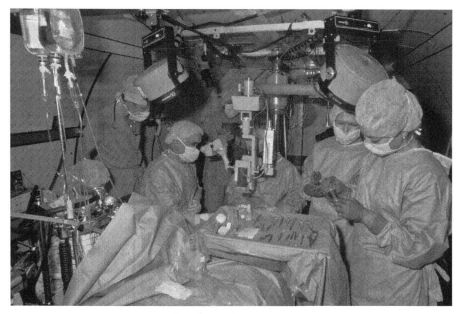

On-board surgery.

The following morning, invited visitors and the press were welcomed aboard. Mrs. George H. W. (Barbara) Bush was our special guest and she was enthusiastic and beaming as the functions of the mobile teaching ophthalmic outpatient eye "hospital" were explained to her. From that day on, she and the President were to remain faithful supporters of ORBIS.

Ellington Field was an inactive airport usually given over to military functions. Our aircraft was parked on the tarmac, not near any terminal, a position in which it would be located on all of its future assignments abroad. The water filtering systems and the generators had been lowered to the tarmac, and the passenger steps had been rolled up to the fore and aft cabin doors to permit visitors to walk through the plane before it was made ready by sterility precautions for surgical procedures. All of the instrumentation was in place, the television system and communications systems were turned on, and the flight deck was open for visitors to examine.

What emerged first and foremost was something that I had never fully anticipated even when visiting the aircraft during its conversion

and that was the awesomeness of standing alongside the huge flying hospital, climbing into it, examining its technology, hearing its
sound systems, watching its television relays, and observing the uniformed crew performing their various activities. Its enormity when
viewed from the ground, its quietly functioning generators, its stark
white paint with the eye of the ORBIS logo on the tail--this was
indeed magnificent, a white dove of peace magnified a million times
over.   Every visitor had the same awed reaction; it showed in their
faces and was apparent in their excited voices. Even usually skeptical
members of the press were generous with their compliments.

For the opening teaching sessions, the classroom on board was
soon filled with medical dignitaries, board members, and staff members. I had invited two eye surgeons from abroad to be our first visiting teachers--Dr. Luis Salazar from Bogota, Colombia, and Klaus
Heilmann, MD, from Munich, Germany. They alternated with Richard Kratz, MD, from California, and ORBIS advisory board member
Francis L'Esperance, MD, from New York--all operating on Houston patients. The only misstep was mine in omitting Dr. Jared Emery—my Hopkins recruit to BCM—who should have been among
those first ORBIS surgeons but I goofed and the invitation was not
extended.

I was not among the surgeons performing on ORBIS, having decided early on not to be one of its surgical instructors. I feared that
to put myself in a show-and-tell capacity on this publicity-dependent
undertaking might raise the question of whether an underlying motivation on my part was showcasing myself doing microsurgery the
world over.   Valid reasoning or not, that was my considered position. The arrangements to allow for foreign and out-of-state doctors
to operate in Houston on American patients had been made in advance. None of them was licensed in Texas but we requested that the
regulations be waived and they were. That permission was not easily
obtained from the state authorities but it was crucial that ORBIS not
offer overseas what it could not do in the United States. Our opening
session, I insisted, had to have foreign doctors operating on American
patients, just as American doctors would be operating on foreign patients overseas.

There was one glitch in the first day's operating schedule. Dr. Kratz was about to demonstrate how a cataract is emulsified when it was discovered that the instrument's power cord had a three-pronged plug that would not fit into the two-pronged sockets of the operating room. The patient's eye was already incised. No one in attendance knew how to come to the surgeon's aid. Thinking quickly, Dr. Kratz called for a hack saw, which he used to modify the plug; he then re-scrubbed and continued the operation as if nothing had happened. Despite the short delay, it was an otherwise flawless procedure and, like all the other operations being demonstrated that day, its outcome was entirely successful.

After several days of dress rehearsals in Houston, the aircraft departed on its first mission abroad on March 1, 1982. The first stop was Panama City. Our Executive Director George Hambleton and I were passengers, along with a full-time crew of thirteen employees: three residents-in-training, three registered nurses, a nurse anesthetist, an audio-visual programmer, a flight engineer, three equipment engineers, several technicians and a purser. Arriving in Panama City, we were greeted by an excited contingent of Panamanian ophthalmologists, plus other medical authorities and city officials. That was to be the first of hundreds of similar arrivals at airports on six of the seven continents of the world.

The real hero of that first mission was George Hambleton, who was largely responsible for the myriad details involved in each deployment. Months before the aircraft was to arrive in any city, pre-flight visits by ORBIS representatives were critically necessary. George and his assistant, Walter Nelson, made innumerable preliminary trips to the city to see that nothing was overlooked during that preparatory phase. Local ophthalmological societies negotiated dates for when ORBIS would arrive and depart, and designated surgical participants were contacted to be sure their patients for specified surgeries were brought to the airport on schedule and escorted to the aircraft. Arrangements had to be made for a noise-free location where the aircraft could be safely parked, with ready access for patients, physicians and visitors. Security and police cooperation had to be assured, water had to be supplied and reliably available airport transportation service, VIP arrangements for special attendees, local press information, aircraft staff hotel arrangements, and instructions as to time and place for meeting with the selected volunteer teachers were just a few of the other items on the agenda that had to be meticulously in place.

Large television screens could be set up in nearby airport facilities for literally hundreds of doctors to watch and through which they could address questions directly to the surgeon or the physician at the podium in the aircraft's classroom. In some countries, annual ophthalmological convocations were even scheduled around an ORBIS visit, and the techniques of their own or visiting colleagues could be beamed into remote lecture halls at those convocations. Live surgical or laser demonstrations of that nature were new to many of the host countries on the ORBIS schedule. All of these matters required strong executive leadership, with no established routines to go by. But common sense and logic extrapolated from hospital-based eye care combined to make the live demonstrations aboard the aircraft go smoothly and safely from the beginning.

The following numbers speak to the project's early and remarkable success: ORBIS remained in continuous operation for 50 of the next 56 weeks, spending several weeks in each of 27 cities in 20 countries, during which time 87 ophthalmologists from 25 U.S. states and 8 foreign countries served as primary teachers. More than 1,200 host country doctors participated in the programs, an average of about 50 doctors a visit. Nearly 1,000 teaching operations were performed on the aircraft and others were performed in local hospitals, increasingly as time passed and microsurgery-equipped hospitals were available. In each case, the teaching program was custom-tailored to the requests of the host ophthalmological societies. The cost of the first year of operation was somewhat over U.S. $3 million.

So it was that ORBIS hit the jackpot from the very start. In the months that immediately followed its initial flight, the aircraft's break-in period passed without significant incident. Later, there would be criticisms of its costliness by individuals genuinely concerned about the optimal use of any available funding for the always urgent needs of the developing countries. We would remind those critics that our operational funding came mostly from corporate donors (either in cash or gifts in kind) and from foundation sources not usually associated with medical philanthropy, supplemented by the USAID grant we received. There were occasional problems with patient follow-up, although it was our policy to leave one crew doctor behind to supervise the recovery of the recently operated patients after the aircraft had moved on. And there were the not unexpected cries of favoritism or exclusivity that can happen when one host group seemed to have more privileges on the aircraft than another.

We made an effort to be fair to all who came aboard, and we tried to function under the auspices of each local ophthalmological society that would be responsible for the choice of doctors who were to have turns in the operating room. Even from my somewhat remote office at BCM, as the Founder and Medical Director I was ultimately the one responsible for the principles and practices of ORBIS. With those titles came grave accountability, of which I was very aware.

The once-dire predictions of certain failure were replaced by the increasingly enthusiastic support of ophthalmologists, both in the U.S. and abroad. ORBIS would always have vigilant critics reminding us indirectly not to allow its inherent flamboyance to overshadow its practicality and original purpose; but the aircraft project was finally born, and it was more than I had ever dared imagine it could be.

CHAPTER TWENTY-ONE

In September, 1982 I joined Al Ueltschi, George Hambleton, my Assistant, Bette Burkett, a former faculty member and highly admired friend, Dr. Dominic Lam, and our Director of Development, Karin Eisele, on a visit to China with ORBIS, the first time for each of us except for Dominic who was born in China. We were there to see for ourselves what the positive impact of ORBIS might be in a country not given to hiding its impressions of foreign praxis. So far, our record was unblemished, in missions to Panama, Columbia, Ecuador, Peru, Jamaica, West Germany, and England. At last it was time to make a first appearance in a communist country, the People's Republic of China. Its reception there would be the project's biggest test yet. Would a proud and independently traditional Asian people, whose medical care was only just beginning to enter the age of technology, find ORBIS as worthy as had our previous hosts? Would the project's purposes be too brazenly boastful of Western know-how? Or perceived as challenging the ancient medicine they had practiced for centuries? As always, the project would succeed only if it were in sync with local mores and manners, and I worried that it might be too much to expect that all of the ORBIS volunteer teachers were sufficiently aware of those important nuances, particularly in a country like China.

We flew from Hong Kong to Canton (Guangzhou) in the ORBIS aircraft, bursting with anticipation. As we approached, a crowd of about fifty people became visible on the tarmac even before we disembarked near the terminal. Their smiles indicated that we were welcome. Chief among them were Dr. Eugene Chen and his wife, Dr. Winifred Mao, undoubtedly the two most famous and now quite elderly Chinese ophthalmologists, once friends of my father's when I was a kid in short pants and Dr.Chen was a visiting fellow at The Wilmer Institute.

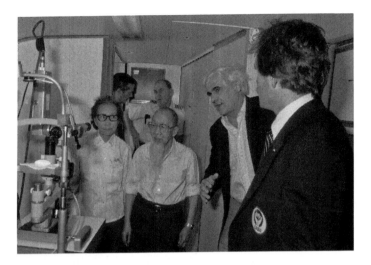

They were the catalysts of a hearty Chinese welcome. There could be no doubt about the enthusiasm our hosts showed us as we disembarked. But still to be discovered was whether the aircraft as a teaching machine would be as exciting and useful to them as it had been to others.

The following day, the visiting Western doctors demonstrated phacoemulsification, IOL implants, and various types of glaucoma operations. There was a talk or two on medical ophthalmology and the use of various new medicaments. Those may have been highlights for the Chinese but for me the highlight was their demonstration to us of acupuncture as the only "anesthetic" used for surgery on the eyes of their patients. It was remarkable to us that during an operation made painless by acupuncture, the awake patient could move his eyes freely, proving that there was no need for the injections Westerners used not just to deaden any surgery-induced pain but, concomitantly, to immobilize the eye. If the muscles that move the eyes are able to move during the operation, the surgeon can determine if enough muscle shortening had been done and, if not, he can fix it right away. The Chinese demonstrations were indeed impressive, in case after case. How do I know that these patients did not feel any pain? Because on that day, I took off a lapel pin used for an airport ID and gently pricked the ankle of one of the patients lying on a gurney with his acupuncture needles in place, ready to become the next case on ORBIS. He reacted to the pin prick with a sharp jerk of his foot. That was not a definitive test of acupuncture's authenticity, but at least it proved the patient was not loaded up with a heavy systemic painkiller.

The visit to China perfectly exemplified what ORBIS was intended to do: exchange expertise between host and visitor for the betterment of eye surgery worldwide. In most circumstances, an ORBIS visit to a host country was suggested to the foreign ophthalmologists when meeting with them at American or international conventions. But there were numerous small countries that lacked colleagues who regularly attended international meetings or in which foreign-born doctors were living. Many countries' doctors have no national medical school or other institutional base at which they can continue their education, yet they have the eyesight of their nation completely in their hands. One such country is Jamaica. At that time some dozen ophthalmologists served the population but they lacked any particular societal cohesiveness. And in 1982, none was Jamaican by birth. We knew that several of these ophthalmologists had expressed interest in our project at one of the annual meetings of the American Academy of Ophthalmology, but they had said they did not know how to go about officially inviting us to come because of our fairly stringent requirements for host country collaboration.

As mentioned, the usual procedure was for George Hambleton to visit the country and make the arrangements through the local ophthalmology society, but since there was no such society in Jamaica and George was heavily scheduled in other countries where there were already-scheduled ORBIS itineraries, I flew to Kingston to figure out the best way to get the aircraft invited. I arrived alone and on a weekend. It was to be a "cold call" exploratory venture, and so I decided it would be smart to start at the top.

I had arbitrarily selected my hotel, a Hilton or Sheraton. Upon arriving, I found the phone number for the Prime Minister, using the telephone book that lay alongside a Gideon's Bible in the drawer of the bedside table. A man answered. Not surprisingly, he said Prime Minister Edward Seaga was busy and could not come to the telephone. He asked the nature of my call. I told him that I wanted to meet the Prime Minister and tell him about ORBIS and seek his help in arrangements for the aircraft to come to Kingston. The man seemed hesitant. Then, after a moment's thought, he said, "Would you speak with Mrs. Seaga? She is so very personally interested in medical affairs."

"I would be delighted to speak with her." The phone went dead for a minute or two. Then, "Hello! MITsy he-ah!" came through the receiver.

I introduced myself. Her chipper British-accented voice rather quickly changed from diplomatically formal to genuinely interested as I described the purpose of my call.

"Why don't you come up to Vale Royal and we can have a talk about ORBIS. It sounds original."

I had no idea where Vale Royal was, or even what it was, but I called a taxi and to my surprise I discovered that it was located on a hill less than half a mile from the hotel and was the Prime Minister's official residence and office, complete with beautiful grounds. At the top of some steps leading to the front door stood Mrs. Seaga, waiting to extend her greeting. She insisted we start with a quick tour of the large, turn-of-the-century mansion.

"Eddie's office is in there. And there's mine." As we went though the main reception room, I asked about the three fish tanks filled with freshwater fish. "He loves those fish," she replied. And then, "Here, let's sit and talk about your airplane."

She was unabashedly intrigued and an expressive listener, both reactive and participatory. After about twenty minutes, she abruptly looked at her watch, stood and said, "Look, join me and the children for a picnic lunch on Lime Key and we can talk some more. But first I have to get rid of an Englishman who is here with his two daughters. He used to live in this house when his father was in the British foreign service. Come with me and meet him and then we can be off." I was only too happy to accept her invitation.

The Englishman turned out to be a 37-year-old public relations executive, a former actor brought up in London's equivalent of the Old Guard Eastern Establishment. Oliver Foot was tall and dark-haired, with a Laurence Olivier-as-Hamlet haircut; he was polite, talkative and pleased to have been allowed to show his daughters the place where their father had been raised during early boyhood.

Foot told us that he currently lived in Manhattan, had attended an American college and was estranged from the girls' American mother, Nancy. He went on to explain that he had been born in Kingston and had lived at Vale Royal when his father, Hugh Foot--later Lord Cara-don--was the British Colonial Secretary, at which time Vale Royal was his designated residence. In fact, he proudly said that his father had spent considerable time teaching him to speak audibly and distinctly by having him practice orating from the second floor balcony of Vale Royal. His father had stood below on the lawn---at some distance from the house---and coached him in the art of voice projection. Presumably the boy was being prepared for a life in governmental service similar to the father's, and also the boy's distinguished uncles, one of whom, Michael Foot, had led the British Labour Party.

Foot was curious as to why I was there with Mrs. Seaga and asked what I had been discussing with her. I gave him a few sentences about ORBIS. He said it sounded very interesting and requested my card, giving me his. I suggested he might want to stop in at the OR-BIS central office in Manhattan to find out more about my project.

When Foot returned to New York, he not only stopped by but was interviewed and soon became a full-time employee in that office. It was apparent from the beginning that he had had much exposure to the rich and famous acquaintances of his family, including the likes of Winston Churchill. I was soon to discover that he signed letters over the title of The Honorable Oliver Foot, based upon familial en-titlement. I knew little more about him than what he had told me in the few pleasantries we'd exchanged in Jamaica, although I did discover, somewhat to my surprise, that he had once been an evangeli-cal preacher. I admired his jubilant ambition and came to enjoy him as a trustworthy friend. He proved to be a born advertising expert and was invariably charming, enthusiastic, and dedicated to his new work in advertising and promotional efforts on our behalf. He most certainly had learned from his father's lessons, for he spoke with clar-ity and ease in front of audiences, his presentation enhanced by his cultured British accent.

However, on that day in Kingston, Mrs. Seaga gave our Honorable acquaintance short shrift. She and her three children, ranging in age from about three to nine, and I bundled into a long black limousine. Three Secret Service agents in dark suits with white shirts and ties came to join us, looking rather fierce and on-duty as they climbed into a separate car to follow our driver for the mile or two to the dock. There a small boat with an outboard motor was waiting to take us to Lime Key. Off we went, loaded to the gunnels--the five of us plus the three young Secret Service men. Each of our rather diminutive bodyguards now wore nothing but an elfin bikini, accessorized by a pistol stuck into its waist band. There was no way that they could have been concealing walkie-talkies or other devices for communication or defense. Apparently on the uninhabited island a short distance away, there would be no need for official guarding.

En route to Lime Key, Mrs. Seaga graciously suggested that she be called "Mitsy" and she agreed to call me "David." That was the start of a delightfully relaxed, chatty, funny, interesting sojourn. As the children played and swam and took care of themselves, I sat on the beach listening to Mitsy describe her life as the wife of the most important person in Jamaica. She had been a Miss Jamaica and was still exceptionally attractive. Her interest in ORBIS and her lively way of talking and teasing and enjoying herself on that small, desolate island off Kingston was enchanting.

After several hours on Lime Key, Mitsy abruptly recalled that she was due back at Vale Royal to serve tea to some dignitaries who were coming to visit the Prime Minister. "What will Eddie think of me? Gracious! I should be there to help welcome his guests ."

Since it was already about 3:30 in the afternoon, we rushed to the boat and a few minutes later we were at the Kingston dock. Mitsy, the children and I leaped into the waiting limousine. When we got back to the residence, Mitsy decided it was already too late to make an appearance at the tea party. Moreover, there was no one on the staff to prepare the tea tray for the guests. We sneaked into Vale Royal through the back door for deliveries. In the huge empty kitchen, Mitsy set about boiling water and collecting the tea tray, cups, saucers, lumped sugar, cream and linen napkins. I was assigned to getting the cream bottle from the fridge, finding the box in which sugar was stored, and folding the napkins to set them on the tray. Somehow it seemed hilarious for us to be scurrying around barefoot in the Prime Minister's kitchen in wet bathing suits making tea for unknown dignitaries who would have no suspicion from whence the tea had come. The butler, white-jacketed and sedate, was called and he disappeared with the loaded tray into the drawing room where Eddie and his guests were waiting.

Several hours previously, I had been an unknown American. Now, as I called a cab, Mitsy had another idea. "Why don't you come for dinner with us, David?" It was an appealing invitation. I felt, though, that I should share some of the hospitality. "Why don't you and Eddie and the children join me for dinner at the hotel?" In my wildest dreams, I did not imagine she would accept that alternative. But, "How very sweet of you! We would love to come." Easy as that.

At the appointed hour of seven p.m., the Prime Minister---soon to be officially "Eddie" to me, too---pulled up with Mitsy and the three children in the limousine. I met them at the door of the hotel. The same security guards that had been with us in the afternoon were now joined by twice their number and all were dressed in the same dark suits, white shirts and dark ties as before. Each held a pistol, finger on the trigger, drawn and pointed upward. As the family and I walked into the dining room, the cortege of guards surrounded us: those in front looking straight ahead, those alongside facing outward and walking sideways, crab-like, and those behind facing, and walking, backward.

They surrounded us in that secure cortege until we reached our reserved table. Then they departed to be seated at another table in the partially filled dining room, far away from where we were sitting. As best I could determine during the meal, they never looked up from their plates as they happily ate the same meal and drank the same wine as I had ordered for the Prime Minister. I hoped that any aspiring assassin would respect their off-duty leisure time. Little did I know then that they were all my guests--vintage wines included---but the evening was worth every farthing.

During dinner, I naturally spoke about ORBIS, answered questions and explained what a success the project had been so far. The Prime Minister was a good listener—at least in the early part of the evening. For a change of pace, I suggested to Eddie that, as Prime Minister of Jamaica, he might consider filling his fish tanks with beautiful Jamaican fish from the reefs off Kingston, rather than freshwater fish from elsewhere in the world. He courteously said he liked that idea. He was a pleasingly stolid Harvard Business School-educated gentleman who lacked his wife's animation but had a modesty I found very appealing. He must have been unusually tired from a long day's work, for as dinner went on, he dozed off at the table despite all the noise surrounding him.

ORBIS not only went to Jamaica a few months later, it returned several more times thereafter. After many years of marriage, the Seagas were divorced. In later years, when Mitsy would come to Houston for one reason or another, she would call me, but as time went on, we lost touch. Wherever she is today, I can imagine that she gives much joy to those who have the pleasure of basking in her warmth and charm.

CHAPTER TWENTY-TWO

In 1980, after my second wife and I mutually decided to divorce, I elected to step down as Chairman of Ophthalmology when the person I thought would be the best successor for my job started being recruited by other institutions. A search committee was set up and, even after a national search, happily, my choice, Dan B. Jones, MD, was selected—a brilliant man with excellent academic credentials, a great sense of humor, and a southern accent better understood in Houston than my northeastern pronunciation.

Life became less complicated. ORBIS was up and running and I was out from under the tasks of departmental and residency management after years of hard work but high productivity in terms of departmental development. Being the responsible faculty and facility builder of a great eye department had been a rewarding opportunity but the time had come for new blood to take over, and Dan Jones was already doing an outstanding job. The doyen of Houston society, Lynn Wyatt, put me on her list for luncheons and various other formal entertainments, and I had fun meeting her friends and acquaintances, from Princess Margaret of Britain to Grace Kelly (Her Supreme Highness, Princess Grace of Monaco) and the charming prima ballerina, Dame Margot Fonteyn. There were also numerous male movie stars, famous mountaineers and African white hunters whose names I was less motivated to remember.

One morning in the winter of 1982 a visitor barged enthusiastically into my office in The Cullen Eye Institute—a full-figured man with matching round eyes, a sort of beardless Santa Claus. Mr. Norman Pennick turned out to be a headhunter from a healthcare employment agency wanting to recruit me for the medical directorship of a brand-new hospital in Saudi Arabia.

"Thanks, Mr. Pennick, but I'm not job hunting and I have no interest in working in a hospital in Saudi Arabia. Nice to meet you but it's not for me." I moved to the door and hoped he would follow.

"Will you do me a favor, then?" he asked, inviting me to be a consultant for his agency in helping him find the right man to recruit to lead the medical staff of the new hospital. Called the King Khaled Eye Specialist Hospital—but referred to phonetically as "K-KESH"-- it was located in the capital city of Riyadh. The hospital had had the keen interest of the late King Khaled, who had been closely involved in its construction, and it was almost ready to become fully functional once it was staffed by thirty-five eye doctors, each with a two-year contract.

Mr. Pennick saw that he had managed to capture my interest, so he continued. "The hospital looks like a futuristic fortress. It was funded by the Saudi government to the tune of more than 700 million U.S. dollars [the equivalent of more than $1.5 billion today], which makes it the largest, most expensive, and soon-to-be the most productive eye hospital in the world."

He went on to explain that the new facility had 11 operating rooms and 236 patient beds, with a medical staff that could potentially number 35 ophthalmologists, an optometrist, an internist, a pediatrician, 4 anesthesiologists and several hundred expatriate nurses, plus countless technicians, aides and interpreters. All medical records were to be in English, and every doctor would have an interpreter at his side whenever needed, since only a few patients would speak English.

"But I really can't leave Houston at this time. It's impossible," I protested. We were both standing at the door to my office by now, with no one budging. "I have to admit that what you say is tempting but I've also noticed that you have quite a way with words. You remind me of Texans, who think everything here is the biggest and the best. Good luck in your search."

"Do me a favor, Doc," he persisted. "You become a consultant for the company, and I'll buy you a first-class, round-trip ticket to Riyadh just to visit the hospital so you can think about who might make a good candidate for the job."

I told him I would consider doing at least that much and he left but, in truth, as I thought it over, what I was already considering was not just the visit but the job as I might fit into it. I could continue my role as medical director of ORBIS, even if it meant traveling longer distances as the aircraft flew around the world. The home office in New York was by now large and competent enough to survive very well without me. And I could use the opportunity to observe ORBIS from a distance, giving me some objectivity as I plotted out the organization's long-term future, for I believed it was not too early to start thinking about how ORBIS could grow. After all, the high annual budget allotted to the aircraft component of our teaching program could not be justified indefinitely; hopefully, effective and independent alternative programs would result from our initial involvement. I wasn't quite sure how to keep ORBIS on an evolutionary trajectory that ensured it would stay on the cutting edge in addressing curable global blindness, but I thought that Saudi Arabia might offer new inspiration. Nearly two percent of the country's population was blind, with hundreds of thousands of its citizens suffering disorders that could lead to blindness. That made the Kingdom a microcosm of global need, combined with the assets for solving it.

Having pretty much decided to say yes even before I visited the hospital, I reassured the ORBIS board and staff, especially George Hambleton and Betsy Wainwright, that even if I did take a job that would transplant me to the Middle East, I would remain in close contact so that I could continue to serve effectively as our project's guiding light. Betsy had become my eyes and ears at the organization and if trouble were to brew either at board level or at staff level, I felt sure I would know about it from her. As chief of public relations, Oliver Foot was becoming the voice of ORBIS, serving much as an ambassador of good will on board the aircraft during its missions to the host countries. To each of these close friends, I emphasized that in no way would I be any less devoted to ORBIS; rather, I would consider my "sabbatical" in Saudi Arabia as an opportunity to become reinvigorated—something every long-term creative leader should seek.

Although I felt slightly ashamed about how much the lavish remuneration that the job offered appealed to me, I also realized that at this time in my life, financial rewards had to become a priority that they hadn't previously been. Even at its most benign, divorce is an effective purgative of bank accounts. So, with these thoughts in mind, I took Norman Pennick up on his offer to send me to KKESH on a visit and within a week, I flew from Houston to New York, and from there, on a non-stop Saudia Airlines 747 flight, to Riyadh.

I recall that flight vividly. It was twelve hours of mostly turbulent conditions, during which the flight crew would periodically lay down prayer rugs and drop to their knees and pray, intermittently pressing their foreheads to the rug while facing the flight deck. I did not notice any of the Arab passengers joining the crew in their ritual prayers but I did note that liquor wasn't served on the flight. Instead, juice was presented in crystal tumblers, and the then-obligatory sticks of chewing gum for popping ears were replaced by wrapped candies that tasted like prunes soaked in soft toffee. I was wondering if the meat course would consist of something on the order of braised camel but to my surprise, it turned out to be strips of prime beef steak cooked to perfection. The Saudis manage well their cultural straddle between East and West—a Muslim country with catholic tastes.

Arriving at the Riyadh international airport, I was met by a friendly twosome of Saudi men in white robes (*thobes*) and checkered "tablecloth" headgear (*gutrahs*)—one from the Health Ministry and the other from the eye hospital administrative staff.

"*Salaam Alaykum*, Dr. Paton. We are pleased to meet you."

It was mid-morning when we drove west from the airport through the outskirts of Riyadh toward the vast barren, rocky desert that lay beyond the city's paved streets. We passed a few clumps of concrete block houses with encircling walls and virtually no planting, until finally there was just dry and dusty land, dotted with an occasional palm tree. Where could the hospital possibly be? Carcasses of cars abandoned by the road made the scene surreal. I began to feel that we were heading into a void. But then a blur appeared on the horizon, perhaps a mile away, transforming from a smudge into an Arabic-style, four-story pantheon of gray marble, bedecked with turrets and boasting a Versailles knockoff of decorative fountains. This was an eye hospital? It seemed more like a fairy tale oasis.

Behind the main building were partially concealed villas and apartment buildings that spread out in a cluster, with fully grown palm trees, masses of bushes and flowers, and criss crossing roads and paths---all forming a giant compound surrounded by an elaborate iron fence with an entrance gate and a guard house attended by uniformed officers. There it stood, in all its considerable glory---KKESH, the King Khaled Eye Specialist Hospital.

When our car entered the hospital grounds, what struck me was the absence of any human activity. There were no people. As we got out of the car, the intense sunlight and the desert's dry heat engulfed us, a reminder of how locale can affect the senses. We entered the main building, where we were greeted by more lavish décor, with a central indoor fountain placed directly under a huge metal-and-crystal chandelier. Prominently displayed on the wall were portraits of the former king, Khaled; the present king, Fahd; and the crown prince, Abdullah. Proceeding from the marble entryway, we toured clinics, eye examination rooms, offices, a kitchen, cafeteria and three floors of patient rooms finer than the accommodations in an average hotel. There were the 263 empty but fully made beds that Norman Pennick had described, but he forgot to mention that almost every one of the eleven operating rooms had a ceiling-mounted, operating microscope, currently wrapped in dust covers prior to the hospital's opening. Each item was spanking new and top of the line. No extravagance had been spared.

A skeletal staff was storing the day's delivery of supplies and bedding. The nurses were mostly Filipinas, supervised by senior ophthalmic nurses from several Western countries, including the United States. The hospital and its support structures could accommodate not only more than 400 in-patients, but also the entire core staff of 400 persons—from professionals and administrators to the guards and gardeners—who would collectively keep the eye hospital alive and flourishing. Their living quarters were located in those large apartment buildings and the long line of individual villas—one for each doctor and his family—that I had seen previously. The facilities also included two large, high-walled swimming pools and a set of hard-surfaced tennis courts.

The largest and most convenient villas would house the director of nursing, the chief administrator, and the medical director, who would also have a car and driver at his disposal. The expatriate staff—such as all the doctors and senior nurses on contract to the Saudi Arabian government—would live within the hospital compound. The superintendent of the hospital (a Saudi pediatrician by training) and the assistant medical director (a Palestine-born Saudi who had been educated in Cairo and London) would live in Riyadh with their families. I saw the setup, met the principals, got a feeling about the hospital's remarkable potential—and made my decision.

Returning home to Houston, I discovered that Norman Pennick had left a completed contract in my office, obviously confident I would be taking the job. I signed it without hesitation. Then, with an ulterior motive, I described the hospital in glowing terms to my son, Townley, stressing its potential for emulating—even exceeding—the audiovisual set-up of ORBIS, whose design and components he had had a large part in providing. At KKESH, the audiovisual provisions would, of course, be on a much larger scale, for there were ten operating rooms and a large conference area, and I was also determined to initiate a teaching program within the hospital. Townley was excited at the prospect of becoming the first engineer, and then the primary operator, of that system, which I managed to make happen. In being the catalyst for him to be hired, I was pleased to do for him what had been done so often for me, and very glad indeed to have him with me on this new adventure.

Within a month I was back in Riyadh with Townley, this time to stay. Saudi Arabia is a recently formed country, extending just two generations from its Bedouin roots. As has become well-known in recent years, there is a strong religious influence over all aspects of its peoples' lives and the religious police, known as *mutaween*, enforce the strict codes of the nation's indigenous beliefs regarding women's clothing, women's subservient roles, the proscribing of alcoholic beverages, the separation of the sexes in public affairs and the call for Muslims to pray five times daily. There is no right of assembly, thus no movie theaters, stadiums, or even public trains or buses. Women are still not allowed to drive cars and if they are not married to the driver, they are forbidden to sit in the front passenger seat. These and other mandates are strictly enforced by the *mutaween*.

These proscriptions offer a challenge to Westerners living there but it is well to remember that the Kingdom's laws and regulations take into consideration the characteristics of a formerly isolated and unsophisticated public that is altogether remote from our understanding or experience. I believe that if we in the West are convinced that we have a better, happier way of living, then it is up to us to show others, rather than tell them what alternatives are available, not in boastfulness but as caring people who are also proud of our culture as they are of theirs.

My life in Saudi Arabia was far from boring. The Kingdom's culture combined the tradition of Bedouin hospitality with an appreciation of the practical advantages offered by technological advances, epitomized by the transporting of camels to the camel market in the back of pickup trucks. Patients at KKESH not only welcomed me as their doctor, the men might kiss my hand and murmur sincere words of gratitude in Arabic. I gradually absorbed many of the ways of my hosts. Arab expressions such as *malesh* ("It doesn't matter") or *inchallah* ("God willing," or "hopefully") became part of my vocabulary.

Male doctors holding hands when walking together with male patients or each other was simply as an expression of brotherly affection and I grew comfortable with it within that culture.

I had never before performed so much major eye surgery, nor seen as many patients with fascinating and often advanced eye disorders that were new to me. I found teaching and leading the beginning residency program to be as important to the needy population as the performance of curative eye surgery, for teaching would leave behind many pairs of hands that could accomplish much more than my own hands could contribute. Since that was a basic tenet of ORBIS, I felt at home away from home and indeed more useful to the world than in the U.S., where I was just another eye doctor among thousands to choose from.

The Arabs have a love for the desert that I could not have fathomed before I experienced it myself. With friends, I would take a four-wheel-drive vehicle out into the Saudi desert at night. Faint breezes replaced the burning sand and sweltering heat of the day, and there was, above all, a vast emptiness. At the right location, lit by the headlights, small sparkles appeared in the sand in front of the car. These are quartz-based, semi-precious gems that are almost as hard as carbon-based diamonds and their color is just as durable once they are mounted in settings by European jewelers who specialize in that work. We would turn off the lights and the ignition of the car and walk along the sand into the emptiness, marveling at a beauty that defies words because it offers such a sensory experience. The moon would provide enough light to make a flashlight unnecessary, and never had I observed so many stars in the sky.

When I arrived in the Kingdom, there was not a single native-born Saudi serving as an ophthalmologist in the entire country. There was a distinguished Egyptian-born ophthalmologist, Akef Al-Maghraby, who ran a private modern eye facility in Jeddah, and his work and that of his assistants was of high quality—which remains true today. But in 1982, when KKESH opened, almost nothing else was being done for eye disorders elsewhere in the Kingdom other than to provide eyeglasses and eye drops as might be needed. A handful of government-salaried expatriate ophthalmologists were spread across the country but they did only a few operations in a year, and none were using modern technique.

I was thrilled to be responsible for changing eye care in a nation in great need of modern ophthalmology and to be able to help literally millions of citizens having a high incidence of eye disorders and a high prevalence of blindness, much of which was curable. It was a job that was personally gratifying at every level. Further—and more importantly---as medical staff was recruited, KKESH was able to provide the highest level of eye care to hundreds of thousands of poverty-level "peasants," without charge. The same outstanding care was available to all Saudi citizens, from the King and his many relatives down to the shopkeepers, camel drivers, and street cleaners of Riyadh. But it would take considerable time and effort to make that happen.

Late in 1982, the Ministry of Health willingly financed a survey of the Kingdom to determine the types, numbers, distributions, and severity of the eye diseases that for many decades had been plaguing the general population. The collected data, showing how widespread the serious incidence of neglected eye disease was, supported my conviction that the only way we could start first-class eye care at KKESH was with the services of recruited colleagues from the West. But the only way such care could be sustained indefinitely would be to start a residency training program for Saudis. That kind of work was very familiar to me. I had long served—in a voluntary capacity--the American Academy of Ophthalmology as Secretary of Continuing Education and, eventually, as Chairman of its Basic and Clinical Science Course, the nationwide program of instruction for all U.S. residency programs. In addition--and again in a voluntary capacity--I had served for over a decade on the American Board of Ophthalmology and there, too, as the eventual Chairman--that being the organization that certifies American ophthalmologists by a tough oral and written examination process. My KKESH contract as medical director did not call for a commitment to train Saudi doctors but, seeing that I was strongly in favor of establishing a residency training program and had the credentials to do so, the Saudi ministry approved my plan. I hasten to add, however, that the bulk of the work in

forming and leading the resulting program at KKESH took place
after I returned to the U.S., in the capable hands of Dr. Khalid F. Tabbara, originally from Lebanon but a well-respected academic ophthalmologist in California when I recruited him to the Kingdom.

Paradoxically, adding a residency training program resulted in a
shortage of funding for a full 35-member staff of recruited eye doctors. When I arrived in the Kingdom, it was not easy to recruit qualified Western ophthalmologists to commit to a two-year contract in
a distant locale such as Riyadh. To many potential appointees, the
Arabic-speaking Kingdom sounded remote, hostile to non-Muslims,
unreasonable regarding the roles of women, unwilling to accept Western mores and even frightening. However, the fact that recruitment
involved the establishment of a residency training program added an
appealing component to the job description. I used whatever blan-
dishments, powers of persuasion and connections I could muster to
sign up, one by one, a group of high-caliber colleagues. Also, with
the aid of a recruiting company, I managed to attract several Arabic-
speaking senior doctors from the United States and Europe who were
capable in their own right but also served as bridges in the medical
family of East and Middle East doctors that was being assembled. In
addition, owing to political upheavals in Lebanon at the time, several
outstanding young ophthalmologists from Beirut joined our medical
staff.

But the money allocated for medical salaries by the Ministry of
Health, generous as it was, fell far short of the amount needed to attract well-paid, top-level expatriate ophthalmologists. So I asked
the Ministry of Health if I could appoint nine "fellows" (doctors who
had recently finished their residency in ophthalmology and wished to
go on to specialize in one of the various sub-fields of ophthalmology)
and they gave me their approval. These young Westerners became
excellent role models as a residency program was laid out and imple-
mented. And they could be paid considerably less than their more
seasoned colleagues, thereby solving our staff salary shortfall.

Not everything went smoothly, of course, and there were occasional unfortunate culture clashes. One of them involved Nora, a
Filipina operating room nurse and American citizen who had been

one of my personal nurse recruits from Houston. One day she was being driven by a local American man named Jim to a supermarket to stock her kitchenette at KKESH. Jim was employed as the pilot of one of the many Saudi princes. Unfortunately, Nora was sitting in the front seat of the car and as Jim was pulling into a parking place at the supermarket, a car with two young Saudi men blocked his space. He tooted his horn in annoyance, as anyone might do when cut off by a rude driver. The religious police arrived and saw that Nora was seated in front. She acknowledged that she and Jim were not married. The *mutawas* opened the trunk of the car and found a case of wine, which was on its way to Jim's royal boss after being purchased abroad.

Now there were two counts against Nora and Jim: a forbidden seating arrangement and liquor in their possession. They were sent to separate male and female jails. One of the few Saudi legal provisions shared with the American system of justice is that each new prisoner is allowed one phone call. Nora called me but was unable to tell me where she was being held since she spoke no Arabic, so couldn't ask. All she could say was that she was in a large room with twenty other female prisoners and a couple of chamber pots for communal use. She had somehow broken her dental bridge and had only the clothes on her back.

The pilot, Jim, called his royal employer and was discharged from his jail within minutes. Nora was imprisoned for six long weeks before I could first locate her and then get the help of a patient of mine, the assistant police commissioner, to have her released from prison. She was not permitted to return to the KKESH compound even to collect her belongings and was sent directly from jail to the airport to be deported to the U.S. in the first seat on a commercial airline that became available. That incident remains an unpleasant memory, certainly, but, in fairness, there is no question that Jim and Nora knew the rules when they broke them. There is also no question that for her crime, she was treated far more harshly than her male companion.

To many Saudi patients from the desert, bedrooms, bathrooms and even hospital corridors were an anomaly. When visiting these patients at evening rounds, I might find the husband in the patient's bed and the female patient on the floor under the bed. And sometimes the patient or the visiting family member would not understand how the toilet functioned, using the bathroom as a mere depository for excrement left discreetly in a corner. One can only imagine the challenge these people were facing in entering an environment so foreign to their experiences, and yet they were uncomplaining, appreciative and invariably far more cooperative than many of my patients in the States.

The princes and princesses of the Kingdom were something else entirely. At times it seemed as if all ten thousand of them had me on call, not because of any special talent on my part but because, as I mentioned earlier, of my status as the hospital's director. That became a problem at night; the Saudis are night owls, even when the religious days of Ramadan are not limiting their eating and drinking to non-daylight hours. Thus, I would receive calls at all hours at my villa to come as soon as possible to see a princess who might have been waiting at least twenty minutes! At first I pictured gorgeous young storybook princesses anxiously awaiting the arrival of the doctor, but in fact most of the princesses looked much older than they were and after removing their protective face veils, revealed deeply wrinkled, sun-leathered skin, uneven teeth and eyes with redness and lid scarring that indicated years of fighting endemic trachoma—like that which I had first encountered in Iran when serving as my father's secretary. They were generally uneducated but very much aware of their royal connection. Of course, many of them were cooperative and kindly, as were most of the urbane and articulate princes.

The taciturn and obliging Crown Prince, now King Abdullah, was a frequent patient. He spent much of his summer in Taif, in the mountains north of Jeddah. If he needed eye care, he, like all the others, called for me, as the medical director. The Crown Prince would send a Lear jet to pick me up at the Riyadh airport, fly me halfway across the country to the nearest landing field in the western province and, after a drive that took an hour or more, I would wait, sometimes for several hours, to see him at a military hospital near his summer palace. This, after a long day of work. I did not remain idle, however, for as many as ten or a dozen members of the royal entourage would arrive with various eye complaints, expecting to be diagnosed and treated that evening. The Prince himself was usually reticent but friendly; his eye problems were not particularly difficult to manage, and his appreciation for my services was expressed merely by a nod of recognition rather than by words spoken directly to me in English, even though I believe he knew the language quite well. My guess is he hid his command of English from those he would just as soon thank by nodding instead of possibly having to deal with annoying questions or requests for royal favors.

After the appointments with the Crown Prince and his family members, I would be taken on the hour's drive back to the airport, then flown to Riyadh, getting me home to my villa with the prospect of only three or four hours of sleep to prepare for the start of a long list of scheduled surgery. Still, VIP obligations were well worth the inconvenient hours, since I viewed it as something of an exotic treat to be flown back and forth across the Kingdom at odd times to see the country's top leadership. Although I never personally examined the eyes of King Fahd, I did have the privilege of meeting him when he came with a large entourage to officially open KKESH. Remarkably enough, I had a far better opportunity to speak with him in Washington, D.C., thanks to Jim Baker who, when he was Secretary of the Treasury, invited me to a state dinner given by President Reagan at the White House in honor of King Fahd on March 12, 1984, while I was in the U.S. for a few weeks of vacation.

Toward the end of 1982, I had a delightful visit from my sister Joan and her third husband (she was twice widowed), who came for a few days to see what life was like in the Kingdom and to check me out—would I be dressed like Lawrence of Arabia, riding around on camels, and gobbling sheeps' eyes at desert feasts? Although they came prepared to tease me about those stale stereotypes, they left completely impressed by the hospital and the magnificent eye care opportunities it offered.

In July 1983, George Hambleton urged me to join ORBIS in Amman, where he had instigated a royal reception for the aircraft, its crew, its visiting teachers and the Jordanian ophthalmologists. The reception was to be given by King Hussein and Queen Noor, the former Lisa Halaby, whose father had been CEO of Pan Am Airways and was thus acquainted with George. Queen Noor was also a Princeton graduate, entering the university in the first class to include females. It was too good an invitation to turn down, for it would be exciting to see ORBIS in action and to renew acquaintance with some of its skillful eye doctors.

A double thrill lay ahead. I was asked by one of my Jordanian friends to assist him in performing a corneal transplant on ORBIS, to be transmitted to local television and witnessed by His Majesty King Hussein. I agreed to assist but only anonymously, in keeping with my resolve not to abuse the aircraft project as a soap box for personal promotion. However, during the operation the surgeon, inexperienced as a teacher and nervous about performing in front of his king, asked me to take over. Since the magnified television transmission from the operating microscope showed only our hands, it was an easy series of moves to change seats and have my hands take over his role as surgeon as he continued describing the operation alternately in Arabic and English. The operation went well. It was the first and only time I would operate on ORBIS, and the kick I got out of doing it remains a bright memory even today.

Later that evening, at a ceremony before dinner, Queen Noor honored me with a second Jordanian medal and citation, the first having been presented by King Hussein almost 20 years previously at the St. John Ophthalmic Hospital in Jerusalem. The new award, entitled the Royal Decoration of the Second Order and given for founding and leading ORBIS, came with a handwritten tribute signed by both the King and his Queen: "To our good friend, Dr. David Paton, with our highest esteem and warmest wishes." George, whose initiative led to that award, stood modestly aside as I received the spotlight—typical of my dear friend. It was the last time that I would see George in the capacity of Executive Director of ORBIS, for he had to resign later that same year to attend to pressing family business obligations.

A year later, Oliver Foot, George's successor as Executive Director, came for a visit to Riyadh. He was accompanied by his distinguished father, Lord Caradon, the latter a personable man in a wheelchair, due to a transient illness. Oliver asked if I would examine his father's eyes, which I did with pleasure, fortunately finding nothing seriously wrong. I enjoyed meeting the man who had taught his young son the art of public speaking at their Vale Royal residence in Jamaica, emblematic of early expectations of Oliver.

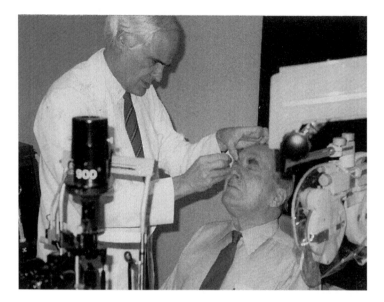

Oliver, like his father, was a natural diplomat of the first order, telling me I was missed at home as he explained that, while in the Kingdom, he hoped to stir up some funding for ORBIS. I facilitated an appointment with one of King Fahd's brothers, Prince Talal bin Abdul Aziz Al Saud, who later contributed half a million dollars to our project, which definitely helped make Oliver's trip to Riyadh worthwhile.

I believed that Oliver saw the relevance of KKESH for me. Not only did I consider Oliver a good friend and an enthusiastic collaborator, but now that he had been promoted to George's job of Executive Director, he was also the key person with whom to discuss the potential evolutionary concepts I had been thinking about for our project. And Oliver had the ear of the board, particularly its chairman, Al Ueltschi, who had by now assumed full command. He seemed to be in an effusive mood in Riyadh and was almost embarrassingly deferential to me. My mother had recently written of receiving a beautiful 8 by 10 inch color picture of ORBIS at a Tunisian airport, with an

inscription that read, "I will never be able to thank David enough for giving me ORBIS," signed, "Oliver."

But when I got him by himself for a chat about the future of ORBIS, his interest in discussing potential programmatic changes was essentially nil. That was discouraging since I considered it my job to warn him that ORBIS's popularity could begin to wane in the near future, as modern ophthalmic microsurgery became more commonplace and modern operating microscopes more available, making Western teaching expertise in developing countries less imperative. In addition, ever-improving audiovisual and telemedical techniques supporting worldwide communications would diminish the uniqueness of the capabilities of the aircraft, which also faced increasingly complicated and tight airport security procedures, regardless of the political stance of the host country. As I saw it, ORBIS could shift the emphasis of its mission to more developed countries and just hammer away at exchanging state-of-the-art concepts with predominantly European ophthalmologists, even if doing that would circumvent the primary purpose for which it was founded.

My comments may have been falling on deaf ears, but I was not done. There was another topic I had initially put aside but now segued into as a natural sequence to thinking about the future. It concerned an American ophthalmologist, Dr. Larry Schwab, who was then serving in an official advisory capacity to the Ministry of Health of Malawi.

He had sent a letter to a dozen or more prominent ophthalmologists and other influential people connected to various ORBIS funding sources and the opinions he expressed were causing a stir at key agencies concerned with the prevention of blindness. Although Dr. Schwab had not been present when ORBIS had gone to Malawi in the spring of 1984, he had studied accounts of the eighteen-day visit, discussed the subject at length with local participants and health authorities, and concluded that the aircraft's expensive teaching program (that, for example, included corneal transplantation and phaco) was not aligned with the needs of that country, or other poor countries worldwide, for that matter. There were only two ophthalmologists working in Malawi, far from a justifiable reason for a costly visit from the aircraft. The basic essentials of examination, management of eye complaints, and prevention of disease could have been provided with only a suitcase containing several hundred dollars worth of equipment to be used by public health workers without need for a medical degree.

While in Malawi, the ORBIS staff had elected to teach eye care assistants to perform surgery—surgery which would have to be approved by the health ministry and would only make sense if the instruction were to be ongoing and the students consistently monitored. Dr. Schwab reported several cases during that ORBIS visit that had experienced post-operative complications. For example, a thirteen-year-old one-eyed Malawian girl underwent a corneal transplant on the aircraft performed by a visiting ORBIS surgeon who was evidently convinced that such an operation would improve her vision. But she had a Vitamin A deficiency that should have been diagnosed, causing dryness of her eyes, one of which was already incurably blind, without any light perception. Furthermore, she lived far from where the aircraft operation was performed. Within two weeks of the aircraft's departure, she was brought to the capital city to see Dr. Schwab, who found a "melting graft," a result both of her nutritional status and clear evidence of insufficient postoperative care. The child ended up also losing light perception in her remaining eye, with no chance for restoration of vision in the future. It was all too obvious that the corneal transplant should not have been performed at all but, once performed, proper arrangements should have been made for her and for all of our project's patients to have full postoperative care.

As ORBIS had grown from concept to reality, I had tirelessly spoken about the importance of pre-assessing each host country to determine if it was a good fit with ORBIS's purposes and whether there were enough qualified local people to justify the expenses involved in providing the aircraft's teaching services. So Dr. Schwab's criticism was enormously distressing to me.

Oliver knew very well how I felt about the importance of this Malawi matter, but he was unapologetic, believing that the visit had nonetheless made a valuable contribution which he felt I could not appreciate, not having been there to witness for myself the enthusiasm of the participants, including surgical assistants, a number of nurses, health care workers, and aides of various kinds. Although I wasn't against allowing assistants to perform certain surgical necessities within well-defined limits, I believed it should be done only where there was near-desperate need and no possibility of obtaining enough residential eye surgeons to provide the hands. My question to Oliver: Did he have a framework in place for the ongoing training of the paraprofessionals we taught that included sustained monitoring of their surgery both during it and while the patients were still in recovery? He had no answer for me.

In discussing all this with Oliver, my principal point was that, as originally clearly established, the Medical Director—me--should be informed about the nature of each anticipated visit and approve it, most especially if it were to a country with only a few ophthalmologists. I then learned for the first time that Dr. Simon Holland, a fine young ophthalmologist who had served on ORBIS as a staff resident, had been given much of the authority of the medical directorship. He, too, had received copies of the Schwab letter and had responded by writing articulate, defensive rebuttal to Schwab's complaint and copying me, which is how I'd first become aware of the problem.

I am not certain that the ORBIS board of trustees was ever fully aware that this outcry was initiated by a sincerely concerned expert in public health and eye care for the poorest nations. Dr. Schwab was not some temperamental critic of ophthalmic evolution being offered in East Africa. He was a member of the Prevention of Blindness Committee of Malawi and of a similar committee serving Kenya. He reported that he was not just speaking for himself but that there was "a general opposition to ORBIS as it was currently functioning in the poorer nations." He asserted, furthermore, that ORBIS had been invited to East Africa by "political coercion" and that there were far too few individuals in Malawi or its neighboring countries who could benefit from the skills taught by ORBIS to justify its lavish, eighteen-day presence.

Schwab strongly asserted--again, rightly, in my opinion---that the expenditure associated with ORBIS' work to benefit so few caregivers was, in effect, an unconscionable travesty. I wondered if he

knew just how much it was costing to keep ORBIS in operation—-
$10,000 daily. On the political front, Dr. Schwab argued that the
ORBIS operation sent all the wrong signals to Malawi's pro-U.S.
government about setting appropriate priorities in a destitute country, which first needed to develop basic medical intervention skills.
I could well understand Dr. Schwab's concerns and was much disturbed by the misguidedly celebratory mood that ORBIS' work in
Malawi had prompted back at New York headquarters. The visit was
being described on the ORBIS website as "triumphal."

Whereas Oliver continued to believe that Schwab's dissatisfaction
was overblown, I viewed it as a warning that our wonderful aircraft
could easily begin to slip into disfavor. To people desperate to find
funding for the simplest of measures in preventing eye disorders, the
enormously expensive display of ORBIS could be seen as being about
as helpful as waving thousand dollar bills at starving children.

Dr. Schwab's letter was merely smoke-signaling a fire that would
ignite if ORBIS continued the misguided direction of the use of its
aircraft. The words he wrote to me in a personal letter cut me to the
quick: *Project ORBIS is not appropriate for ophthalmology in the developing
world because of the transfer of inappropriate skills of high technology. It is
not cost effective as a therapeutic delivery instrument. The elitist image of OR-
BIS and of the U.S. is paternalistic and smacks of ophthalmic imperialism. It
creates the impression that surgically curable blindness is being eradicated by
its {ORBIS'} activities. That there are 65,000 preventable and surgically-
curable blind in Malawi alone is masked. Your organization is entrusted
with the opportunity, and you, the Medical Director, with the ethical responsibility to stop wasting precious human and financial resources in blindness
prevention activities in developing countries.*

Finally, Dr. Schwab referred to the work of ORBIS in African nations with the most disrespectful of all intra-professional
terms, "buccaneering," a term originally popularized by my former
colleague at Wilmer, Dr. George Weinstein. It meant   "recklessly
unconcerned for the good of the patient." This assertion, too, was
driving my determination to convey to Oliver the need for our project
to gradually become more land-based and supportive of sustainable
eye care units in the poorest of nations with the help of American

volunteers. But he was so put off by my evident distress that he simply terminated the discussion. Little did I know that the ORBIS board even then was having conversations with Oliver and aircraft companies as to whether ORBIS should graduate to a larger aircraft and expand its on-board activities.

I had one more suggestion to make to Oliver, which I later related in a letter covered with diagrams. For the sake of improved international collaboration among non-governmental eye care organizations, I said it would make sense to develop an international council of the leading blindness-related agencies, to avoid turf and program overlap. That didn't go over too well either, and I surmised it was due to Oliver's fear of the possibility of ORBIS losing its independence, if part of such a council. It would be the better part of another decade before the founding by the World Health Organization and the International Agency for Prevention of Blindness of Vision 20/20: The Right To Sight, whereby multiple agencies working to prevent or cure blindness joined to exchange ideas and for collaborative task sharing, the approach I had urged Oliver to initiate.

Since Townley was living in his own quarters in another section of the hospital's employee residence and had made many friends his own age, my constant pal in the evenings was an African Gray parrot named Chakoo, the only word he knew when I bought him and his birdcage at a booth in the souk. I guessed it to be an Arabic word, but no one seemed to recognize it. Because it is impossible to determine if an  African Gray is male or female without an examination under anesthesia, I simply assumed that the bird was male, making our co-habitation in keeping with the "no mixing of the sexes" rule for unmarried people within the compound. Sometimes caged, sometimes flying free, Chakoo made it clear he much preferred to be at liberty to perch anywhere he found convenient or comfortable. One evening when an internationally acclaimed visiting professor from Houston came to my villa for a drink, we were scarcely seated in the living room when there was a flapping of wings and, bursting into the room from the kitchen came Chakoo, who headed straight for my visitor. Startled, having not be forewarned about my bird, he flung his arms up in front of his face protectively. Chakoo lit on his lifted forearm, perched there for a second or two, ruffled his feathers, then came out with "Bullshit!" in exactly my voice, followed by a large dropping, as if punctuating his tactless remark.

Chakoo's main social blunders had to do with his inappropriate bathroom talk and bathroom habits. When a "drop" happened, I would utter an "Uh-oh," and soon Chakoo picked up the habit of saying "Uh-oh" whenever he dropped. Often I could hear him say it when I was in an adjoining room, or even upstairs, as if he were alerting me to rush in and clean up the mess. But the bird was like a child whom one loves in spite of his misbehavior, and I never had the heart to put the black sleeping cloth over his cage to censor his remarks. Before leaving the country, I "willed" Chakoo to U.S. Ambassador Walter Cutler, who promised him a comfortable nest in the Embassy. I heard later that Walt taught him to whistle the "Star-Spangled Banner."

I returned to the U.S. soon after Oliver's visit, with Townley scheduled to return some time later. Among other priorities after returning to patient care in Houston was a resolve to meet a certain widowed woman who was held in great esteem by Jim Baker. As much as I respected Jim's evaluation of women and was grateful for his referral—to express it in mathematical jargon--she was still an unproven hypothesis rather than a statistical likelihood. But it was time to see for myself.

CHAPTER TWENTY-THREE

I returned from the Kingdom quite spoiled by the leadership role it had offered and the uncomplicated manner in which high-volume, first-class patient care could be provided without the heavy overlay of paper work necessitated in the U.S., as in other Western countries. Those hints of what might be ventured at home were in the back of my head as I reckoned with the fact that the years ahead were only a blur of imagination, with nothing yet of any material substance to build upon, other than a concern for how ORBIS might mature and evolve in the years ahead. The BCM eye department really did not need a returning former department chairman hanging around like an old sea anchor possibly dragging against the flow of my successor's intentions. I did return to patient care, and seeing many of my former patients meant reconnecting with dear friends, most of whom seemed able to see better due to the surgery I had performed, one of the gratifications of patient care continuity. Meanwhile, Dr. Dan Jones was providing the eye department with his own academic goals, appropriately stemming from passions that were his but not necessarily mine. That is what makes for a healthy medical school department. His ready grin and chairman-like comfort indicated to me that he was in full control of the department I had entered thirteen years earlier as a stranger from Baltimore. It was time for me to take stock as to where I was and where I wanted to be. My personal and professional "gear system" for living happily comes down to change, curiosity and creativity.

So, in a thoughtful but unfettered state of mind, I turned my attention eagerly to meeting the woman Jim Baker had been urging me to meet. She had worked for him during the presidential transition from the Carter to the Reagan Administration and they had remained friends and political colleagues during the years that followed.

To introduce us, Jim and Susan Baker invited us to dinner at their home in Washington. But on the appointed Saturday evening, the

Bakers were astonished to find that I, having somehow gotten the date wrong, remaining in Houston. My mind was apparently more fettered than I had thought.

As luck would have it, the lady in question was willing to give me another try. We agreed to meet one January evening a few weeks later at a restaurant in New York, where we both were expected at the same nonprofit's annual board meeting and dinner. I picked her up at her apartment, where her daughter, Lauren, a lovely young woman, met me at the door. Then Diane Johnston Brokaw appeared behind Lauren, with a smile as warm as the sunshine of Hawaii and cerulean eyes that danced with happiness.

I was smitten straight away, exactly as if shot with an arrow from Cupid's bow, as corny as that sounds. Meeting her became the moment when the past received a period and the future, an exclamation point. My dreams of the perfect woman had just materialized.

It is easy to make decisions when heart and mind are in sync. I asked Diane to marry me later in the evening and went to sleep feeling very certain that her acceptance was as serious as my proposal had been. That was a Thursday evening. We spent much of the weekend with a couple whom we both knew, Dr. and Mrs. Burton J. Lee. Burt was later to become the White House physician for President H.W. Bush. A Yalie, he considered our precipitous decision to marry a dreadful, typically Princetonian kind of impetuousness, and he warned Diane against untested assumptions and possibly dangerous risk-taking. Well intended as it may have been, his advice was worthless and futile.

At the end of the weekend, I had to return to patients in Houston. I called my widowed mother from the airport: "Ma, I'm going to be married!"

"Oh, for Heaven's sake, David." Pause. Audible intake of breath. Continued pause, a cough, and then, "Which one is it?"

"You haven't met her, Ma. Her name is Diane Brokaw. I met her three days ago."

My mother was appalled. Two failed marriages and now an instant commitment for a third attempt! I told her that it was already settled and assured her that she would love Diane. I promised to arrange for them to meet within a few weeks.

As predicted, when Diane and my mother were introduced, it took only an awkward moment or two before they became comfortable and, in just a few weeks, completely devoted to each other. I know that my father would have loved her, too. Interestingly, we discovered that she had shaken hands with both of my parents at a social function a few years earlier. Small, wonderful world.

Diane's son was teaching school in Hawaii and Townley was still wrapping things up in Saudi Arabia, so it took a few weeks to make arrangements. We "finally" had a church wedding in Manhattan on March 9, 1985, officiated by a part-time auctioneer, part-time minister, whom we particularly liked because he had met and married his wife on similarly short notice. My first wife, Janie, and her husband, Clint, also attended the wedding. Janie told me that she, too, had been thinking that Diane and I should meet.

Diane is five years my junior, gorgeous, a gourmet cook to whom food is an art form, a show of love, an integral part of being at home. Both fun-loving and serious, she is the world's most organized, executive director type—only a lot more fun-filled and down to earth than that rather austere title suggests. She attended the Punahou School in Honolulu, later to be made famous by the president known then as Barry Obama. She married Hawaii's favorite dentist, seventeen years her senior with two daughters who came with him, then he and Diane had two more children, a boy and a girl. They eventually divorced, and Diane moved to New York where she met and married a Princeton classmate of mine, Bill Brokaw, who had five children by his first marriage. He was one of the most engaging and entertaining of all of my college friends, but he struggled for years with a severe bipolar disorder that eventually led to their separation. Then, quite suddenly in October 1984, he died from a heart attack.

Under three Republican presidents, Diane served as Executive Director of the President's Committee on the Arts and Humanities, a presidential appointment. She commuted several times a week between offices in Washington and Manhattan, her primary home being in New York. Well-read, she does the Sunday *New York Times* crossword puzzle every week, and was to become a Life Trustee of the Institute of International Education, which has offices in 31 countries and headquarters in Manhattan.

After Diane and I were married, it was easier for me to be the spouse who changed a home address, so I resigned from Baylor and moved to New York City. Fortunately, change has never been something that I have avoided at the expense of an enticing opportunity. Some of the ideas I had shared with Oliver Foot that had not been of the slightest interest to him were very much on my mind. I had suggested that ORBIS should begin to establish land-based facilities to sustain the work of the project if the aircraft were to be discontinued or encountered prohibitive factors related to global threats to aircraft security. I was determined to launch what I had in mind, hopeful that when it was sufficiently developed ORBIS would take on its non-profit purpose.

Manhattan was a good hub for developing the new bifid corporation I had in mind, OcuSystems, which I hoped would soon become fused with ORBIS, perhaps even evolving into an organization that would eventually lead to the aircraft's honorable retirement. It was to be an altruistic undertaking but with a for-profit component on the American end that would bring in sustained financing for the non-profit component in the developing nations.

I had founded the company while finishing my tour of duty in Saudi Arabia, inspired by the work of Dr. Govindappa Ventkataswamy at the Aravind Eye Hospital in Madurai, India. He used the income from private patient care to supplement the cost of care for those who could not afford it. It might be called a Robin Hood scheme—although Dr. V. did not steal from the rich, he merely charged them enough to support care for the poor. I knew that extensive domestic travel would be necessary to accomplish the launching of my version of this approach and the Northeast was a convenient place from which to define, establish and help finance another, but very different, kind of corporate venture.

OcuSystems' intended initial phase would be the first and only time I was ever involved in a commercial relationship with medicine. As I was envisioning it, the company would offer for purchase privately-owned ambulatory eye surgery centers, inspired by ORBIS and, in1985, more advanced than the existing state-of-the art surgical centers.

Architect's renderings of proposed for-profit
ambulatory surgical center prototype.

Each center would contain a waiting room modeled on the interior of a passenger plane, with an office setup offering audiovisual
communications by earphones and a screen at each seat for patient
communication and registration, along with instructional television
programs and the same kind of seats for family members. The centers would be outfitted with the necessary, uniformly identical equipment, instrumentation, disposable supplies, maintenance and training manuals for jobs at each staff level. Thus OcuSystems would be
assuming the multi-task challenges of building virtually identical,
code-compliant, free-standing facilities for eye surgery, along with
equipping them and maintaining them with the benefit of economy
of scale, thereby also relieving the owner-ophthalmologists of many
responsibilities that were beyond their interests and know-how.

The all-in-one package of an OcuSystems surgicenter would bring
income from several parts of its patient-care facilities. A portion of
that income would go to the for-profit company owners (not including me), but most of it would be turned over to ORBIS, to be used to
grow and sustain a separate system of replicated eye care units in developing nations. If the two-network concept worked, there would be
enough income from the American units to support, at least in part,
a network of small, replicated, efficient, inexpensive, prefabricated,
fully equipped and standardized surgical eye care units for combat-
ing curable blindness in the poorest nations. Those who owned the

American centers would be encouraged to become periodic voluntary instructors in the surgical units abroad. Thus, the so-called Robin Hood plan of Dr. Ventkataswamy and the replication and multiplier concepts of ORBIS would be combined and updated--as all models must be if they are to keep up with the times.

But the company's struggling corporate management was tenuous, at best, and, in order to survive, it was more geared to the promise of investor profit than to financing the network of surgical units abroad. We tried hard to persuade other eye care professionals—specifically, optometrists—to join the venture, the idea being that they would work with OcuSystem's ophthalmologists and refer patients, as had been successfully done with individual owners of existing ambulatory surgical centers. But, to put it in a nutshell, that did not turn out to be a viable financial arrangement for OcuSystems, and my efforts as a catalyst for the ophthalmology-optometry interface led to much derision, including some from a few of my favorite colleagues.

Yet even though the OcuSystems experience was not productive and we soon had to close down the company, I continue to believe the original concept of a for-profit company designed to support a not-for-profit company is well worth re-exploring, and I hope that others dedicated to philanthropy but more skilled in business will follow through someday. They are welcome to my architectural plans.

The concept of volunteerism has been intriguing to me ever since I had my first taste of it in Newfoundland as a medical student. In fact, I am proud to say that I am credited by officers of the American Academy of Ophthalmology with suggesting that the Academy should start a program of free eye services (including surgery) to be offered by member ophthalmologists to the poor in this country. That idea was developed as EyeCare America, which has become the largest program of its kind in American medicine, helping over 880,000 people since its inception in 1985 through the voluntary services of more than 7,000 ophthalmologists. It has been recognized by three U.S. presidents and endorsed by 50 state ophthalmological societies. I didn't play a role in making that program happen, but it gives me pleasure to think that I came up with the basic idea.

In December of 1985, Oliver Foot, in his capacity as Executive Director, invited me on behalf of the board to join the ORBIS contingent of staff and volunteer doctors going to China in January, this time to Beijing rather than Gangzhou. I did assert seniority in saying, more than asking, that Diane would be joining the group,

Diane, Oliver, Al, Dr. Lam and Dr. Dodick

making it our long-deferred honeymoon. Also with us was Dr. Jack Dodick, one of the finest cataract surgeons in the United States and a good friend of mine, and Dr. Dominic Lam who had been with me for the first ORBIS visit to China and was now an entrepreneurial scientist of rare merit living in Hong Kong and representing the finest admixture of Chinese and American mentalities—therefore, an ideal observer of ORBIS in action.

Foot & Ueltschi

Our trip coincided intentionally with the First Chinese International Ophthalmologic Conference, which had drawn some eight hundred registrants, all nationals. The ORBIS attraction was a sidelight to the conference but it almost stole the show. Hundreds of doctors paid visits. Their enthusiasm was undisguised. The enormity of this scientific creation, with its surround of technical paraphernalia, still had the arresting impact of a majestic abstract art form at first sight, raising the adrenalin that kept being pumped as the host eye doctors climbed into the aircraft and participated in its various programs. ORBIS was for intellectual advancement of eye physicians but its visual impact— even for non-physicians--constituted an undeniable seduction

Once the day's programs of surgery and lectures began, the senior doctors and the various contributing local teachers were given the prime seats in the aircraft's forward classroom. I stayed there with its tell-and-show programs while Diane visited the Forbidden City and other sites of interest. On ORBIS that week, the full program went well—which is to say, uneventfully--and the attendance over- flowed into the terminal building's waiting areas, which meant that the teaching was getting through to hundreds of colleagues from all over China, inspiring them by a show of futuristic eye care that their country could easily adapt and further develop. It was a joy to be with something that was functioning so beautifully, without a hitch that I could observe.

However, when I returned to New York, I became aware of con- tinuing repercussions from mishaps resulting from other ORBIS sur- geries, and I will never know how many of these were received in the central office and not forwarded to me. The criticism I heard came to me directly from the person complaining, not from Oliver or the board. For example, while the furor over the Schwab-prompted complaints about the aftermath of ORBIS's visit to Malawi was still ongoing, another doctor, Arthur Lim, a distinguished and highly re- spected colleague on ORBIS's medical advisory board, wrote to me from his office in Singapore about a report on an eighty-year-old sur- geon and senior professor who had had surgery on board ORBIS in Sri Lanka. He had long ago lost his right eye but had managed to get around with the vision in his remaining eye. Surgery was done on that eye by an ORBIS surgeon and, apparently due to insufficiently attended complications after the operation, his post-operative vision had become reduced to bare light perception—in that, his only eye. It was a disturbing case, and I was further distressed that I had not heard about it through the ORBIS office.

Those letters of complaint made it evident that while I had been in Saudi Arabia there had been a breach of trust in choosing where ORBIS would be deployed and in the mandates for its responsibility to see that qualified care was given to every patient as long as the operated eye was still in uncertain condition. I told Oliver once again that I must reassume the authority I no longer felt I had as Medical Director to oversee all medical aspects of what was being offered overseas. But he persisted in asserting that Dr. Schwab's, and now Dr. Lim's, reports to me were exaggerated and relatively insignificant in the great stream of ORBIS's much-heralded successes. He was the Executive Director with full board support and, astonishingly, I had lost whatever access to the board I had had in the past, due to the chronic and intermittently severe health problems that kept Betsy Wainwright away from her intermediary role with the New York power center. But it was true that in general, ORBIS continued to be a great success, and therefore I persuaded myself that discussing these issues with individual staff members was all the contact I needed.

Moving on from bankrupt OcuSystems, I decided to return to academic ophthalmology and accepted an appointment as a professor at Cornell Medical School, close to where Diane and I were living in New York. There I opened a departmental office intended primarily for international patients. I was enjoying my work and the faculty there until I heard that Cornell's affiliate, the Catholic Medical Center, was seeking a chairman for its ophthalmology residency—a challenging job that meant taking on a depleted department without much internal support. But I viewed the challenge as an opportunity and got the job.

In 1986, when I started as Chairman of Ophthalmology at the Catholic Medical Center of Brooklyn and Queens (CMC), the bedroom communities in which its five widely separated hospitals were located covered regions of the city that were racially overwrought and plagued by drug addiction. "Bed-Stuy" in particular was a notoriously dangerous part of the city for white passersby or stalled drivers, and that slum—then only in the very early stages of gentrification---lay between two of the hospitals served by the ophthalmology residency program. On occasion I had to visit those hospitals at night to assist the residents with difficult patients, so as a safety measure I painted over the blue-and-white emblems on our little gray BMW. Of course, the hospital parking windshield sticker read "doctor" and that, plus the emblem paint-over, still led to the inviting conclusion: "Doctor's car with drugs on board!" But doing it somehow it made me feel safer.

Drugs went with the territory. On my first full day of work at CMC, an employee of a private ophthalmology office a few blocks from my designated office at Holy Family Hospital was fatally shot through the eye by a disgruntled student. And before dawn on a Saturday morning, a thirty-seven-year-old, drug-crazed Brooklyn resident was brought to one of our hospitals, where he slit his wrists in a failed suicide attempt, then tried to gouge out his eyes with his fingers--also without success.

The executive staff and faculty of the CMC hospital system was an intriguing group, predominantly Italian Catholic, as distinct from Irish Catholic. At my first executive staff meeting, a heated argument took place between the Chief of Surgery and the Chief of Family Practice. It got so heated that, in fact, I feared they might come to blows, but they quieted down and after the meeting, I noticed the two of them walking arm-in-arm from the building. The Italian strains in their blood may have boiled up but friends were friends.

The Family Practice Chief was in charge of two trailers permanently located at JFK airport, each containing several tiers of stacked hammocks. Airport police would bring suspected drug "mules" to the trailers, where they were given strong laxatives and kept under guard until the medication took effect with the release from their bowels of sealed condoms loaded with crack cocaine or other dangerous and addictive substances. The men and women had separate trailers, for inter-gender privacy, but I could just imagine the stench and the agony of the laxative-affected inmates sitting on floor pots in the trailer as guards monitored their productivity. If that monstrous purge proved negative, I wondered how—or if---the cops apologized for the inconvenience and gratuitous humiliation.

Over time, my office was moved from its first location to another, and finally to St. John's hospital in the borough of Queens. For the small working staff—consisting of my invaluable assistant, the administrator,

a nurse and a technician---our eighteen-member residency was over-
loaded with teaching responsibilities and initially undernourished
with contributing faculty. We had a good group of voluntary practitioners helping with the teaching load, but much of the weight of
responsibility fell upon the young shoulders of the only other full-time
ophthalmologist, Dr. Andrew Danyluk. Andrew was the official vice-
chairman and in that capacity he did everything, consistently functioning with quiet excellence. I could not have carried on without his
input, especially as time went on and I began losing my energy.

Some former patients from Saudi Arabia, France, and a few other
countries contacted me for appointments in my new office location.
The Saudis would call from their private jets to confirm an appointment and would later arrive in stretch limousines. These patients
were invariably taken aback by my little office and the simplicity of
the surroundings. Sooner or later they drifted back to the care of doctors in Manhattan, where there were convenient hotels and luxurious
offices to help assure them they were receiving high-quality care. I
couldn't blame them, for I probably would have succumbed to the
same prejudices had our roles been reversed.

What pleased me most about the CMC years was that they were
spent in my own backyard's Third World, a place where doctors and
teachers---and especially teaching doctors---were much needed. The
CMC residency received no support from Cornell Medical School, to
which it was affiliated in name only. Thus, sustaining the CMC residency program called for ingenuity. It was immediately apparent to
me that there were far too few African-Americans becoming ophthalmologists, nationwide. I made a personal vow to help remedy that
deficiency, although the Bishop of the Brooklyn diocese and other
Church leaders kept wanting to draw my attention to a few of their
former altar boys as good candidates for the eye residency. That aside,
there were six residency positions and I needed more ophthalmolo-
gist-teachers than were available to fulfill the residents' basic educational needs. My intention was to admit three African-American
candidates each year; the other three residents would be foreign-
trained medical graduates (FTMGs) who had finished their ophthalmology training abroad and had completed an internship in the U.S..

To become certified by the American Board of Ophthalmology required U.S. training, but no residency elsewhere was likely to accept foreign graduates.   And since the FTMGs were already living in the U.S., I would not be adding to the brain drain from their native countries. The fact is that there were outstandingly well-trained and enthusiastic candidates for those residency positions.

Although the actual number of African-Americans in our program never reached the goal I'd set, that was partly because of my eventual retirement from CMC and partly due to the fact that my successor, Dr. Cono Grasso, had no reason to follow the same path but instead chose to shape the residency in his own manner, which he did with patience and notable expertise.

One resident in our program was a fine-looking young man from the West Coast who was personally appealing and had more potential for success as a general ophthalmologist than most of the others. I liked his attentiveness and his apparent good manners, but he had a disturbing behavioral characteristic whereby once he made up his mind about something, there was no changing it. One day in the operating room, when I was assisting him with surgery on an eye into which a piece of wood had been lodged, I directed him to remove it in a certain way. He said he had decided to do it another way. I repeated what he was to do. He refused. At that point, I took over and managed the extraction of the foreign body as I had instructed him, then spoke to him after the operation. He admitted he had a fixation on doing things his way--which in this case would have been the wrong way.

On the basis of that incident and other difficulties he had been having, a psychiatrist diagnosed him with "personality trait disorder." The upshot was that I felt obliged to fire him from the residency for disobedient behavior during a major eye operation. When he left, I felt very sorry for him but it was evident he had a problem that needed attention.

Firing a resident or faculty member had not been required of me before that, with one exception. In Houston, a female resident in my department at BCM was on call one night at the local veterans' hospital when she was contacted by a night supervisor of nursing to come and see one of the postoperative eye patients, who was having pain without known cause. The resident refused, saying she did not think it was necessary, after checking with her faculty advisor (each resident has one), who agreed she did not have to get up, get dressed and drive to the VA hospital to answer the call. Later I was told that checking with her advisor had been easy enough, since he had been just a pillow's length away that night.

I was not concerned with social etiquette or resident-faculty affairs. What bothered me was that she had refused to examine a patient after being officially requested to do so by the senior nurse. One thing about the medical profession that does not seem to apply to business or even to law is that compromise in rules cannot be condoned when patient care is concerned because lives can be at serious risk. There had been other issues raised regarding the doctor in question, sufficient for me to recommend to the medical school's disciplinary committee that she be let go, and she was. She subsequently brought a law suit against me and the medical school for what she claimed were inadequate grounds for dismissal. Her case—which she eventually lost--was financed by a feminist organization in Chicago (as if her professional misconduct had anything to do with gender) and did not cost her a penny but, as I recall, the amount demanded by that young woman's lawyer far exceeded in millions the amount of reimbursement my insurance would have provided, had I lost.

That was the only time in my life that I was sued, despite a long medical career with many thousands of surgical cases, despite working in Baltimore, Houston and New York, cities where lawsuits against doctors were quite common. I think the main reason for that much luck was that I dictated all of my patient notes while the patient and his or her family were in the room, then provided the patient with a copy of them before he or she left the office.

Life at CMC was filled with the routines of patient care and the teaching responsibilities of any residency program. It was an interesting experience to fit into an institution so far removed from the sophisticated academic entities of my prior years, but highly appropriate for the communities it served. The change provided a refreshing interlude, a good way to earn a living, and an ideal place to begin laying out the specific plans for ORBIS' promising future.

CHAPTER TWENTY-FOUR

On the morning of February 12, 1987, I was opening mail at my desk at the Catholic Medical Center. A full and varied day of patients and academic responsibilities lay ahead. Life was on an even keel and everything was copasetic.

"Phone for you, Dr. Paton. Mr. Ueltschi is on the line."

"Thanks. Hello, Al. What's up?."

"Um, yuh ... David, this is Al Ueltschi." Silence. Then, "We're calling to get your resignation from Project ORBIS."

I was dumbstruck.

Seconds ticked while I digested what I'd just heard. In those first moments of stunned disbelief, I stood up, as if sitting down were too casual for this conversation. My hand holding the receiver was shaking. So, I noticed, was my other hand.

Then a second blow hit me like the aftershock of an earthquake, the realization that no one but Oliver--my charming, admiring, enthusiastic, supportive *friend*, the man I had personally introduced to ORBIS--could have set this in-house coup in motion.

"My resignation? What the hell are you saying, Al?" Again, silence. "You're not serious!" Longer silence. "What's gone wrong?"

"Hold on a moment, I've got other people coming on the line. Operator, can't you get the damn connection right!"

In over a decade of collaborative dealing with Al Ueltschi for Project ORBIS, there had never been a disagreement between the two of us. Curt and usually humorless despite his unconvincing smile, he had conducted the job of fundraising and board management in a manner that I had had no reason to criticize. Lately, he had even gotten caught up in the excitement of ORBIS and was basking in its recognition. In my view, we had always treated each other with an appropriate degree of deference and respect.

Ueltschi had the call under control now. Mac McCollum, as Chairman-in-retirement, and Peter Mullen, as Board Secretary, had come on the line with him, Mr. Mac in Houston, Mullen in New York. Ueltschi paused for me to say hello to them.

"Let me get this straight," I went on, in part just to delay whatever Ueltschi intended to say next. "Mr. Mullen is your personal lawyer, isn't he? In fact, I know he is!"

"Well, he's a lawyer but he's with us on the line as Secretary of the ORBIS Board." Then, impatiently, aggressively, Ueltschi confirmed my suspicions. "David, the situation we're calling about is as follows: Oliver Foot will resign as Executive Director unless you resign. Now we're not going to give you much time on this. Oliver is essential to us. Our project is in his hands." Then, even more resolutely, "Mr. McCollum and I are requesting your letter of resignation."

All sorts of thoughts and questions raced through my mind, a disorganized reaction to shock, focused on cause rather than resolution. Can a volunteer for an organization based upon the work of volunteers simply be cast aside, after devoting nineteen years to its creation and operation? By a phone call? An this was all due to the overweening ambition of a person who had never said a critical word to me directly, Oliver Foot?

I knew instantly that the alternative Foot had given--"him or me"--meant that they were speaking to me with the equivalent of a gun pointed at my head. If he quit, it would take months to train a green successor for the well-paid executive director's job. The project could not risk that kind of down time, with the resulting cancellations of its obligations abroad. Foot was safely perched in the catbird's seat.

During the call, Peter Mullen--serving as Ueltschi's supplementary mouthpiece---spoke briefly and crisply to underline the seriousness of the call. He should know, for he was arguably at that time the most distinguished hostile takeover lawyer in the nation, if not in the world. That made this call all the more scary. My good friend of seventeen years, eighty-four-year-old Mac McCollum, (who unwittingly referred to Oliver as "Oliver Twist"), offered an occasional echo of support for Ueltschi. But we all knew that Mr. Mac was no longer able to be a force in that telephone call and I could not harbor any ill will toward him; he was a kindly person whose career had been highlighted by contributions and generosity, but he was no longer himself.

Suddenly another voice chimed in---a shrill, high-pitched sopra-
no recognizable as Eleanor, Mr. Mac's Born-Again wife. She had no
official relationship to the board or to ORBIS in general, except as
the wife of the original chairman of the board. Many were the times
that, as a guest in the McCollum home, I had sat holding hands with
them around the dinner table during the monologue of improvised,
pre-prandial grace which she would offer in a tremulous high-pitched
voice, sometimes even breaking into song as she looked around the
table at each of us, bound together in religious obeisance. Eleanor
had also been a patient of mine with a difficult eye problem and I had
always been available to her, no matter when the need arose. "Oh,
David, you have so many, many things you are interested in. Just give
us your resignation and it will be good for everyone concerned," she
now implored me.

It seemed that "someone" had told her I was tired of ORBIS. Who
could have created such an impression? The answer was all too obvious. In what I had thought to be private conversations and personal
letters, I had evidently provided Oliver with enough material about
future planning and admonitions about proper post-operative care to
turn the lay board against me. No doubt he had also exaggerated
my thinking and distorted my reasons for creating OcuSystems, and
suggested that I was becoming a counter-productive influence simply
because he didn't share my vision for the future of ORBIS. And in
demanding my resignation, the board--or at least its executive committee, along with Oliver Foot—had obviously decided that it was
better not to get into a policy debate and just keep to an arbitrary
dismissal that required no explanation other than Oliver's ultimatum.

Interrupting Eleanor, who was still chirping on about one thing
or another, I asked Al to give me time to collect my thoughts, justify
my position and request his reconsideration. Moreover, I asked him
to put his demand into a letter to me. He did not respond to that,
probably on the recommendation of his standby lawyer, but merely
repeated that he wanted this matter to be concluded as quickly as
possible. He said he would call again in a week.

In that interval, I realized that there had been warning signals
in the past that I had chosen to ignore. By means of subterfuge and

whispered innuendo, other ORBIS people had been forced out, if not
overtly, then by sustained pressure. First there had been Oliver's dismissal of my niece's husband, Bill Post, the unfailingly thoughtful
and kind person who began working for ORBIS as a volunteer book-
keeper. George Hambleton had departed of his own accord to take
care of family needs, but later said he had felt pressured for his resignation. He was followed out the door by the skillful, evidently all-
too articulate Director of Development, Karin Eisele, who had not
been entranced by Oliver's reign and had said so. And, finally, it was
all too obvious that Oliver had persuaded the board to move Betsy
Wainwright to the board level, where her commanding voice would
be muted by the surround of powerful laypersons with whom she
was always the very picture of good manners and respect. Oliver, like
others, had chafed under her unintentionally imperialistic approach
when she was trying to get things done.

Needless to say, a week later I was no more prepared to resign than
when the original call had come through. I had asked to meet first
with the full board, then with the executive committee, then at least
to talk by telephone with Oliver. All my requests had been denied or
ignored, without excuse and without apology. Since the board chair-
men, McCullom and Ueltschi, had insisted that no doctor—not even
the Founder—would be permitted board membership, I had no opportunity for direct appeal. I wrote a long letter to the board, asking
for reconsideration.

A single response to my request to meet with the board came
from Charles Lord, then Vice Chairman of the board. I considered
him, Betsy Wainwright's old friend, a friend of mine as well. In fact,
at one point I had, at his request, written a letter of recommendation
to Jim Baker, then President Reagan's Chief of Staff, asking his help
in getting a government appointment for Charlie in the early days of
that administration.

Now, in response to a long explanatory letter I had written to him,
imploring him to arrange for me to meet with all the board members,
Charlie invited me to lunch at his Manhattan men's club. But, over
sandwiches, he, too, insisted that I resign, without a meeting with
the board or any kind of hearing with others present, explaining that

those measures would not be in the best interests of the organization. He repeated what Ueltschi had stated, that my resignation was Oliver Foot's condition for staying on, and that was that.

I had not heard a word from Betsy, and although we met from time to time in later years we did not discuss ORBIS, for now we were on separate, undefined sides of what was presented to me as a power grab by one man, supported by Mr. Trippe's daughter, whom I had thought was surely the most loyal of all my ORBIS friends.

After the lunch with Charles Lord, I continued to delay writing the farewell letter demanded of me, but when Al Ueltschi's next impatient call came, I glumly agreed to send him my resignation as Medical Director of ORBIS—and I did so. Neither at that time nor in any of the years that followed did I hear a whisper either of regret or apology, no calls to ask "how-ya-doing?," no cards---nothing from Al Ueltschi or any member of his board. As for Oliver, despite all his surreptitious aggression I remained convinced that he was too well mannered and sensitive a person to be without conscience, and I kept wondering how he managed to keep it under wraps.

ORBIS was about the global need for improved eye care, and not about me. But the precipitous and dishonorable means used to reject its Founder and Medical Director definitely was about me. If I were to describe the circumstances of my resignation in a manner more circumspect than I have, I would be failing to convey the sudden sense of career catastrophe that overcame me in those dark early months of 1987.

CHAPTER TWENTY-FIVE

By the time of Ueltschi's call, ORBIS had become an important presence in the realm of voluntary medical services deployed in what might be referred to as global ophthalmology. As such, it was my favorite credential—indeed a growing global "ID"—that to a modest degree emulated what my father had created with the first eye bank ever established. There was no point in pretending that I had simply stepped away. Moreover, I felt weakened by the loss of a crutch that had brought a degree of implied credibility to any new idea that I wished to persuade others to consider. What was even more disturbing, though, was the implication that the various recognitions I had received as the founder of ORBIS were at least partially invalidated by my involuntary departure. If I raised a ruckus, the organization, which was dependent upon charitable support, would be tarnished by a significant sign of inner conflict; if I did not complain, my own reputation would be damaged by the inference of misdemeanor, or worse.

Being fired was a new experience and it took a toll. In the weeks that followed, I became aware of an increasing feeling of exhaustion, boredom and professional disinterest. I fretted about the various inconveniences of commuting and became annoyed by doctors in other specialties with whom I shared committee responsibilities. Everything seemed to be an effort, and I complained about my work after I came home at night. Diane urged me to just close the ORBIS book and turn my focus elsewhere, but she had not gone through two decades of its development and its eventual deployment.

The summer of 1987 was for me the beginning of an unproductive period of being an empty shell-like presence at CMC. The old fire in the belly turned into burnout. Conducting the residency program became a bothersome nuisance, then a burden and, finally, each administrative requirement in a day's work seemed a huge imposition. Teaching was a troublesome exercise, rather than a welcome challenge. Worst of all, my ability to perform eye surgery—one of my greatest pleasures in ophthalmology—began to deteriorate with the onset of a sometimes incapacitating "intention tremor," variably present but damnably threatening to the performance of ophthalmic microsurgery when it struck.

That tremor, which was caused by a loss of self-confidence and manifested most markedly when the pressure was greatest, would come at the point in the operation of greatest risk to a patient's eye, making proper precision difficult, if not impossible. Starting in mid-1987, it led to one of the most humiliating circumstances of my life: namely, having to pass routine surgical cases to others. I was the head doctor, and I was losing my hands, as well as my head.

One day, several months after the ORBIS dismissal, I scheduled a one-eyed, middle-aged woman for a cataract operation that included sliding an intraocular lens into the eye after the phaco stage of the operation was completed. My hands became tremulous. The lens implant got installed but not in the right position. Post-operatively, I could see that the implant would have to be repositioned in this lady who was wholly dependent upon her only eye and who had complete trust in my ability to care for her. Easy as that would ordinarily have been to accomplish in only a few minutes of operating time, my confidence was so shaken that I referred her to a distinguished eye surgeon in Manhattan, who did the repair without any trouble. Dr. Danyluk could have done it just as easily, but I needed to pretend to myself that it was a job for a senior colleague having extraordinary skill. Fortunately, the eye was fine.

Andrew and the residents who assisted me in surgery had to have been aware of my technical decline. During operations, Andrew had been tactfully providing more and more assistance while never commenting on my unsteadiness. Still, it was obvious that my ability to maintain a strong teaching and administrative presence in the department was dwindling and my surgery was becoming impaired. Something had to be done. Every medical doctor has to assess the safety of his work and deal with undue risks before patient care is jeopardized.

I gave up eye surgery.

I was approaching the " kills," the narrows that one passes through in almost any life that becomes dysfunctional. What do some men do when they are frustrated and unhappy with the direction of their lives? Some grow a beard, a way of hiding out for a while. I grew a luxuriant muff of white hair around my lower face, emblematic of the discomfort and insecurity that came from what I felt was publicly recognized failure.

Yet even before the beard arrived, two honors—needless to say, without any impetus from the ORBIS board or its Chairman—came my way, lifting my spirits. Never mind that good friends facilitated both of them. On September 15th, 1987, I was inducted into the French Legion of Honor by order of President François Mitterand of France. The French ambassador to the United Nations, the Honorable Claude de Kemoularia, and his aides arrived at the Catholic Medical Center hospital in Queens and, in a roped-off street ceremony that

commenced with a recording of the "Marseillaise" and then "The Star-Spangled Banner," the Ambassador hung a medallion around my neck, followed by the traditional, two-sided, French air kiss. I owed this delightful honor to his wife, whom I had operated on in Houston a few years earlier. Both she and her husband had become my good friends and they went to bat for me after hearing of my misfortune.

Then, on November 9, 1987, in an Oval Office presentation by President Ronald Reagan, I became the first medical doctor to be awarded the Presidential Citizens Medal. The medal is the second highest civilian award given in the United States, in recognition of an American citizen who has performed exemplary deeds or services for his or her country or fellow citizens. The President read a tribute, lauding

ORBIS for its unprecedented contribution to the world, to the reputation of our country and to the fight against blindness, which needed recognition and resources. He then hung around my neck a large, gilt-and-enamel medal embossed with the Seal of the President of the United States and handed me a box containing a tri-colored lapel pin and a medal engraved with my name. Could there be any doubt that my college roommate, Jim Baker, was the instigator of that honor?

After the "hit" was completed, Oliver Foot was promptly promoted to a new position, President of ORBIS, becaming a member of the board. He remained active with the aircraft project, extending greetings to dignitaries and political leaders in many countries and continuing to do an indisputably fine job as a promoter of the project and an enthusiastic fundraiser. Over subsequent years, the DC-8 was replaced by a DC-10, and the teaching functions were likewise expanded, as was the annual budget. Various land-based programs were added to its activities, still dependent upon ophthalmologists' volunteerism, as originally envisioned.

On October 27, 2006, nineteen years after his coup, Oliver sent a letter explaining that the reason he had not been in touch with me in all that time was ". . . because I just didn't know how to begin." He went on to ask if I would meet with him, saying, "I have been waking up at night and wondering how to thank you for giving me the greatest opportunity of my life, serving ORBIS. . . I know I have made mistakes and I have learned a great deal from those over the years, but I just hope and wish that some day our friendship can be rekindled." He finished his short letter with, "Even if you never want to meet me again, I would like you to know that I hold you in the highest esteem." That last was so Oliver.

I was surprised and pleased to hear from him after almost two decades of silence. In my response, however, I reminded him that he was asking me to turn the other cheek without the slightest expression of repentance on his part. I reminded him of the facts surrounding our friendship's sudden collapse and said that before I would agree to meet, I felt he owed me an apology, at the least for making sure I was not permitted to defend my position before the ORBIS board.

He then sent a second and final note that was brief and to the point: "Thank you for your letter. I am so sorry you feel the way you do. There is no need for further communication, Sincerely, Oliver."

The Oliver Foot story entered a sad final phase in 2007. I had heard rumors from ORBIS volunteers that he had had a few unexplained absences from his job. Shortly after ORBIS's celebration of its twenty-fifth anniversary at the United Nations in New York City on March 2, 2007, Oliver apparently disappeared again. A few days went by before he informed the board that he would return only briefly before permanently leaving his job but remaining on the board. Less than a year after that, on February 6, 2008, Oliver died at 61, his death promptly attributed to a familial heart disorder which had also killed his late brother. Glowing tributes to him poured in, many in leading newspapers in the U.S. and U.K.

I wrote condolences to his widow, Gail Foot, and copied my letter to Al Ueltschi. I did not hear back but no reply was necessary. As I said in my letter, I sincerely believed, and continue to believe, that Oliver's death was a big loss to the project. He was a complex individual with a troubled dark side I did not know about until reading blogs about him on the Internet after his death. His troubles had started in adolescence, when he was arrested for stealing jeans from a shop, prompting the headline, "Peer in Hot Pants Drama." At his subsequent trial for theft, his father stood up for him, blaming himself.

I did not know until informed by the blogs that Oliver considered himself not only an evangelical but a Born Again Christian or that in his unpublished autobiography he "constantly refers to the 'demons

of temptation' and his failure in living a life that reflected his beliefs."
In an article in London's newspaper, *The Independent*, Oliver's wife is
quoted as saying, "He could mix equally with aristocrats, prostitutes,
drug addicts and thieves." If Oliver had a drug or alcohol addiction,
I knew nothing of it; nor, I suspect, did his ORBIS employers. But
on August 7, 2008, a coroner's court in Southwark, England, cor-
rected the previously attributed cause of death with the report that
Oliver Foot was an "alcoholic and frequent user of cannabis and crack
cocaine, " the latter being the actual cause of his death.

CHAPTER TWENTY-SIX

There was more unhappy news to follow. At 77, Betsy Trippe Wainwright DeVecchi's illnesses eventually overtook her and she died quite suddenly in April, 2009. She deserves--and was given---much credit by those at ORBIS and by her many friends for her hard work soliciting support from philanthropists, encouraging the interest of ophthalmologists, and helping to organize the project's infrastructure. Based upon what her husband, Bob DeVecchi, has told me, it was her ill health that prevented her from speaking up on my behalf. What I shall always remember above anything else is the enormous contribution her efforts amounted to in the genesis of ORBIS.

Similarly, I believe I have figured out the motivation that caused Oliver Foot to act as he did. He and I were driven by similar ambitions, both seeking to justify ourselves as we followed in the wakes of prominent fathers. There was never any doubt that he wanted ORBIS to be an outstanding agency, not only on behalf of its global mission but also as his own stepping stone toward knighthood. I believe he hoped to achieve for himself what his father and uncle had been granted by the Queen, and he probably came very close to reaching that goal with ORBIS. After a rocky start in adolescence, and after various undertakings had failed to lead to a lasting career, he found ORBIS serendipitously through my introduction. It turned out to be the right medium for his compelling stage presence, his refined English accent, and his promotional talents. But at a certain point, he needed me out of his way. My sojourn in Saudi Arabia provided the opportunity for him to build personal control of the clinical work while promoting the idea that ORBIS should become a much larger aircraft, such as a DC-10. I, more than most, can understand how it is that--for whatever reason--some offspring need to prove themselves to their parents in order to earn their independent self-respect.

Until recently, Al Ueltschi's mode of interpersonal conduct remained less   comprehensible to me than Betsy's silence or Oliver's
takeover, so obviously fueled by vaulting ambition. But I came to an
eventual understanding of the Chairman's actions by observing comparable conduct on the part of some very successful and powerful men
in two other organizations that have also meant a great deal to me
over the years. In brief, my dismissal from ORBIS, as orchestrated
by Al Ueltschi, amounted to an act of institutional imperialism pro-
tected by the legal safety zone of a nonprofit entity—in legalese, a
no-fault white collar misdemeanor--which is better termed an act of
arrogance. Arrogance is not something to be taken lightly. Simple
arrogance can be the cause of serious difficulties created inadvertently
in nonprofit organizations by powerful people.

As one of the nation's most successful businessmen, Al was conducting our nonprofit, ORBIS, as if it were his own for-profit company—while, I hasten to say, contributing large amounts of money,
as well as volunteering his unique intellectual services for the betterment of the organization. But in running ORBIS his way, with
a board he tightly controlled, he was acting without the restraints
that are customarily maintained within such charitable organizations,
where infrastructure is necessarily far less ironclad than it is in the
business world. Powerful volunteers are not to be herded, questioned
or contradicted. No one still reliant upon the essential contributions of such leaders, however imperial they might be, can risk saying
what I'm saying here. But since I'm retired, I can be frank, while at
the same time acknowledging that those leaders of nonprofits most
likely to behave arrogantly are often the ones who are the most needed—and wealthiest—members of their nonprofits' boards. They are
always oblivious to their occasional serious but unrealized missteps
which can lead ultimately to a forgiveness for not knowing what
they do.

To further explain this never-mentioned dichotomy, not-for-profit
organizations can all too easily provide a safe haven in which wealthy
and powerful donors can indulge their whims without fear of being censored, maintaining a businessman's focus on affairs within the
corporation rather than a nonprofit's focus on its outreach. No one is

likely to protest since those of us in academic careers are dependent upon, and enormously indebted to, the generous donors who give millions of dollars to sustain and enhance our institutions and service agencies. But when some among those powerful persons allow their egos to trump common sense or common courtesy, what occurs is not just a violation of social ethics but, all too often, irreparable damage to the very institutions they serve. What's worse is that the damage may be done before the cause has been diagnosed. Arrogance is like halitosis, in that it is easily detected by other people even though the victim himself has no awareness of its presence. Moreover, no one wants to alert the offender to his problem—and in the case of an arrogant leader, who wants to look a gift horse in the mouth? But without the diagnosis there is little hope of cure for the afflicted. Note that I offer no quarrel with the right of the board, and Mr. Ueltschi in particular, to dismiss whoever had fallen from grace, but the means by which it was done demonstrated the kind of underlying imperiousness that could have been circumvented had an awareness existed of nonprofits' mores and their susceptibility to harm from a business counter-culture.

In some circumstances arrogance is far more damaging than in managing the expectations and ego of a single person. For example, the sort of arrogance that felled me at ORBIS has more recently been exhibited on the part of the governing boards of Baylor College of Medicine (BCM) and its principal adult hospital, The Methodist Hospital (TMH), and has resulted in grievous harm to both institutions.

These contiguous partner institutions within the Texas Medical Center had functioned inseparably and efficiently throughout the half-century of Dr. DeBakey's full (BCM) and virtual (TMH) leadership of both. However, in 2004, the two institutions' boards of directors, each composed of individuals of imposing wealth and/or position, began a power struggle stemming from a dispute over the ownership of mutually occupied property. My reading of the public media's reports is that they behaved like cosmopolitan versions of the Hatfields and McCoys, far less excusable in today's Houston than it might have been in old-time Kentucky. Each board—influenced by its leaders—was narrowly focused on its own interests rather than on the overall common good, or upon pursuing the eleemosynary purposes those entities had long served with indisputable excellence.

The presumptuous obstinacy that prevented the boards from settling their differences led to a now notorious financial calamity and a serious blow to healthcare at the preeminent Texas Medical Center. BCM was forced to commit to building a new hospital and a clinical office building requiring hundreds of millions of dollars, much of which is still to be raised. Further, the new building would have to be located in a relatively inconvenient site for the medical school's faculty. Construction got under way well before the current national economy put a stop to the work's completion, with much funding still to be sought. TMH, by far the richer of the two institutions, also had to find a substitute medical school in order to enable the administration to create a new residency training program, thus permitting them to apply for grants that would be unavailable without a medical school's authority. Finding no medical school within Texas willing to affiliate with such an independently-minded private hospital, TMH ended up agreeing to pay $100 million to sign an extended contract with the Weill Cornell Medical College in New York City.

Regardless of the distorted logic of such a merger, Cornell University's medical school in New York is now the medical school for the Methodist Hospital in Houston, despite being 1,500 miles away and comparably separated by state licensure and institutional culture. Meanwhile, The Cullen Eye Institute (CEI)—co-owned by BCM and TMH and home of the department of ophthalmology I spent a decade helping to build--has been dragged into a quagmire of confused identity and financial uncertainty.

Collectively creating an expenditure in excess of $500,000,000 of not-for-profit dollars has been an unimaginable two-institutional calamity. That cost, and the degradation in reputation and excellence of each uncoupled institution, would not have been necessary had intelligent decisions been made without the blinders of arrogance impairing the judgment of members of both institutions' boards. This is the best example I know of how arrogance, pure and simple, can markedly diminish two great institutions.

I do not presume to know a good solution for the BCM-TMH divorce, other than re-marriage and redistribution of the facilities and personnel so that they are once again a single medical school closely tied to its principal hospital. Breaking apart those two institutions was like separating a pair of Clydesdales, then having to look for quarter horses to fill both huge empty harnesses. However, I feel quite certain that sooner or later more objective, wise and caring board members of those institutions will find a way to reunite and therefore further empower the two nonprofit entities. But it will take humility for such conciliation—a most discomforting challenge for people who take pride in being valuable instigators and honored citizens.

Figuring all this out finally enabled me sincerely to forgive Al Ueltschi—and to have learned a valuable lesson that can be passed on to others in straddles between for-profit and nonprofit institutions. His working culture was that of the aggressive business world, with the for-profit motivation that is essential to our nation's economy and within which arrogance is not a risk to effective productivity. But when arrogance is carried into the nonprofit environment, it becomes a yellow flag to be carefully watched for signs of potential disturbances. The particular circumstances will determine what obligation one has to intervene on behalf of the entity at risk. But prevention is infinitely preferable to having to seek a remedy.

After my ORBIS dismissal, it was months before I began to recognize that my work as a teacher and surgeon—work I had once found so stimulating—had progressively become reduced to being a conscious drudgery. I was depressed for the first time in my life. Perhaps churchgoers might have found resolution for this kind of unhappiness in the hope and charity provided by their faith, but for me that would be a cover-up instead of a cure. In retrospect, I needed psychiatric intervention as much as my father had needed it after Pam died, but despite having had a psychiatrist in the family—my grandfather—neither he nor I had an inkling that we would benefit from outside help.

Help for me finally came from finding relevance in an ophthalmic report written by a man of God. While still in the foggy days of my depression, I discovered certain parallels in my situation to how

blinded soldiers reacted to the trauma of their complete loss of eyesight. In no way do I mean to equate what happened to me with the
plight of those who are blinded in battle, but any major permanent
"deprivation" has a similar kind of emotional impact. In the 1960s,
a Catholic priest, Father Thomas Carroll, who had studied recently
blinded soldiers, noted that all sudden loss of vision is followed by
a period of dazed awareness and considerable confusion. Some soldiers—possibly reinforced by their training to be brave—resolutely
committed themselves to accepting their blindness without a whim-
per, a "stiff upper lip" response to calamity. These exceptional individuals were heralded by all who knew and met them, not only as
heroes but as wartime martyrs. But, interestingly, Father Carroll observed that these soldiers could never be properly rehabilitated from
a visual to a tactile world, for they lacked the incentive to acquire a
new and different approach to their impaired lives.

The majority of blinded soldiers had a more realistic response.
After the initial stage of dazed shock, they entered into a phase of
depression lasting from a few months to several years, an indication
that they were dealing with the irrefutable truth of permanent blindness. Only after acquiring that mindset did they become receptive to
the difficult process of rehabilitation training. In a sense, it was their
depression that facilitated their progress.

I, too had gone through these stages: First, shock and confusion
after the phone call from Al; then a prolonged period of depression
as I came to accept the new reality of life without ORBIS; and, finally, an eagerness to bring into focus some of the blurred vistas of
past years for future use. Once one has reached "a certain age," any
remaining creativity is likely to be a re-visiting of one's longstanding
interests and convictions with the welcome perspective of experience.

And so it went. In 1989, while I was still at CMC, I started the
EXCEL Foundation, intended as another means of encouraging new
approaches to global eye care and bringing attention to generic issues
of healthcare delivery. One of its purposes was to sponsor a Sabbatical
Professorship for the Advancement of Ophthalmological Services in
the Third World, consisting of a generous stipend to be awarded to
an established American doctor for full-time attention to whatever

eye-related project attracted him or her in the general field of public health and eye disorders. The 1990 recipient was my one-time critic, later my good friend, Dr. Larry Schwab, who used that year to update with a third edition his valuable textbook, *Eye Care in Developing Nations;* a fourth edition was to follow in 2006. My beard gradually faded away.

In June of 1990, I organized a two-day symposium, sponsored by the EXCEL Foundation and CMC, for the consideration of how health care delivery can keep up with increasingly costly technology, expanding populations, and the need for preventive measures---not only for the eyes but for all aspects of healthcare. At that time, the overall topic was only rarely featured in academic faculty discussions and seminars directed toward understanding and possibly addressing the dark clouds gathering above the medical profession's means of providing its expertise. There were 30 speakers and an attendance of over a hundred registered physicians with expressed interest in health care delivery systems.

My talk was titled, "Academia's Role in Health Care Delivery," which at that time was far from a common consideration. Its thesis was that academic physicians should devise and test various methods for improving the efficiency, quality and availability of medical care at affordable costs—for if the physicians themselves are not the prime movers in necessary change to meet the costs of modern technology and medications, then the government will address the matter primarily from the viewpoint of finance, which will not be in the best interest of either patient or doctor. Unfortunately, I believe that is what has happened in the ensuing two decades and I rarely hear a political debate that seeks consideration of the medical doctor's input. The conference itself, with numerous authoritative and influential speakers, was enthusiastically received by the audience; but it may have been a case of whistling in the wind, for I have no positive fallout to report. Sympathetic colleagues told me I was pushing too far ahead of the times, a refrain I've heard all too often over the years.

In 1998, when Diane and I faced retirement--she from government employment, I from Weill Cornell and its affiliate, CMC--I got permission from the EXCEL Foundation's board to fold its assets into

the brand-new East Hampton Healthcare Foundation, one of whose
founders, Dr. Jerome J. DeCosse, was also a former Markle Scholar.
That organization, dedicated to improving healthcare for all who live
in our town, became my principal medical interest beyond serving on
five nonprofit boards and several institutional committees related to
ophthalmology. Retirement for me still meant not-for-profit involvement but only if conducted in the nearby presence of my perfect and
forever wife.

In March, 2008, I was invited to return to Riyadh to help celebrate
the King Khaled Eye Specialist Hospital's twenty-fifth year since its
doors first opened when I became its first medical director. During those intervening years, KKESH had become—as projected---
the leading modern eye hospital in all of the developing countries,
with a thriving American-type residency training program. Hundreds of thousands of cataract operations had been performed at the
hospital, as well as thousands of corneal transplants with corneas invariably imported from other nations, possibly the largest volume of
corneal transplants in any nation during that interval. Thanks to the
excellence of a series of American medical directors who succeeded
me, and in combination with the genuine commitment of the Saudi
government and Saudi-trained ophthalmologists, KKESH had become a potential international powerhouse of academic ophthalmology, lacking only a suitable partner to take it to the next step in its
maturation.

Upon returning from that visit, I was asked by the hospital's Executive Director, Dr. Abdul Elah Al Towerki, to find an American
academic institution to be that partner. It took no flash of genius to
suggest The Wilmer Institute and, after almost two years of discussion and extended negotiation, that affiliation has been agreed upon.
The arrangement, for which I was happy to be credited for proposing
and helping to catalyze, stands to strengthen the rapport between
Saudi Arabia and the U.S. as these institutions work together to create a valuable outreach of our profession to the developing world and,
beyond that, to all nations seeking applicable systems and techniques
in state-of-the-art teaching, research and patient care.

As for the benefit of having a dyslexia-adjusted brain, I want to add—perhaps immodestly—that in 2008 the Johns Hopkins School of Medicine awarded their Distinguished Alumnus Award to this fellow with the learning deficiency, unable though he was to analyze statistics for any medical paper he ever wrote. What one does not have can be much less important that what one does have, which in my case was always a love of my profession and my work, plus an innate respect for the abilities of others. Anyone who minimizes the importance of those reality-based primary assets will fail to find the kind of success I so thoroughly enjoyed.

In April of 2010, in New Haven, Connecticut, I organized a symposium sponsored by the nonprofit agency, Unite for Sight (UFS), that included three other younger—and, I admit, sharper---speakers with similar interests. Our topic was "The Principle of Replication as Applied to Eye Care in the Developing Nations," with each of us emphasizing separate applications of that principle, mine being how the efficiency of the multiplier effect can be applied to high-volume patient care. I reiterated one of my favorite admonitions for global healthcare: the benefit of "thinking big" and only compromising the bigness down the line if it becomes mandatory to do so. I also took pains to point out to an audience of predominantly young persons considering careers in health care that, with sufficient motivation, determination and commitment, anyone—including persons such as myself with routine testing results below top levels--can make important contributions to whatever he or she envisions as a worthwhile cause.

Diane and I live on Long Island, New York, but spend four months of the winter on the Big Island of Hawaii—thus dividing our time between two of this country's largest islands, as distant from one another as any two points within the U.S. and equally far apart in cultural background and environment. The contrast makes our life together all the more interesting. In Hawaii, at almost 3,000 feet on the slope of Mauna Kea, we have a small condominium featuring a fireplace, a large bookcase, a huge double bed and a breathtaking mountain view. On Long Island our house lies between a meadow and a woods, about a mile from the sea.

One day a few years ago on the Long Island side of the U.S. I received a heavy jolt, literally and figuratively. I was driving home from the post office when a speeding Jaguar barreled through a stop sign and smashed into my Jeep, flipping it upside down and spinning it 180 degrees. The next thing I knew, someone was calling through the broken right front window, "Anybody alive in there?" It was a fair question.

"Yes, me. I can't move much." In fact, I was imprisoned inside the diminished car by a tight seat belt and crushed doors. There were shards of glass covering my hair, face and body and my neck hurt from the sudden impact. The man outside the window asked—rather ominously, I thought--if there was anyone I wanted to notify. I gave him our home phone number, he dialed it, then reached in and held his cell phone for me to speak to Diane. She arrived on the scene a few minutes later and found my wrecked Jeep surrounded by police, firemen, and an assortment of curious observers. I had failed to tell her that I had been talking to her from within the wreck. She watched as the jaws of life freed me from the crushed Jeep and I was hoisted into an ambulance, then followed us to the hospital, with full siren accompaniment. After the shards were removed from my body, I passed my X-rays with flying colors and was dismissed from the hospital.

A picture of the totaled Jeep was later to appear in *The East Hampton Star*, being the most photogenic accident of the week.

Lucky as I was to be alive, I would have to replace my well-preserved Jeep with the skimpy Blue Book amount offered by the insurance company. When I heard a day or two later that the Jaguar driver had been indignant that the police delayed him at the scene of the accident, I could sniff the arrogance I've been describing as easily as a bird dog points quail. The Jag driver was sent on his way without even a ticket for speeding through a stop sign because it was an unwitnessed collision without a fatality. The police chief explained to me a few days later that technically and legally it was a "no-fault" violation. That sounded to me something like a hostile takeover without redress.

The accident was more than a reminder of faults that are no-fault within the law, for it also reminded me that life has capricious ways of zeroing out, and there were thoughts I wanted to share about shaping one's career to capitalize on strengths and minimize weaknesses—and to describe the thrills of being an ophthalmologist. Hence this book. In thumbing through its pages, I see that my mood seems to evolve as the story unfolds from the lightheartedness of an ingenuous would-be doctor, to the committed focus of a resolute physician and, finally, to the less bottled up approach of a retired opinionator--weathered, tested and no longer constricted by the inhibitions that those who are still "in office" must abide by.

A few weeks before finishing this final chapter, I heard that ORBIS had had a series of staff and board replacements and that the chairman of the board (upon which I had been denied a seat simply by virtue of being a doctor) was a highly respected British ophthalmologist, Robert L. Walters, who had served as a volunteer surgeon on the aircraft and had been found to have the skills of leadership and professional knowledge so essential to the guidance of a medical agency. I contacted him by email; we met briefly when he was visiting New York City shortly thereafter. I subsequently met with another person of singular importance to ORBIS, Mr. Jack McHale, its acting CEO and President—followed by a chat session with some twenty persons of the agency's multi-skilled staff at the New York headquarters. Most knew my name but that was about all. I am delighted to add that this is soon to change. On December 20, 2010 I received a letter from Mr. Walters (as all British surgeons are called) generously describing my past founding relationship to ORBIS and including a resounding sentence: "It gives me great pleasure to welcome you back to ORBIS."

Everyone at ORBIS with whom I have met has made me feel warmly welcome. Moreover, there is to be a celebratory dinner held in my honor at The Century Club where I am a member, as was my father, great uncle and grandfather.   I hope by that time in April 2011 this book will be available to present to all who attend. It just may become the most memorable evening of my life in the world of eyeballs.

This return to the ORBIS family is like re-entering the life of one's beloved child after two decades when he has become fully educated, mature and worldly--and deeply engaged in his career. In this case the child has changed body as well as mind, for ORBIS is a DC-10 and soon to graduate to an even more ideal aircraft by 2012. Like a proud absentee father, I identify genetically with the success of this half-human, half-mechanical creation whose important work has been broader and more voluminous than I could have dared imagine. Since 1982, its far-flung legion of workers in aircraft-based and land-based sites have carried out more than 1,000 programs in 87 countries, trained over 6,000 doctors and more than 33,000 nurses, technicians, paramedics and rural health workers; performed more than 156,500 eye surgeries; and has been responsible for treatment of more than 9,000,000 blind and visually impaired people. And while accomplishing its missions, I feel certain that the ORBIS aircraft has been visited by more heads of state and ministers of health than any other health-related mobile entity—anywhere, ever. Such visits, in themselves, cannot fail to inspire attention to the international needs of the blind and partially sighted.

ORBIS is still not without its occasional critics. It is an expensive undertaking that requires effective fund raising among several leading industries and from the generosity of a host of donors. And it is only fair to say that despite whatever personal issues I had with him, until his recent retirement Al Ueltschi has firmly coordinated the various components of the ORBIS missions' financial needs and provided a hard-nosed CEO capability for decision-making and implementing the purposes of his agency. He deserved and has received many honors for such contribution.

Furthermore, paradoxically, I now realize that during my prolonged absence from ORBIS, the tasks of fundraising, promoting, and international medical deployments had been accomplished exceedingly well, perhaps largely as a result of the enthusiasm and moxie of the late Oliver Foot in his capacity as the voice and face of the organization.

Meanwhile, over those intervening years, I was able to work on other original undertakings, plus a hodgepodge of new and existing medical commitments, while also enjoying a home life far less encumbered by work responsibility than had I been at the medical helm of a burgeoning international project like ORBIS. Then, too, as Diane would be the first to point out, I am a big-picture person, not given to the minutiae that make up the continuum of an organization's achievements. Every life is earned by its successes and taught by its losses. I realize with the benefit of hindsight that ORBIS today is undoubtedly more prosperous, better staffed and more diversified by means of its permanent eye care centers in several countries than had I remained its medical leader over the past two decades. But there is always room for new ideas, modified approaches, and the benefits of steadily improving technology to keep the aircraft's programs well suited to the needs of eye care and at the cutting edges for populations of all sizes. Looking forward, it is exciting to think that I may still have some usefulness in the evolutionary process of this extraordinary profession. My focus today is not just upon the flying eye hospital but upon the full emergence of global ophthalmology as a legitimate subspecialty of ophthalmology. That should keep me quiet for a while.

I have frequently mentioned the sense of privilege that a medical life affords. There has been, for me, no greater appreciation of privilege than the thrill of restoring sight to the blind or, less dramatically but more resoundingly, preventing impending blindness. Having been the primary enabler of several education-based nonprofit agencies that have helped cure or prevent blindness for millions of people has brought the unbeatable sense of professional completeness.

But personal fulfillment of that nature comes with a broader realization that, whatever the undertaking, it is only accomplished by the collaboration of many heads and hearts working in unison. That togetherness of purpose for helping to improve eye care in diverse nations is the very essence of global ophthalmology—and that turns out to have been the greatest passion in my work over the years.

Each of us sufficiently positioned to make career choices has the chance to shape his life as best fits his abilities, and to help make his chosen field better than it was when his work began. And each eventually will know only by the extent of his personal satisfaction whether he has met that mark.

POSTSCRIPT

During the several years it took to produce this memoir, the tedious-ness of writing about myself would sometimes sink from *ad infini-tum* to *ad nauseum*. Whenever that happened, I would come up for a breath of oxygen and a dose of relativity, pausing to wonder, Who is that ingenuous guy masquerading as me while making light of ex-periences abroad and maybe even misconstruing the real heft of the medical profession? More shades of gray seemed needed to convey intended meanings and I found it frustrating that my inexperience as a writer prevented me from being able to come up with the pixels needed for better resolution. Perhaps this is why so few medical doc-tors choose to write their memoirs. We are trained to take histories, not to give them.

But I have been a teacher and I have lived during drastically changing times in a healing profession that these days is generally not regarded as highly as I believe it deserves, possibly because a technology-laden, robotizing barrier has increasingly come between doctors and their patients. Because of that, we may seem ever more remote while being even more essential to the care being rendered than were our predecessors in previous generations. The physician's first-hand interpretations and choice of options can never be replaced by rote systems; and doctor-patient communication will forever be a vital component in amplifying the effectiveness of our applied technologies.

Therefore, I believe that we physicians should do what we can to humanize our profession by offering candid and informative views of what makes us tick and how our diverse personalities handle chal-lenging situations while still attempting to adhere to our profession's code of ethics. But when personal interests are at stake, and the stakes are high, then even in our placid, polite, usually politically correct medical profession, a great commotion can be stirred up and we physicians can begin to growl and show our teeth to one another in a rather unbecoming way.

In one prolonged period of being fed up with the first person singular, I put aside the memoir to write about someone else—a contentious medical activist all but wearing a sandwich board to publicly protest his independence while creating one hell of a ruckus within the eyeball world's inner sanctum. In personality and native abilities, he I were as different as any two contemporary doctors could be—except perhaps for untamed ambition. Not surprisingly, we disliked each other even before we met, for I functioned within medicine's academic systems and he chose to circumvent the likes of me. Viewed initially—and superficially—as a medical dilettante by the Old Guard of his specialty, this young upstart put the question to the gray beards of what constitutes "fair play" when the playing field itself is under reconstruction. For better or worse, he was sharply cutting at the cutting edge of his profession's technical renaissance that was just beginning when he and I were children and was at full tilt by the time we were approaching our years of greatest productivity. What he did in his way had an enormous impact upon what I did in my way. Therefore, I have included the essay I wrote during my time-out as an extended postscript to my own story.

TROUBLE WITH AN UPSTART

He was a small man, possessed of grandiose ideas and appetites. He was a young doctor in his thirties—as was I--and an aspiring inventor. He had the outlandish purpose of wanting to change completely the way cataracts were operated upon in order to facilitate the patients' recovery from that surgery and to improve the vision he would be restoring. Mind you, he was trying to interfere with a common eye procedure being performed worldwide by hundreds of thousands of eye doctors operating upon many millions of persons every single year. That is a bit much to leave to one's own devices, especially if those devices are represented by mind-blowing gadgetry used in unmonitored research by a self-taught inventor. Moreover, his very persona drove the medical authorities to despair and distraction. That reaction was prompted by his craving for publicity, his offbeat ideas, and his defiance of any semblance of mannered protocol. But—and here comes the crowning blow to his credibility as a physician--he was also a would-be Pied Piper; for him the instrument of choice was a saxophone, which augmented the already brassy overlay to his medical facade.

In the late 1960s and thereafter, Charles Kelman's brash intrusion into the traditionally sedate field of ophthalmology was viewed by his profession's hierarchy as unprofessional and unseemly. But his doings were uncommonly eye-opening at a time when the rest of us ophthalmologists presumed that our eyes were already open wide enough.

For quite some time, I have thought about telling the Kelman story from the perspective of those of us who were his strident critics. Were it told otherwise, the intensity of the controversy he instigated might be diffused and the tale left buried in the antiseptic annals of medical history.

Because his is a story involving cataract surgery, it deserves to be told as much for the contemporary cataract-prone public as for the current and future generations of the profession that was so shocked and outraged by this errant inventor. Almost from the start, he had his followers who, spared the technical details of his controversial work, were so besotted with his charm that they could scarcely wait to give him their cataracts as talismans of their devotion. It was that intense. You could easily detect the arrhythmia and bruits affecting the stout hearts of his professional contemporaries. At the time, anyone with any kind of caution knew that blind faith in a madcap inventor was bound to end up disastrously. The better part of valor was to take any discordant influence under advisement—by the way, handy metaphors are the right tonic for one's self-assurance in foisting protest against such an out-of-line miscreant. Any significant offense—and he was definitely offensive—needs a ready defense.

There was another element to that caution. For many decades, cataract surgery was customarily a delicate but readily mastered operation that restored eyesight quite successfully and provided most ophthalmologists with a major portion of their income. Those facts alone are clues to the personal distress felt by many established eye surgeons who reckoned that if Kelman's hare-brained ideas about changing the surgery for cataracts were to prevail, the surgery would become a far more difficult operation, one that many of them would be unable to master. Understandably reluctant to advertise this fear, they instead bemoaned not only his allegedly unmonitored research but also his "inappropriate" social behavior with horn and microphone. There are various ways for a vulnerable group to express its collective disapproval, and everyone naturally gravitates to the way that is easiest: "He's a flash-in-the-pan troublemaker! He's an embarrassment to the profession."

As might be expected, Kelman's critics consisted of the conventional ivory tower academics, joined by a power-vested old guard from the various ophthalmic societies, plus many mostly senior practitioners who were comfortably set in their ways. As the profession changed with valid new innovations, there was no need to change its mores and standards which were the rightful responsibility of the vested academic leadership. With some exceptions related to personal idiosyncrasies, the Kelman conflagration was a microcosm of Town vs. Gown, which in the last half of the past century was a far more widespread demarcation of medical identities than it is in this century. I should admit from the start that being an academic ophthalmologist, I entered into the Kelman hostilities from the ranks of his all-but-sworn enemies – a "gown."

The academics felt secure in the certainty that no world-shaking scientific invention could be created by just one person working alone, carrying his idea single-handedly over the long pathway from raw concept to proven achievement in order to protect it from the medical kleptomania that may happen when research is shared in its period of development. But that was Kelman's chosen course. He also worked independently because he had more confidence in his own mental resources than he did in the opinions of others. He was not only cheeky but brash. And it did not take much intent on the part of critics to cut their parlance from brash to rash and thereby raise the specter of felony from a whiff of misjudgment. That is the way it goes in high stakes' risk prevention.

It is a fact that in those days, research in the trial-and-error approach to modifications of surgical technique was considerably less regulated. Some of Kelman's ideas went directly from his laboratory experiments into the hospital operating room, where he tested their usefulness on patients without an invited *eminence grise* looking over his shoulder. Those authorities, however, picked up on half-whispered anecdotes passed around in hospital corridors implying that this whippersnapper was a surgical risk-taker. It did not matter that he had already proven he was good at inventing useful modifications for other eye surgery. He was a misfit, plain and simple.

Even his natty off-hours wardrobe didn't fit the mold. Everybody knows that those inventors who reach the world stage tend not to be the life of a party. Rather, they are apt to be eccentric wallflowers possessed of unkempt hair, bushy eyebrows, Birkenstock sandals and modest voices emitting abstruse equations. This did not describe Charles Kelman. But his dapper appearance aside, the luminaries of the profession sized up his project as a complex daydream that would lead nowhere, mired as it was in the mind of an investigative neophyte who was way, *way* out of his league. We academics had clearly in mind that "big-time research" was in our bailiwick, not his.

Kelman's ardent obsession with secrecy in his research, combined with his safe-to-assume surgical vigilantism behind operating room doors, caused him to be repeatedly called to account for his clinical investigations by the suspicious governing officers of his hospital. His supporters--invariably other townies--might point out that life's outliers invariably get picked on, to which the gown men would counter that many of them richly deserve what they get.

Adding fuel to the fire, Kelman was a high-energy operative who needed to be stoked by public approbation. When mentally exhausted from experimental surgery on cats and rabbits or from the tensions facing the harassment of hospital administrators or prying colleagues alleging inappropriate experimentation with surgical ideas in the operating room, he would take time out for gigs – yes, *gigs* -- as a Dorseyesque saxophonist with a perpetual smile whose flexing hips kept time with the melody and whose petitioning eyes sought nurture from the audience's lavishing rapport. When his lungs needed a rest from blowing, he told jokes with innate timing, and sang his own songs, hoping that at least one of his songs would be picked up and popularized by a famous singer. He said as much. There was no subtlety to his makeup.

Beyond question, in the early 60s Kelman's musical and related performance abilities were enrapturing crowds from Manhattan to Atlantic City and beyond. Sure, he could spew charm as if atomizing snake oil, rain it upon spellbound audiences and transform them into grownup groupies, but would you want such a variant of medical doctor to be the surgeon operating on one of your eyes? It seemed obvious that he could not be taken seriously by his profession when his name was appearing in the entertainment section of newspapers and his face was becoming familiar on folksy television programs. His office on the 34th floor of the Empire State Building was, in itself, a showplace of modern décor and technology. In those days, for a doctor to be known for anything but his word-of-mouth reputation was, frankly, considered anti-Hippocratic.

Kelman made no bones about wanting to be somebody, but not just somebody, *somebody!* Medicine and music were the two inseparable pillars of his brain and he sought greatness, recognition and fame in both. That fused duality made him somewhat like the famous con-joined twins in P.T. Barnum's circus, in that nutrition of either ben-efited both, and they managed to marry separate wives and each have their own children, inconvenient as that may seem to those without such duality. Kelman exploited his duality to the nth degree. He expected the major part of his fame to come from his inventions, with the series of miscellaneous "performances" that comprised his public life showcasing his social talents. To that end, he took singing lessons, practiced his saxophone with distinguished musicians and wrote songs with his own melodies that he piped into his office's waiting room. Yes, he wanted to help mankind, but there is an old bromide about actions speaking louder than words—and his actions were not speaking but shouting in the opposite direction.

Charles Kelman depended upon himself for his advancement in life more than anyone else I have ever known. This may have come, in part, from the voice of his late father ringing in his ears. His father had been a part-time inventor and semi-successful businessman who listened carefully to his teenaged son's music, then told him flat-out that he was never going to be a great musician— a really, really great musician. Therefore, the boy's path to distinction must be as a doc-tor. So Kelman became a doctor as a second-choice career. He studied medicine in Switzerland, learning French, befriending a blind man who inspired him and enjoying a succession of women without per-manent roots—femmes de la nuit, as they are called in Paris. The details are not germane, but even then he was essentially his own boss and a practiced loner. After finishing his basic medical training abroad, he returned to the U.S. and took his ophthalmology residency at one of the finest programs in the country, The Wills Eye Hospital in Philadelphia.

Upon becoming an ophthalmologist, Kelman entered solo private practice in Manhattan. He knew his specialty well and he had rock-steady, as well as dexterous, surgical hands, possibly as a result of high-speed hand-brain coordination on the saxophone. His life, day to day, was stimulating and frenetic, yet incomplete. He said as much in autobiography published in 1985, *Through My Eyes. The Story of A Surgeon Who Dared to Take On The Medical World* (Crown Publishers,

Inc. New York). I don't recall any other physician writing his memoirs before retirement, but that was Kelman. By then, he had a wife and children, a growing income from surgery, a mind full of ideas and a developing public image as a two-for-one cultural phenomenon. Yet he needed more, even much more.

Thus, in the late 1960s and lasting for no less than a decade, this possessed performer--of operations, research, and entertainment-- became the number one pariah in the world of ophthalmology. What he wanted second-most in this world was to reverse his miserable reputation within his profession–although not at the cost of what he wanted most: nothing less than to come up with the biggest breakthrough in 20th century eye care. He did not consider himself a modest man, and his aspirations were not modest. He was dead set upon exploiting every ounce of potential to maximize his resourcefulness, a man who self-made and self-propelling.

In today's savvy world, the public most certainly knows that a cataract is the lens of the eye that has lost its transparency. As a result, when the patient's vision becomes problematic, the cataract has to be surgically removed. There is no alternative. What is not common public knowledge is how the operation is performed, so here is a quick tutorial, as it lies at the crux of this man's history.

By Kelman's time in the past century and for many decades before, traditional cataract extraction was a procedure often performed under general anesthesia and always performed in the U.S. on patients who were hospitalized. The operation required a large, circumferential incision into the eye at the base of the cornea, typically three quarters of an inch in length, which is a big gash when we are considering eyeballs. After the cataract was removed through that opening--like extracting a pea-sized pellet of hard tapioca encased in an envelope of soft cellophane--it was customary to close the large incision with five to eight stitches. There was considerable post-operative lid swelling and eye discomfort that remained until the stitches could be removed a few weeks after the surgery. A prescription for eyeglasses was provided four to six weeks later. The glasses were thick and heavy and recognizable as belonging to a cataract patient. Alternatively, the patient could use hard, and later soft, contact lenses that required some manual skills. Techniques were evolving. Slowly and yet steadily.

In the 1960s, cataract surgery's orderly evolution was the result of work by many eye doctors abroad and in the U.S. Some surgeons, including Kelman, were breaking up the cataracts within the eye and removing them piecemeal, but even that required a large incision to do completely and cleanly. In the latter decades of the 20th century, intraocular lenses (IOL's) were just beginning to be placed within the eye after cataracts were removed. There were dozens of variants of those plastic lens implants. In fact, Kelman was to develop IOL models of his own, at least a few of which became popular commercial products.

Over several years of self-devised research adjacent to the animal facilities at The Manhattan Eye, Ear and Throat Hospital on East 64th Street, Kelman had developed a number of important contributions to the methods of cataract surgery. Even those of us who were his critics would readily acknowledge that as fact. But he wanted to go for the gold ring. What his research was addressing was the invariable "large incision" that had always been used for cataract extraction surgery since the beginning of enlightenment eons earlier. Kelman's mission was to reduce the length of the incision, not just a little but a lot, despite the fact that every ophthalmologist knew from his earliest training that when a cataract incision was too small it led to severe complications in the process of the cataract's removal. One of the ABCs of teaching surgery was and is to stress the fact that surgical safety must never go upside down with surgical innovation. *Period*.

With that fact presumably set aside, Kelman theorized that if cataract surgery could be done with a much smaller incision, the patient's vision would be more rapidly restored; general anesthesia and, most particularly, hospitalization would no longer be needed. Cataract surgery would become an ambulatory procedure. The resulting overall efficiency, lessened need for sustained post-operative care and the greatly improved effectiveness of the surgery would have immense worldwide significance for hundreds of millions of patients in just a few years. The truth is, Kelman had an idea of potentially enormous significance. But so what? Anyone could imagine anything, like dating Marilyn Monroe or pretending to be Thomas Edison.

By 1967, after a myriad of attempts to fulfill his surgical goal, the frustrated investigator was at the point of desperation as the third and final year of a supportive research grant was about to expire. Quite suddenly and unexpectedly, serendipity brought epiphany. While he was at the dentist's, a buzzing probe was used to clean his teeth. The buzz was from the probe's ultrasonic vibrations that softened the teeths' plaque so that it could be washed away. That buzz turned out to be Kelman's sonic boom. Why, he asked himself, couldn't ultrasound work similarly to dissolve cataracts to the point of becoming a pulp that could then be sucked out of the eye through a tiny tube inserted through a tiny incision? Yes! That was *it*! He tore from the dentist's office and sprinted to his hospital laboratory with the dental bib still around his neck and a borrowed tooth-cleaning unit under his arm.

Thousands more hours of bench research, animal experiments and tentative applications to human eyes lay ahead. He found that the ultrasound could indeed emulsify the lenses of animals but there were many impediments to doing such surgery safely and easily on humans. Unquestionably, the operation being derived from his basic concept required the kind of precision provided by the surgical microscope. Only a relatively few ophthalmologists in the 1960s and '70s were familiar with the use of the surgical microscope, and Kelman was one of them. So was I and others in the younger generation of eye surgeons, many of whom were still in training.

Despite proving to be a great advantage, microsurgery was, for the first time in the history of any surgery, a technique that could not be learned by means of lectures, photographs, films or mere trial-and-error experience in the animal laboratory. It required hands-on teaching by an experienced micro-surgeon instructing each student how the hands are positioned and manipulated when seen as fingertips under high power in a three- dimensional surgical field whose magnification would make the motion of a toothpick look like the wave of a semaphore. Beyond the basics of microsurgery, what Kelman envisioned for his new operation was a brand-new layer of manual expertise piled upon the already demanding basics of microsurgery.

Dr. Kelman's imagined new microsurgical procedure was developed with as much privacy as if he were developing a nuclear weapon in his laboratory. Whereas no one would argue the need for the secrecy that surrounded the original wartime Manhattan Project, Kelman's Manhattan project was merely a medical doctor working benevolently for the good of mankind. So why the war-like secrecy of closed door surgery? That earlier reference to medical kleptomania is not without validity when it comes to important discoveries. Charles Kelman was certain that, given the chance, someone would steal his concept and his surgical technique from him before he could brand it as his own. His natural paranoia was fortified by his conviction that one of his earlier inventions had, in fact, been stolen. Never again would he allow that to happen. He knew that his new idea was so hot that it was intellectually incendiary; thus only his trusted assistants were allowed in his laboratory or, later, in the operating room when further refinements had to be made on human eyes.

It was in 1971– the year I became an ophthalmology department chairman at Baylor College of Medicine in Houston– that Kelman's research was heralded in the lay press as an historic medical "breakthrough." Chatty columnists gave considerable inches to his interviews: "The invention of a formidable electronic machine for a new method of cataract extraction by a talented young ophthalmologist named Charles Kelman who also mesmerizes audiences with his musical magic ..." Well, you can surmise the gist of the press coverage, not to mention the increased thralldom of his public.

Never before those mid-century days had publicity for an individual physician been condoned by the American Medical Association or any other official authority. Just the mention of a physician's name in the press--even unsolicited--had formerly been considered a flagrant violation of medical mores. Then, in the 1970s, the Federal Trade Commission and state regulatory bodies began loosening their restriction on marketing and advertising by doctors and lawyers. Many traditionalist physicians considered that change of policy to be a dreadful mistake, for advertising and marketing by their very nature would lead to the brink of exaggeration--and sometimes beyond. No matter, the regulations were changing and Kelman was ostentatiously in the vanguard of the new "PR" permissiveness. More-over, the press revelations of his alleged research success appeared in print before any report appeared in a refereed medical journal. This was-- despite the new attitude about medical advertising--a medical faux pas as grievous as holding up a third vertical finger in the face of ophthalmology's academic leadership.

However, the press wasn't lying. The gowns were beginning to wrinkle, if you get my drift, so critical attention shifted to his instru-mentation. As Kelman's cataract extraction project came into its first exotic bud at the end of the 1960s, it was the titanic machine he was using to accomplish his purpose that stirred the bile of the practical traditionalists. The instrument's bulk and its outlandish complexity for a "lil ol" eye operation was to become the convenient Achilles heel used in attacking Kelman's surgery as an unreasonable and impracti-cal procedure that therefore needed no further comment. Vested au-thority in any organization has a tendency toward haughtiness when confronting its junior members. It's just human nature—similar to the way those with stars on their shoulders deal with buck privates.

That logical stance was soon fortified by fresh ammunition pro-vided by hospital snitches--bless them for their tireless tasking in what one might call "factual improvisation." They leaked informa-tion alleging that Kelman was having failure after failure in his post-operative results on human beings when using his big machine. That leakage soon became the we-thought-as-much refrain for a chorus of opponents on the academic side of a frustrated profession. Neverthe-less, it turned out that Kelman had indeed contrived a machine that used ultrasound as the force to emulsify cataracts into a lumpy slime that could be sucked out of the eye through an incision just $1/10^{th}$ of an inch in length! But hold the applause.

It was true that the incision Kelman used was only $1/6^{th}$ the size of the conventional cataract incision. However, for the operation to be accomplished through such a tiny opening, the outsize machine was as vital to his operation as the iron lung had once been to the live of patients with "infantile paralysis." Did such mechanical massiveness make sense for an eye operation? Industrial bioengineers had helped solve a few of the machine's technical glitches and had managed to fit the whole caboodle into its prodigious stainless steel encasement. Still, in its first iteration, the machine was a sledgehammer manu-factured to crack a nut. That preposterous sledgehammer would cost $40,000 (an amount exceeding $230,000 today), with an additional cost of $85 (then) per operation for disposable supplies, while the traditional cataract operations were using instruments that cost only a few hundred dollars and had limitless reuse.

Specifically, the Kelman machine as it arrived on the scene was a 320-pound Goliath sitting on four wheels and containing 129 cubic feet of internal and external Rube Goldberg gadgetry. A computer-ized system for everything but the surgery itself! The front surface of the console was dotted with flashing signal lights and flickering indi-cators and was adjusted by adjacent knobs that were manipulated by the indispensable standby technician who would be stationed along-side the machine and at the shoulder of the surgeon.

Suspended on a pole above the top surface of Kelman's machine were two dangling plastic bags of fluid, delivering their contents to a computer-regulated process within the great steel console. Hence, their tubing extended outward, along with the wiring of the ultra-sonic power supply. During the process of grinding—or emulsify-ing--the cataract with ultrasonic bursts at 40,000 vibrations per sec-ond, the surgeon had to hold and intricately maneuver a cumbersome four-pound hand piece that was the ultimate "secret" of the surgery. It emitted ultrasonic liquefaction at the hollow bore, irrigation-asper-ation tip of the hand piece, whose fluid exchange was controlled by the console's computer. Using two hands, one holding the hand piece and the other holding a metallic probe, the surgeon coordinated the oh-so delicate process of sucking away cataract-turned slime while avoiding potentially permanent damage to eye tissue that lay within a fraction of a millimeter of where the working tip of the instru-ment had to be placed to get the job done properly. Cables reached from beneath the elephantine contraption to foot pedals used by the surgeon to instigate the intermittent firing of the ultrasonic bursts with one foot while the other foot controlled the lighting on the surgical field, the positioning of the microscope's viewing angle and the magnification needed for the various sequences of the operation.

While responsible for these variants, the surgeon also had to be certain that the amount of irrigating fluid delivered to the eye to maintain its shape was exactly equal in volume to the fluid and lens material that constituted the cataract extraction. As happens with computers, the one within the console could falter in its crucial task. The busy surgeon also had to be prepared for such sight-threatening contingencies for the eye receiving the surgery.

Kelman named his new operation "phacoemulsification"—-with "phaco" coming from the Greek word for lens. In common parlance, the operation itself was referred to simply as "phaco" or "the Kelman Operation." It hit the profession before the great majority of eye surgeons were prepared to use a surgical microscope as anything but a novel operative adjunct too cumbersome for routine procedures that could be done with a loupe alone. Lucky for Kelman that he had good surgical hands and many, many hours of animal eye practice before he began his actual patient surgery. He went so far as to proclaim to those who would listen that through that little bitty "Kelman incision" he could slide specially designed IOL's into the operative eye and thereby restore his patient to perfect vision without glasses. The trouble was, this often-expressed claim was not yet supported by any rock-hard evidence.

Kelman's initial clinical procedures were performed only on patients who had one totally blind eye with no possibility of vision restoration. They agreed to have him remove the eye's cataract as a means of testing his new operation—the "Used Talisman Syndrome" extended pro-bono by devoted believers. The first operation lasted four hours, including one full hour for the ultrasonic blistering of a cataract that got emulsified only after severe damage had been done to the surrounding eye tissues. Word of the misadventure got out, despite the fact that there had been a sign on the operating room door that read in large lettering CONTAMINATED ROOM. DO NOT ENTER. (Any posted inference of a hospital infection is like warning of serious radiation exposure to virginal X-ray technicians still looking forward to motherhood.)

The darkness surrounding the so-called "Kelman Operation" continued to feed his tormentors' conjectures about the legitimacy of his patient care. We academics believed that all medical research should have transparency and full disclosure--working by the books was our byword. In fact, hospital records finally revealed that Kelman's first fifty cases had racked up an ominous number of troubles. That proved to his critics that the skill requirement was too high and the machine too unreliable. How could anyone blame either the old-timers or the academic establishment for their raised eyebrows, dire predictions and, finally, for what they rationalized as necessary humane interference with the inventor's further clinical research for the good of humanity? The operation had outgrown casually malicious cafeteria yakking. It was not a matter to leave for its own resolution. It had become everyone's business--no longer just Kelman's.

Before long, the Board of Surgeon Directors of the Manhattan Eye, Ear & Throat Hospital where he worked voted to bar Kelman from scheduling more than five cases in an operating day, not only to prevent him from usurping operating room time but also because it was predictable that, were he to be reined in, he might want to find alternative hospitals in which to do his mischief. Skepticism about his surgery was further evidenced when the Advisory Council for the National Eye Institute in Bethesda, Maryland, officially disapproved it, based upon an unidentified ad hoc advisory panel of academic eye doctors who felt obliged to intervene in that manner. Thus, as a result of the Council's opinion, Medicare insurance was disapproved for phacoemulsification, and when Medicare balks, other health insurance carriers eagerly follow suit. Since the majority of cataract surgery cases were Medicare-dependent, this was a serious blow to the operation's acceptance, and its implications meant more promotional trouble for Kelman.

Despite the trouble, by 1971 Kelman actually began teaching courses at his hospital to qualified microsurgery-trained ophthalmologists eager to learn the technique he had filmed and was lecturing about, wherever invited. Those who took his courses were bold young men (only men) who were not in academic positions. They came from many parts of the country and had to pony up $1,000 (equivalent to almost $5,000 today) as a registration fee for the privilege of learning what the guardians of the faith--those of us in the long white

coats—considered a specious and dangerous technological extrava-
ganza carried out within the microscopic dimensions of a flea circus.

By this time, even the ever-ebullient Dr. Kelman would have had
to admit that the persistent dusting up from establishment high-
brows was seriously affecting him. One doctor crossing the street
with him in Manhattan warned him to watch out for a fast-approach-
ing motorcycle. Kelman responded that the likelihood of his being
struck by a motorcycle was far less than being run over by an ophthalmologist. Even more indicative of the degree of victimization he
felt was that he told one of his earliest phaco trainees that he feared
he might receive a letter bomb (as some as yet unidentified sicko had
been mailing anonymously to various recipients at that time), and he
discussed the steps that should be taken with his work by his trusted
colleagues were he to be assassinated. Call it paranoia, but Kelman
was viewing the academic leadership of the "gowns" and their presumed henchmen in the context of professional terrorism.

The inventor's steadily expanding support among lay persons remained his essential source of nourishment. Thanks to his own im-
modest proclamations of the promise offered by his new operation,
combined with his well-publicized image as a saxophone-playing,
song-and-joke eye surgeon, Dr. Kelman was being deluged by patients seeking his services. Yet, even though with each passing month
both the tweaking of his machine and the developing surgical technique were leading to less difficult surgical manipulations, his already fragile reputation within the profession as a properly cautious
eye surgeon was continuing to erode.

The hospital board finally got its wish. Charles Kelman quit his
Manhattan hospital and began sending patients to a New Jersey hospital about 80 minutes' drive from his Manhattan office. The drive
was too long for the busy surgeon to make: therefore, he took time
off for a few weeks to learn how to fly a helicopter, purchased one,
and used it to transport himself to and from the New Jersey hospital
from a landing pad in Manhattan. His surgical patients were ferried
by limousine between his office in the Empire State Building and
the suburban hospital and, after surgical discharge, were returned
to Manhattan. This bit of transportation creativity and its fallout of

showmanship made him even more of a public fascination and even more of the profession's pariah--a light-weight whirly-boy with a new plaything.

But Kelman continued to progress in his various pursuits, not only in the further development of phacoemulsification and in a bourgeoning private practice, but also in his musical associations. The profession's increasingly talked-about inventor befriended and performed with Dizzy Gillespie and Lionel Hampton. He appeared on programs hosted by Johnny Carson, Barbara Walters, Merv Griffin, Oprah Winfrey, and David Letterman. His patients now included the most famous of the famous: opera star Jan Peerce; actress Hedy Lamarr; and Prime Minister of Israel, Golda Meir. Many, if not all, of these individuals became part of a virtual cheering section he could count upon as succor against the disaffection of his profession's leaders, who were being driven to new heights of distemper by the publicity over the incorrigibly ostentatious inventor.

The issue Dr. Kelman posed went well beyond being just a scientific spat; it was the rumble of a volcanic eruption that potentially involved big money, big reputations, big men, commercial interests and unprecedented advertising--all prompted by a "nobody." That was the very term with which Dr. Kelman flagellated himself as he pushed himself onward and upward. By 1973, he reached the zenith of his reputation as the eyeball establishment's most renowned troublemaker and the Peck's Bad Boy of physician-requisite decorum. The standoff between town and gown--between power and populist—continued to heat up.

Meanwhile, I was a typical white-jacket confederate, an increasingly enthusiastic microsurgeon performing a moderate number of weekly operations using the microscope with an otherwise traditional technique. The nature of my work in academia had also brought me into roles with various national organizations, such as heading up the program in continuing education for all American ophthalmology provided by the American Academy of Ophthalmology & Otolaryngology (AAOO). Private practitioner Kelman and I were like the repel of two magnets that had misaligned poles, but our disparate forces constitute, nevertheless, the essential yin and yang of the medical profession. Happily for me, those two sometimes-repelling forces are accommodated through the vested authority lying on my side of the divide—teachers trump students like paper wraps stone. Moreover, Kelman was a loose wheel, and I was a cog in a system. His progressive ideas seemed too abstruse for safe employment. With his public acclaim and his support within the young microsurgeons using his operation, he was unequivocally becoming a presence too formidable to spurn or ignore.

A year passed, during which a gradual ooze of doubt began to seep into my academic correctness. To speak frankly, I was similar to Kelman in being a person who enjoyed and sought out new and different ideas; I often found the status quo far less inspiring than alternative concepts. By 1972, an inclination to reassess my opinion of this unusual man led me to go with several associates from Houston to New York to take his course in the use of his phaco machine.

The course began with Kelman in the operating room, doing what appeared to be surgical sleight-of-hand as he lectured from behind his mask. This almost magical demonstration was not what I had expected. We watched as his machine worked flawlessly. Every case was different but every cataract outcome was the same—-mind-bogglingly beautiful eyes, as if no surgery had been performed! After his demonstrations, as he walked into the teaching classroom I remember having an eerie feeling, as if the previously unseen Wizard of Oz had suddenly materialized as flesh and blood. When we met, he ventured a half-smile. Aware of each other through the grapevine, we shook hands tentatively. Dr. Kelman knew where I was coming from, but the question in his mind had to be, which way did I intend to go?

His training course next moved into his enthusiastic and effective laboratory teaching of phaco, from its basics to its subtle microsurgical details of technique. I had to give him this: His patience, as well as his determination to share the 'how to's' of even the most minute manual manipulations, instilled in all of us--his students--that we could indeed conquer the surgical conundrum of small incision cataract surgery.

It had become plain to me that bad-mouthing a reputedly eccentric surgeon before actually meeting him was much easier than replacing the dismissive term "eccentric" with an alternative term such as "uncommon" or "unique." Dr. Kelman was an effective teacher, a deeply involved enthusiast and a sincere believer in what his machine could make possible for all cataract surgeons young enough, flexible enough and dedicated enough to learn his operation. What had not come through in the hearsay about him was that he was also a man fully in charge of his choices and capacities. His independence was merely the liberating force behind everything he did, freeing him to follow the strong convictions that continually fired his engine, seemingly inexhaustibly.

Within months, our residency training program in Houston became the first of many beyond Manhattan to teach its trainees phaco surgery, and Dr. Kelman came to Houston to lead one of the hands-on instruction sessions. Dr. Jared Emery, my fellow faculty member in Houston, was our department's principal phaco advocate—and, like me, a full-time academician whose phaco-centric curiosity had been increasing. No matter what one had previously thought about Dr. Kelman's flamboyance and headline-seeking, his complex surgery could produce an eye that, within a few hours of the operation, looked to the critical observer and felt to the patient as if it had not even been operated on. And perhaps even more stunning, the eyesight was likely to become normal in a matter of hours, after having been in slow decline for decades.

The overriding bias of my thought had originally come not only from the group-think of the establishment, but in particular from my former professor at Johns Hopkins' Wilmer Eye Institute and most influential mentor, Dr. A. Edward Maumenee. Arguably, he had contributed more important ideas to the profession's advancement than any other ophthalmologist I had ever met or even heard about. He was a magnificent surgeon and an inspiring teacher for legions of colleagues. Maumenee, the academician, is now remembered by many of his peers as the greatest ophthalmologist of the 20th century. He was not about to be won over by phaco's bumptious inventor.

Dr. Maumenee's wisdom and his respect for orderly and studied process were inviolate. And he was not alone in his views. Among Dr. Kelman's many other critics was an internationally acclaimed Manhattan eye surgeon, Dr. Richard C. Troutman, who, despite being an early convert to microsurgery, remained an outspoken critic of phaco as being an operation too risky to endorse for patient care. Ironically, he could not have foreseen the pivotal role that his own surgery, combined with others', would play in the future of the Kelman operation.

Professor Maumenee maintained a broad academic perspective. Whenever he discussed Dr. Kelman he would point out that there were tens of thousands of eye surgeons whose livelihoods could be damaged by prematurely switching to a surgery that would not overcome its existing risks if the learning curve turned out to be too steep for the general run of ophthalmologists. Millions of patients might be at risk of increased complications if new surgery was performed by hands that were less than sufficiently skilled. Beyond patient safety, the cost of the surgical care could skyrocket; and there might be a redistribution and reduction of the average ophthalmologist's access to his bread-and-butter cataract surgery. Acceptance of a potential paradigm shift has to take into consideration such far-reaching and serious implications. Kelman himself pointed out that phacoemulsification was a young doctor's surgery, requiring cool hands, a cool head, and the enthusiasm needed to learn new work with new technology. Even with those qualifications, severe complications of phacoemulsification were definitely happening from some of the surgeries performed by several of the trainees Kelman had inspired to undertake his technique.

One day in the latter half of 1972, Dr. Kelman heard from one of his loyal informers that the AAOO was forming a committee to investigate the validity and safety of phaco. The AAOO was territory he identified with me and my relationship to its educational programs. Worried about the known opponents who were to serve on that committee, he asked Dr. Emery and me to collect information from as many experienced phaco surgeons as could be identified so that their surgical results could be compiled to determine if phaco's results were competitive with those of traditional surgical outcomes.

The collection of data was undertaken by Dr. Emery, who obtained the information from 300 surgeons reporting a total of 2,875 cases. The data showed unequivocally that, in well-trained hands, phaco was safe. That was forceful evidence, but did the numbers prove that the Kelman operation was as safe as traditional eye surgery performed with the operating microscope? Jared Emery thought the proof was evident and he became what I believe to be the first full-time academic fully committed to phaco surgery. I, too, was definitely--if surreptitiously--continuing to lean in that direction.

Then came a near-perfect academic storm. In February 1973, Miami, Florida, nearly became Kelman's ophthalmic Waterloo. High among the popular and authoritative sources of continuing education in modern ophthalmic surgery were the biennial clinical "congresses" organized by a good friend of mine who was a strong Kelman opponent, Dr. Robert B. Welsh. The four-day meeting had an attendance of more than 700 ophthalmologists eager to hear about eye surgery's most talked-of controversy--and whether phacoemulsification would receive mercy-killing or forbearance from the high authorities. Professor Maumenee was the most senior panel member and, as always, the most articulate and influential. Over the course of the meeting, phaco was being consistently targeted. I was one of seven full-time panelists designated to discuss each paper after it was presented. It would be natural to surmise that the very positive data that we had collected and that was reported by Dr. Emery would tip the scale toward a landslide of acceptance of "phaco for all." But that was not the upshot.

On each day, the Miami program had an hour given to "Phacoemulsification: Publicity and Catastrophes." Although the papers themselves were recorded for subsequent publication, the discussions of phaco were so highly critical that they were considered confidential and remain to this day a memory for only attendees to recall. There was plenty of highfalutin' academic bitching, mostly by senior practitioners who knew they could never master phaco and felt intimidated by its apparent success in younger hands . Moreover, the program included an invited talk by the immediate past-president of the American Trial Lawyers Association, who spoke on "Legal Aspects of

Phacoemulsification, Its Publicity and Lack of Scientific Investigation." His talk covered precautions regarding malpractice, liability and slander in the context of performing surgery disapproved by the profession's leadership.

To top off the atmosphere of animosity toward phaco, someone had stationed at the entrance of the meeting hall three patients whose eyes had been seriously damaged by phaco surgery—not performed by Dr. Kelman himself but by several of his Florida trainees. Registrants entering the hall were urged by the patients themselves to examine their blind, tearing and painful eyes. One patient held a small flashlight to assist the examination by any doctor inquisitive enough to wish to look at his eye with better illumination. Never before or since have I encountered a medical program so heavily loaded against the validity of a technique and its proponent.

When Dr. Kelman got word from his informers of an unwillingness on my part to speak up against Dr. Maumenee's criticism and to give no more than a meek expression of support for phaco, he was incensed. In a letter, he told me that I had disappointed him, reminding me of all the teaching he had provided to me personally, both in New York and later in Houston. He had a point, but at least he knew that I was increasingly coming over to his side, Dr. Emery having been a strong influence on me in that regard.

Later in 1973 I returned to Manhattan to watch Dr. Kelman in surgery once again. On that trip, my position in respect to phaco and its pilot-inventor was finally transformed as I was drawn into a better understanding of what made him who he was. The initial basis of that understanding came from the fact that I was heavily involved in an admittedly flamboyant project of my own that, like his, was a creative endeavor—ORBIS. From it I was learning in spades that creativity in medical affairs often requires public as well as intrinsic medical support; and, what's more, originality within a profession is not always as welcome as the inventor might imagine it to be. In short, I was finding out first-hand that the achievement of a project requires much more than just the good idea that got it started. It can take blood and guts to stay alive to fight forces based upon conventional wisdom. Kelman was such a fighter, but was I ready to join his battle in switching sides?

It was a Kelman-piloted helicopter ride to the hospital in New Jersey that filled in the missing pieces for me. I discovered that we were flying over Manhattan, the Hudson river and then New Jersey--heavily occupied air space--without a registered flight plan. It turned out that his avoidance of such a plan was typical, known by his close friends to be his custom on other trips as well, whether to New Hampshire to visit his daughter in summer camp or ferrying a visiting colleague back to LaGuardia airport. On the one hand, that flight plan omission seemed unduly risky, if not downright illegal. On the other, I truly believe that his flaunting of the rules was a deliberate act of autonomy signaling an ingrained compulsion to reject control and restraint. He simply could not be productive if he had to consider himself one of life's herded lemmings.

I had fully accepted the data that Dr. Emery assembled, and now the inventor himself had become too real, too thoroughly understood, and too convincing to be denied or reproached. Some might say his rare ability to invent was a function of genius. But I have my doubts about genius as his fundamental asset. He had a rare determination fortified by a colossal ambition to achieve that were heaped upon his native skills. As he had written unabashedly in his memoir, Dr. Kelman's basic goal was to become famous and to that end he had worked harder, longer, with more direction and with greater dedication than few of us can even imagine. His drive to succeed was as evident in his music as it was in his medicine, and these forces came together in a unison of purpose to rise to fame as an eye surgeon and inventor of surgical technique.

So, to aid in pursuit of his project's goal, he capitalized on the challenges that arose--in particular the opposition of the ophthalmological establishment--to arouse the fury of self-justification that was a key factor in sustaining his relentless initiative. To my enlightened way of thinking, this astonishingly unique man prevailed in his quest for distinction by force of character, by liberation from conventions, and by the effective unification of all of his native assets into a nurtured cyclone of well-studied abilities. In today's explanation of human energy sources one hears the medical mention of "dopamine spurts." In retrospect, one could say that Dr. Kelman's ability to achieve was a dopamine addiction fueled by his sky-high ambition to be, as he said of himself—"somebody," meaning somebody very special.

My pilot host and phaco instructor was more than generous to me in his outreach, truthful in expressing evidence-based conclusions and strikingly committed to making sure that he mastered what he conceived in each of his activities. The ultimate proof was in the case-after-case of complication-free surgery that I again witnessed on that second visit with him in New Jersey.

My phaco-ambivalence ended as I got my head around the enormity of phaco's contribution to our profession, rather than focusing on its initial growing pains. Moreover, once one is convinced that an inventor is legitimate in purpose and sincerely dedicated to finding "a better way," then one can better understand, without bias, the roles of personality and modus operandi that underlie rare achievements. There is something intellectually rewarding in discovering the key to a rare mind. I believe that I found that key for Dr. Kelman. He was now Charlie. My friend, Charlie. And I recalled with regret any pejorative adjectives I had previously used to describe him during my gratuitous condemnations of what eventually proved to be a revolutionary achievement.

Official approval of phacoemulsification--its true turning point--came with the report of the Cataract-Phacoemulsification Committee of the AAOO in October, 1974, at its annual meeting held that year in Dallas. There the highly respected Dr. Troutman added his own surgical results to the data of 400 ophthalmologists, amounting to 5,870 cases of traditional cataract surgery. The results were compared to the data from the 300 ophthalmologists' reports from 2,875 cases of phacoemulsification that had been previously reported by Dr. Emery and myself at the Welsh Cataract Congress earlier that year. According to a statistician's scrupulous analysis of these two techniques, phaco proved at least as effective in restoring vision as the standard operation performed by Troutman and those whose cases were included in his collected data. Troutman himself was chairman of the AAOO's reporting committee. He had been one of Dr. Kelman's longstanding scoffers and now, with admirable frankness, he acknowledged that, although unanticipated by him, the proof was indeed in the pudding.

As subsequent models of the phaco machine became smaller and more manageable, significant improvements in the Kelman surgical technique were to make the operation ever safer in the surgeons' hands. However, phaco could not exist without microsurgical skills, and those skills in turn were also being applied to the majority of other eye operations. The importance of the lessons learned from Charlie and the impact of his work on my own efforts in ophthalmology intensified even more my appreciation of a fearless inventor with an unwavering conviction. Ironically, Charlie's achievement became an important asset for ORBIS, the gradually materializing concept I had been struggling with since 1968. To a considerable degree my project, including as it did, the teaching of microsurgery by hands-on instruction within a teaching aircraft, was spurred by the global interest of ophthalmologists in learning phaco; and phaco, in turn, was benefited by its official recognition as an ideal cataract procedure in locales where its instrumentation was affordable--and where it was taught by ORBIS.

ORBIS was a "gownish" idea but over the forthcoming years it was dependent upon the teaching skills of ophthalmologists primarily in private practice, most of them from the United States--in other words, "townies." In keeping with the vital mix of practitioners and academics in the health and growth of our specialty, two uniquely different projects once combined created international benefits greater than either could accomplish alone.

Then, at the start of the current century, due to increasingly prevalent teaching of microsurgery and the popularizing of phaco worldwide, something quite extraordinary began occurring. Inspired by Charlie's operation, alternative operative techniques were derived from phaco in a number of developing nations, achieving successful cataract extractions with incisions almost as small as phaco's but with ingenious, inexpensive instruments. Today, although the Kelman Operation remains the preferred method if cost and training in its skills are not an object, the availability of Charlie's basic approach with small incision surgery is unequivocally the method of choice worldwide. That means that Charlie's concept is being used in well over fifty million cataract surgeries every year. His goal of revolutionizing cataract surgery across the world has been fully achieved.

In 1978, Professor Maumenee referred a doctor on his staff with a traumatic cataract from Baltimore to Houston for Dr. Emery to perform the necessary surgery with phacoemulsification. The greatest of all teachers–again I speak for many of us in this field of medicine–had finally come around. Moreover, from the inspiration of phacoemulsification has come laparoscopy, arthroscopic surgery of the joints, and similar small-incision management of operations on almost all of the organs and soft tissues of the human body. It would be incorrect to credit phaco exclusively for that surgical revolution, but it would also be wrong to fail to mention the primary influence phaco has had throughout the various surgical specialties.

In 1999, Charlie was diagnosed with lung cancer. Despite surgery and chemotherapy, the cancer recurred in 2003, becoming widespread and inoperable. The last time I played golf with him, early in 2003--just the two of us on his Atlantic Club course on Long Island--he was not on his best game. Toward the end of the round when his ball found a bunker he managed to hit it out, but his footing was insecure and his strength seemed sapped. I reached out a hand to help him back to solid turf. His dismissive glance at my hand--who needs your help?--was followed by the sudden Kelman smile that needed no translation. He grabbed hold, and out he came, propelled by the power of conjoined magnets. That hand-to-hand moment of human relationship may not have been as spiritual as the one pictured on the ceiling of the Sistine Chapel, but it was my personal, sincere and admiring farewell to this incredibly talented man who once was widely seen by us in academia as a maverick of dark purpose and selfish ambition.

That golfing afternoon was the last time I saw Charlie. He died of his cancer on June 1, 2004.

The transformation of the way he appeared to academia--always staying in plain view as his image morphed--put me in mind of Oscar Wilde's portrait of Dorian Gray in reverse, the Kelman portrait metamorphosing from quirky, publicity-seeking inventor to international medical hero. I have tried to write about Charlie within the framework of that kinetic perception. My viewpoint is almost identical to what other academic physicians of that era could relate, were they so inclined. I have had to draw upon numerous metaphors and bromides to recreate old illusions in telling it like it was.

One consolation for Charlie was that in the end he received numerous awards for his world-shaking contribution to ophthalmology. In 2003, he was honored for his distinguished work by his specialty's citadel, the American Academy of Ophthalmology (ophthalmology's half of the AAOO that had split into two separate organizations in 1979); he received its highest honorary title, Academy Laureate.

Yet the one prize he most wanted to receive, the Albert Lasker Award presented for "the most distinguished research contributing to a major advance in medical care," eluded him. Then--the last straw--four months after his death, the Lasker Award was extended to him posthumously. That tardy attribution seemed a final rebuke to Charlie for having done things his own way in starting a valuable new departure for a profession overwrought by change. Despite his unique characteristics, Kelman's troubles came not from being wrong but from being right—the near-miraculous startup accomplished by the once maligned upstart.

MUCH GRATITUDE IS OWED

This book has no index, and the persons named on these pages are limited to those whose identities were necessary for meaning or accuracy in describing these slices of my life. It is now my final opportunity to capitalize on what I have learned from dyslexia. My odyssey's "nobility of names" follows in jumbles rather than in alphabetical lists. Why such disregard for convenience and convention? Because with the necessity of reading every name comes the certainty that it will get the recognition they deserve rather than being passed over by the eyes of fast readers in their habitual race across pages when small groups of words have a subconsciously anticipated alphabetical sequence. I am forcing the necessary visual thoroughness of dyslexia upon every reader curious enough to browse these last pages.

Each name is special to me, yet with an increasingly careless mind I know for certain that others of equal importance will remain overlooked until the wee hours of future nights when their omissions dawn on me and I will curse myself for inexcusable oversight—while imagining in customary optimism that a second edition will correct the mistakes.

First, I am deeply indebted to one of my heroes of Medicine, **Dr. Jeremiah A. Barondess** for the quality of his tone-setting introduction, for the concepts he expresses with eloquence, and especially for the kindness of his words.

Mentors: R. Townley Paton MD, Ludwig von Sallmann MD, A. E. Maumenee MD. These men live in many hearts and minds, as they shall for a long time hereafter—and in mine for this lifetime.

Special friends whose role was important in the writing process: Bruce E. Spivey MD, Susan and James A. Baker III,

Michael Wagoner MD, Barbara Elias, Dan B. Jones MD, John & Natalie Spencer, Susan Senft MD, Dr. William S. and Alice Lea Tasman, Kathy Spahn, Dominic M-K Lam PhD, Victoria Sheffield, Richard A. Weiss MD, Sheila Weinstein, George B. E. Hambleton, Harvey Loomis, Sheila Rogers, Larry Schwab, MD, Alfred Sommer, MD MPH, John Lillard,.

Readers whose valued opinions were sought: Douglas D. Koch MD, Edward & Frances Barlow, Patricia Kyle, W. B. McHenry, David W. Parke, II MD, Eugene M. Helveston MD, Gail Williams, Bette Burkett, The Hon. Walter L. & Isabel Cutler, The Hon. William H. & Jane Donaldson, Judith and Alexander M. Laughlin, David J. Noonan, Richard N. Furlaud, Karen F. Eisele, Donald Rice, Ann W. Chapman.

Advisors for the Kelman Essay: Ann Kelman, Sheila Weinstein, Jared M. Emery MD, Guy E. Knolle, Jr. MD, Richard P. Kratz MD, Henry Mitchell, Herve M. Byron MD, Jack M. Dodick MD, Diane Spiro, Cheryl Jalbert, RN, Robert M. Sinskey MD, William M. Aden MD, David J. McIntyre MD.

Friends and acquaintances who had key input or inspired if not actively contributed: Robert Lacey, Morton F. Goldberg MD, John R. Kennedy (deceased), Peter J. McDonnell MD, Richard A. Lewis MD, Robert F. Munsch MD, Robert W. Butner MD, J. Wright Rumbough Jr., Allen Ellis, Patricia & Yves H. Robert, Marcia & George W. Gowen, Norval E. Christy MD, The Hon. George H. W. and Barbara Bush, Alice & Allan Ryan III, Lynn & Philip W. Hummer, Louis D. Pizzarello MD, Michael J. Wolk MD, Karol Musher, Peter Michalos MD, Stephen J. Ryan MD, Henry Wrong, Peter W. Kunhardt, Philip B. Kunhardt III, Nathaniel R. Bronson MD, Shaul Debbi MD, M.Bowes Hamill MD, Abdul-Elah Al Towerki MD, H. Dunbar Hoskins MD, Henry L. Murray. James E. Standefer MD, Ronald E. Smith MD, Robert C. Doherty, William T. Butler MD, Matthew E. Farber MD, D. Hunter Cherwek MD,

George O. Waring MD, John B. Cotter MD, Gustavo E. Gamero MD, James P. Gills MD, Mohamad S. Jaafar MD, Ahmed M. Trabelsi MD, Sheraz M. Daya MD.

Those whose fundamental assistance can never be forgotten: Monica Morgan, Emily Pogue, Bette McAninch Burkett, Louis Schlanger, Eula Mae Childs, Donna Park Frye, Chantal Nicolas, Barbara Perry

Creators of the book's website: D. Townley Paton (to whom this book is dedicated) and Scott Sawyer; Lauren McMillan recording secretary

Editors: Consecutively, Stacey Donovan, Mari Edlin and then Nancy Hardin who deserves 95% of the credit for any special readability the book's shrunken paragraphs may have. Nancy has taught me a new dimension of hands-on instruction as her firm hand forced mine to cut and slash a lengthy octogenarian memoir into an almost microsurgical remnant of its original size, then condensed the remainder by another third—insisting that my better writing has smaller packaging. Although I have not yet met her in person, she is a lurking presence reducing--even now--what I had intended to say of her unique skills.

Credits: The four Hill School photographs are published with the permission of The Hill School's Alumni Office. The photographs of King Hussein publication permission from Mr. Rod Bull, CEO of the St John Eye Hospital, Jerusalem, Jordan. The hypothetical cartoon appearances of a mobile eye clinic, the proposed teaching aircraft, and a projection of telemedicine for the Cullen Eye Institute and were drawn for me by the late Barry Baker in the medical art department, Baylor College of Medicine. The photograph of Dr. DeBakey, myself and Mr. Ted Bowen was clipped from a Methodist Hospital Bulletin published in the early 1970's. The photographs of ORBIS in flight and photos of person celebrating its forthcoming maiden fight from Houston, etc, and were provided by ORBIS representatives several decades ago and are now published with permission from Mr. Jack McHale, CEO of ORBIS International. The image of the King Khaled Eye Specialist Hospital is published with the permission of its current Executive Director, Dr. Abdul Elah Al-Towerki. The photograph of Dr. Schwab was taken by Bonnie Timmons and provided by Dr. Schwab. The two renderings from the plans for a prototype OcuCenter are published with the permission of Mr. Michael Gordon of Gordon and Associates, Architects P.A. in Mount Dora, Florida. The Oval Office photograph of myself with President Reagan was taken by a While House photographer. The photo of the flipped and wrecked Jeep station wagon was given to me by The East Hampton Star. The photograph of Charles Kelman was provided by the Dr. Charles and Ann Kelman Family Foundation. The author's photograph on the back cover of the book was taken by Brooke Hummer, a free-lance photographer in Chicago. The remainder of the book's images were photographs I took or were taken by others using my camera.

My family's cheering section of in-laws and out-laws by direct or indirect influence: Appropriately first come David Townley and Shannon White Paton and most recently Cricket who cheers sublimely but in tongues. My remarkable sister, Joan P. Tilney, is kindness and love personified, and she has passed on that enviable disposition to her talented offspring: Bernard Peyton, Lin Peyton, Robert Olney, Tina Olney; and Bill Post whose extraordinary wife, Pamela, died from complications of cystic fibrosis a few months before this is published. I want to give special mention to Townley's mother, Jane, and her husband Clinton Gilbert, for I gave her some rough teasing in Chapter 7, and Clint was indispensable during the OcuSystem struggles for survival. I have much love for my step-children who, for example, withstood the self-indulgence of a memoir writer pounding the keys when he could have been a more useful household parent: Garrison Franke (abroad), James Beardmore, Lauren and Brian Ivanhoe and--far from least--their inimitable Beylie.

Finally, most important of all who have inspired and sustained me, contributing in countless ways to the genesis of this book is my wonderful, beautiful, funny, serious, sensible and loving wife, Diane Johnston Paton. Am I ever the luckiest person on this planet!

RELEVANT REFERENCES

Paton D: Project ORBIS: Medical Education for the Eyes of the World. Report of Phase I. 1980; 50 pp. Unpublished monograph, available on request to author.

Paton D: Ophthalmology Aloft: teaching enters the jet age. Journal American Medical Association,245:1712,1981

Paton D: Project ORBIS: International continuing medical education for ophthalmologists. Cardiovascular Research Bulletin. April-June, 1982. 20(4) pp 71-77

Paton D: Present and future training of foreign ophthalmologists in USA: The perspective of the American Board of Ophthalmology. Ophthalmology 90:2, February, 1983, pp 73A-74A

Paton D: Project ORBIS: Interchange of concepts and surgical skills for the eyes of the world. Transactions of The Second International Cataract Congress, Florence, Italy, June 1981, pp 23-25.

Paton D, Hambleton GBE, Munsch RF, Pelavin SH and Quick SJ: Project ORBIS: an international experiment in the efficacy of skills transfer by "hands-on" teaching exchanges. Proc. XXIV Internat. Congress Ophthal. Henkind P (ed.) vol II, pp 1374-1376, J.B. Lippincott, Philadephia, 1983.

Paton D: Skills transfer by hands-on surgery: the ORBIS experiment. Current Concepts in Cataract Surgery (Emery JM and Jacobson AC, eds.) pp 190-191, Appleton-Century-Crofts, Norwalk, Conn., 1984.

Tabbara K, Paton D, Badr I et al: National Survey of Eye Disease and Visual Impairment. Findings and recommendations. Kingdom of

Saudi Arabia. Publication of the King Khaled Eye Specialist Hospital, Riyadh, Saudi Arabia, 1984. Abstract: Ophthalmol.91(9S) 141, 1984.

Paton,D:Systematizing ophthalmic practice. Proceedings of XXV International Congress of Ophthalmology, Rome May 4-10, 1986. pp 750-753. Kugher Publications/Ghedini Editore, Amsterdam, Berkley, Milano 1987.

Paton D: Potential international benefits from the evolution of ophthalmic practice in the United States. Proceedings of the International Ophthalmologic Conference in China (IOCC), Guang zhou, China, November 1985. 151. Paton D: Preparations for eye care in the 21st century. AMA Arch Ophthalmol, 1986. 104:1290-1293.

Paton D: Systems development for ophthalmic care in appropriate nations: An American approach. International Ophth. Clinics,30: No 1, Winter 1990. pp 61-63

Paton D: Special Article: The imperative for change in health care delivery: An ophthalmologist's approach. AMA Arch Ophthalmol, vol 108, pp 937-938, July 1990. Abstracted: Key Ophhalmol 6:No1, 1991.

Paton D: R. Townley Paton 1901-1984. Chapt VII. In Corneal Transplantation. A History in Profiles. Mannis, M J and Mannis A A (edits) Hirschberg History of Ophthalmology. The Monographs. Vol 6:238-263, 1999. J P Wayenborgh, Belgium

8421856R0

Made in the USA
Charleston, SC
07 June 2011